American Automobile Workers, 1900–1933

SUNY Series in American Labor
History
Robert Asher and
Charles Stephenson, Editors

American Automobile Workers, 1900–1933

JOYCE SHAW PETERSON

State University of New York Press

Cover photo courtesy of The Archives of Labor and Urban Affairs, Wayne State University.
Some of this material was originally published as an article in the *Journal of Negro History*, LXIV, (Summer 1979), 177–190. Used by permission.
Some material previously appeared in *Labor History*, 22 (Spring 1981), 213–236 (used by permission) and in *Detroit in Perspective*, 6 (Fall 1982), 47–71 (reprinted by permission of The Detroit Historical Society).

Published by
State University of New York Press, Albany

© 1987 State University of New York

For information, address State University of New York
Press, State University Plaza, Albany, N.Y., 12246

Library of Congress Cataloging-in-Publication Data

Peterson, Joyce Shaw, 1939–
   American automobile workers, 1900–1933.

(SUNY series in American labor history)
   Bibliography: p. 201
   Includes index.
   1. Automobile worker—United States—
History. I. Title II. Series.
HD8039.A82U66 1987   331.7′6292′0973   87–1942
ISBN 0-88706-573-2
ISBN 0-88706-574-0 (pbk.)
10 9 8 7 6 5 4 3 2 1

*To My Parents
and
Grandparents*

Contents

Tables

Preface

With the sit-down strikes of 1936 and 1937, automobile workers flash into sharp focus in our mental slide show of twentieth century labor history. We see the men leaning out of the windows of the General Motors plant in Flint, Michigan, greeting their wives and children, and smilingly declaring themselves ready to stay as long as it takes. Inside the factory we see them playing cards and reading newspapers, reclining on the very automobile cushions that they made and installed into cars. Finally, we see the auto workers jubilantly claiming victory, waving the newspapers whose headlines attest to their courage and determination, rushing to rejoin their families, and telling all who will listen that their lives will never be quite the same again.

These are moving and dramatic scenes. But once we move back before 1936, the auto workers recede into the background, and the focus is sharp on Henry Ford and William Durant, on assembly lines and machinery, on large factories and large profits. It is hard to find the workers at all except as occasional stolid figures standing beside their machines. Until very recently, historians have concentrated their attentions upon company histories, biographies of automobile inventors and executives, and histories of the automobile industry as an economic enterprise.[1] In the last ten years, however, some labor historians have begun to turn their attentions toward auto workers as historical actors of weight and substance even before the emergence of the United Automobile Auto Workers (UAW). Roger Keeran has studied the Communist Party influence in the auto workers lives; August Meier and Elliott Rudwick, the special experience of black auto workers. While both works focus on union building, they also begin to fill in the picture of some aspects of pre-union history. Stephen Meyer, in examining the labor relations policy embodied in the Ford Motor Company's $5 day, focuses on the workers' experience at the workplace as their work underwent great technological changes. As he examines Ford's attempt to mold immigrant workers to the pattern required by the newly reorganized Highland Park factory before 1920, he uncovers much about the industrial experience of the workers themselves. David Brody has consistently reminded all labor historians that the story they are telling is one of power, of attempts by workers to get power and by employers to keep it. David Montgomery has directed our attention to a specific aspect of that struggle for power, using the concept of workers' control to define workers' attempts to maintain some power over production through day-to-day workplace struggles both overt and covert. The time seems propitious, then, for an overall survey of the automobile workers' experience during the industry's early history and especially for an understanding of the 1920s as the decade when the new industrial system was in place and running smoothly. I intend this book to contribute to that exploration of auto workers' (and by implication many other industrial workers') experience of modern industry. Throughout, my focus is on the workplace. I think that understanding the factory is crucial to understanding the particular interaction that took place there between workers of different ethnic backgrounds and previous work experiences. It is the defining, unifying experience.[2]

That the automobile industry has been favored with a great deal of scholarly attention is not due to random choice. It was a model of twentieth century mass production techniques, managerial organization, and labor relations. Auto workers are crucial to understanding modern industrial life. They worked within a pivotal industry whose economic health or sickness was vital to the overall economic health or sickness of the nation. They were workers in a new industry that rapidly transformed itself into modern mass production means of production. By the 1920s, the auto industry was already mature. Studying the men who made automobiles reveals a great deal about the nature of modern industry, how it affects the daily lives and work of its employees, how its workers see themselves as individuals and as members of an industrial working class.

The first part of this book sets auto workers in their historical setting. It briefly describes the history of the auto industry, describes the kinds of people who became auto workers, analyzes the particular nature of work in auto factories and the wages and conditions that accompanied that work. The next part of the book looks at what the auto workers made of their situations, the communities in which they lived, the ways they managed to shape their work experience, and the unions they created. Finally, I examine the impact of the Great Depression as a pivotal experience for auto workers.

In writing this book, I have received help from many people. Paul Glad gave advice and encouragement at the beginning. Over the years, my colleagues at Florida International University, Howard Kaminsky, Darden Pyron, Mark Szuchman, Howard Rock, Eric Leed, Rich Klimmer, and Tom Breslin have made critical comments that helped to shape various segments of this book. Milton Cantor read an early version and made detailed suggestions for revision. Bob Asher has done his best to force me to answer some difficult questions and to tighten my writing style. His encouragement has sustained me.

Everett Kassalow and Richard Wilson arranged for me to attend a meeting of Local 400 UAW retirees. I am grateful for the opportunity this meeting provided to talk with a few workers who had been in the auto industry during the period covered by my study. Joseph Oldenburg generously provided me with a copy of his article on the Ford homes. Lois Steering typed the tables, and Grace Holden typed several chapters. Erik and Lars Peterson endured the tedium of helping me proofread the numbers. Judy Green has lightened my workload at many points over the years.

Final research and considerable rewriting was accomplished while I was attending a National Endowment for the Humanities Summer Seminar at Wayne State University. I am grateful to the Endowment for its support and to all the seminar members for their encouragement and critical reading. In particular, Kathy Aiken shared with me her knowledge of the United Community Services case files and alerted me to the presence of auto workers therein. Stephen Meyer gave valuable encouragement and advice and shared with me his book on the $5 day while it was still in galleys. Robert Zieger, as seminar director, asked disturbing questions and influenced my final conclusions. He also provided a setting for stimulating discussion of twentieth-century labor history that did much to help this book progress.

As always with historical study, librarians and archivists merit gratitude for doing their jobs with unfailing competence and courtesy. I particularly thank Warner Pflug, Roberta McBride, and Dione Miles of the Archives of Labor History and Urban Affairs, Wayne State University; Edward Weber of the University of Michigan's Labadie Collection; J. Parker Huber of the University of Michigan's

Michigan Historical Collections; James T. Bradley of the Detroit Public Library's Automotive History Collection; and Wyn Sears and Dave Crippen of the Ford Motor Company Archives. The interlibrary loan personnel at the University of Wisconsin and at Florida International University helped provide many needed materials.

One of my grandfathers was a Scottish immigrant who worked in the silk mills of Paterson, New Jersey. My other grandfather earned his living fishing the waters of Long Island Sound. Both were working men of integrity and dignity whose stories were my first introduction to working-class history. My father was a Baptist minister devoted to a social gospel theology and practice that included the rights of workers to self-determination and human decency. None of them are alive to see this book. If they were, they would know that my interest in studying the history of working-class people owes much to them.

Brian Peterson has listened to my ideas, contributed his own understanding of German working-class history in the early twentieth century, and provided me with a valuable comparative perspective. He gave equally of his lively and critical intelligence and of his warm encouragement and support; I value them both, and more besides.

Chapter One

The Automobile Industry in the Early Twentieth Century

The history of the automobile industry is one of the great, dramatic, success stories of American industrial life. The industry's rapid rise from the intimacy of the inventor's shop, with its seemingly impractical although intriguing product, to the smoothly running efficiency and modernity of the automobile factory, with its seemingly essential product, caught the imagination of the country and the world. Both the gleaming product and the mechanized assembly lines that produced it became symbols of American affluence and American technological advancement, stirring envy and admiration in cities as diverse at Buenos Aires, Moscow, and Manchester. By the 1920s, foreign visitors to the United States who wanted to see firsthand the meaning of America for the modern world, gave a perfunctory wave to the Statue of Liberty and eagerly pushed on to Detroit where Henry Ford's new Rouge factory demonstrated American technological genious magically creating the product that the world admired. Nineteenth-century England had drawn those who wanted to see the industrial revolution in concentrated form to the factories of Manchester; twentieth-century United States drew similar pilgrims to Detroit for a distilled experience of the modern. In both the cars and trucks moving off the final assembly line and onto the growing network of streets and roads and in that assembly line itself, much of modern life could be summarized.[1]

1

Measured by size alone, the importance of the auto industry stands out. By 1925, it was the largest industry in the nation. But its significance goes far beyond the number of vehicles produced, wage earners employed, or profits amassed. The automobile industry had a far-reaching influence upon the entire industrial, geographic, and social development of the twentieth-century United States. It stimulated the growth of numerous other industries; it influenced the particular pattern of urban growth in the United States; it became a model of productive and managerial organization; its activities became a chief indicator of the health or sickness of the American economy as a whole.[2]

Economists Paul Baran and Paul Sweezy have termed the automobile an "epoch-making" invention; that is, an invention which has the effect of changing the complexion of economic activity and creating outlets for investment capital far beyond any capital directly invested in the production of the invention itself. The automobile industry was responsible for growth in the glass, rubber, paint, metals, and machinery industries. In addition, it was the major reason for expansion of the petroleum industry and associated industries, such as oil pipes. Filling and service stations accompanied the movement of automobiles across the country. Road construction opened a whole new pattern of living and working that stimulated the urbanization of the United States, simultaneously creating suburban residential areas separating the arena of work from that of living for many Americans. The industrial health of the United States in the 1920s was centered around the automobile and its attendant industries from petroleum to construction.[3]

Much that is taken for granted in production and marketing techniques was associated historically with the automobile industry. Mass production, with its large scale production of identical items, interchangeable parts, and sequentially ordered moving assembly lines, was symbolized for the world by Henry Ford's Model T. Consumer financing, product obsolescence, and stimulation of desire for the newest model through advertising, all were features of the automobile industry by the mid-1920s.[4]

Automobile workers themselves received much less attention from an admiring public than did the products they made, the factories they worked in, and some of their more dramatic employers, Henry Ford chief among them. Where they were noticed, the reality of auto workers' lives was often transformed into myth. In employers' literature, automobile workers were highly paid, highly satisfied harbingers of a new industrial era of peaceful labor relations. To those few—mostly socialists—who dared to criticize the quality of this new industrial era, auto workers were robots, dehumanized zombies stripped of their freedom and wills, simple cogs in the automobile factories' carefully engineered machinery. The history of the men who made automobiles is the subject of this book; some knowledge of their historical setting in the industry's development is a necessary introduction to the workers themselves.[5]

The automobile changed rapidly from an inventor's toy to a product suitable only for those wealthy enough to indulge in an expensive fad, to a mass-produced product geared to a mass-consuming public. The development and growth of the automobile industry took place during those early decades of the twentieth century during which the United States has been judged to have lost its innocence and moved reluctantly into a more modern, complex, and increasingly technologically oriented world. The ability of the auto industry to turn an invention into a highly profitable product and to do so by means of highly efficient machine production attempting to make human labor as planned and orderly as the machines themselves, came to stand for changes in modern America both heralded and feared.[6]

The story begins in 1897. Previously, only a few automobiles had been produced in the United States. In 1897, the Pope Manufacturing Company put Columbia electrics as well as a few gasoline cars on the market; the Stanleys began commercial production of steamers; Ransom Olds and Alexander Winton formed companies to manufacture gasoline engine automobiles. From that time until 1929, the auto industry's record was one of the almost continuous growth in the number of vehicles produced and in the number of workers employed.[7] (See Table I-1.)

Alfred Chandler has suggested a three-stage approach to the early history of the automobile industry. The first decade of auto history was one of experimentation, slow but steady growth, and many small producers who managed to launch companies with little capital and experience. The chief problems to be mastered were those of automobile design itself. Proponents of steam-, electric-, and gasoline-powered vehicles competed in the marketplace and in the shops to perfect the automobile engine's technology. The early automobile manufacturers were primarily assemblers of automobiles: putting together the finished product from parts and components bought from outside suppliers.[8]

The second stage of auto industry history began in approximately 1908, the year in which William Durant formed the General Motors

TABLE I-1
Growth of the Motor Vehicle Industry

Year	Number of Establishments	Number of Motor Vehicles Registered	Number of Motor Vehicles Made	Number of Wage Earners	Total Wages Paid (in Dollars)
1899	57	8,000*	3,723	2,241	$ 1,320,658
1904	178	55,290	22,830	12,049	7,158,958
1909	743	312,000	127,287	75,721	48,693,867
1914	1,271	1,763,018	573,039	127,092	101,926,874
1919	2,830	7,576,888	1,934,000	343,115	491,121,373
1921	2,359	10,483,666	1,683,916	212,777	318,752,665
1923	2,471	15,102,105	4,034,012	404,886	659,877,336
1925	1,655	20,068,543	4,265,830	426,110	713,931,334
1927	1,477	23,303,470	3,401,326	369,399	612,955,061
1929	1,398	26,704,825	5,358,420	447,448	733,082,618
1931	1,118	26,093,968	2,389,738	285,515	350,526,346
1933	823	24,159,203	1,920,057	243,614	252,106,467
1935	946	26,526,126	3,946,934	387,801	545,414,168

* 1900.

Figures compiled from: U.S. Department of Commerce, Bureau of the Census, *Census of Manufactures: 1914, 1929, 1939* (Washington: U.S. Government Printing Office); U.S. Congress, *Report on Motor Vehicle Industry*, House Document No. 468, 76th Congress, 1st Session, 1939 (Washington: U.S. Government Printing Office); Alfred D. Chandler, Jr., *Giant Enterprise: Ford, General Motors, and the Automobile Industry* (New York: Harcourt, Brace and World, 1964), pp. 3–4.

Corporation and in which Henry Ford first began to produce the Model T. The auto industry produced 65,000 vehicles in 1908; 126,000 in 1909. The rise of the automobile industry can be seen in its own figures of growth and also in those of decline in the carriage industry. The peak year for the carriage industry was 1909; each year following brought a steady decline in the value of products of the carriage manufacturers. Some carriage makers were successful in converting to automobile manufacturing; others turned to building bodies for the auto industry; still others simply went out of business with many of their workers going into the new automobile factories. In addition, several parts suppliers for the carriage industry directed their efforts to supplying the auto industry.[9]

Before 1908, the market for automobiles was limited to the wealthy few who could afford the initial high prices plus the continuous upkeep of generally unreliable machines. In addition, the lack of adequate roads contributed to the nature of the automobile as a luxury item since it could not be depended on for general transportation. Many trips were simply impossible due to the lack of connecting roads. One of the great advantages of the Model T was its ability to manage "unimproved" country roads. With the advent of the Model T, the market for a cheap, sturdy vehicle within the means of farmers and working men became clear, and the possibility of selling large numbers of automobiles became a stimulus to expansion of the industry.[10]

The importance of the Model T to the growth of the industry was enormous. It changed the automobile from an item of luxury consumption for the wealthy to one which might be widely purchased by ordinary people. Producing for a mass market, the concomitant price reductions, and the attendant development of assembly lines and interchangeable parts were the decisive developments in the automobile industry before the 1920s. That automobiles became genuinely popular articles between 1910 and 1920 is clear in the following figures. In 1910, one car was found for every 19,000 persons in the United States; by 1920, one for every 11 persons; by 1930, one for every 4.5 persons.[11]

Even the Model T, however, needed better roads if automobile ownership was to expand and encompass long-distance travel. Leaders in the automobile industry soon understood the necessity of improving and expanding the highway system. They threw their weight behind the Good Roads Association and Carl Fisher's Lincoln Highway Association; they successfully lobbied for a gasoline tax and for the Federal Road Aid Act of 1916 and the Federal Highway Act of

1921. From 1910 to 1920, the mileage of surfaced roads increased by 81%, from 1920 to 1930 by 88%, and from 1930 to 1940 by 97%.[12]

During this second stage of auto industry history, from 1908 until just after World War I, the chief challenge facing the auto manufacturers was how to produce more and more cars at lower and lower costs per unit. As producton moved into the assembly-line characteristics of modern mass production, manufacturers sought to lower the cost of each automobile by increasing production as much as possible. Efficiency thus became the great goal and a necessity for remaining in an industry that had become extremely competitive and marked by a large number of failures each year.[13]

By the 1920s, the greatest challenge in the industry was no longer production, but competitive marketing. The industry entered into its third phase by recognizing that the public had already been persuaded to buy its first car; it now had to be persuaded to abandon that car and buy a new one. By 1924, most people who were going to do so had already bought their first cars. Sales had achieved a steady level of 3.5 million cars a year, a level which was not permanently exceeded until after World War II. Body design, differentiation of product to provide for different tastes and budgets, annual model changes, mass advertising, and consumer financing became weapons in the competitive marketing battles of the 1920s.[14]

Two forms of concentration, one geographic and one economic, also came to characterize the industry in the early twentieth century. Automobile production quickly became centered in the Midwest, particularly in Michigan. (See Table I-2.) Early automobiles were also produced in New England and New York, so the increasing concentration of the industry in Michigan (more than 50% of all auto workers in the country worked in Michigan from 1914 on) requires some explanation.

Michigan had long been the center of the nation's carriage and wagon industry and many wagon plants were converted to the manufacture of automobile bodies once the auto industry took off. Michigan also boasted a thriving industry in marine engines whose skilled production workers were well prepared to build automobile engines. Natural resources in iron, copper, steel, coal, and timber were adequate in the surrounding territory, and, by a quirk of history, the inventive human resources of several early automobile inventors were also concentrated in the state. These resources combined to give the state the needed momentum; once a small concentration was achieved, the presence of the industry tended to be enough to

TABLE I–2
Concentration of Automobile Industry in Michigan

Year	Average Number of U.S. Auto Workers	Average Number of Michigan Auto Workers	Percentage in Michigan
1904	12,049	2,735	22.7
1909	75,721	25,444	33.6
1914	127,092	67,538	53.1
1919	343,115	175,985	51.3
1927	369,399	209,458	56.7
1929	447,448	214,368	47.9
1935	387,801	238,845	61.6

Figures compiled from: U.S. Department of Commerce, Bureau of the Census, *Census of Manufactures, 1914, 1929, 1935* (Washington: U.S. Government Printing Office).

draw an increasingly larger presence. In addition, Detroit employers were firmly committed to the concept of Detroit as an open shop city, a commitment that was institutionalized by 1902 in the form of the well-organized and effective Employers' Association of Detroit.[15]

Not only was the industry geographically concentrated, it was economically concentrated as well. A clear pattern emerged early as fewer and fewer firms produced more and more automobiles, either due to the failure of some companies in the early years or due to purchases and consolidations. (See Table I–3.) The concentration of the industry in the hands of a few giant corporations had increased so much by 1935 that the big three auto makers controlled 90% of all sales. Such concentration was a condition of productive life conducive to high profits, continued technological development, and the ability to absorb fairly high wages for low-skilled workers.[16]

The first three and one-half decades of auto industry history produced an industry whose basic characteristics were certain to have an impact upon the workers in the industry. The industry's ongoing growth combined with its Midwest concentration created a continuous work opportunity and gathered auto workers in large factories in one part of the country. The great success of the industry made it at least possible that high wages would become associated with it. The particular advances in production technique that spelled out

TABLE I–3
Percentage of Passenger Motor Vehicles Sold by Different Manufacturers

Year	Chrysler, Ford, General Motors	Hudson, Packard, Nash, Studebaker	Total	All Others
1911	37.74	15.34	53.08	46.92
1913	51.61	9.52	61.13	38.87
1915	46.11	6.48	55.59	44.41
1917	53.65	4.32	57.97	42.03
1919	60.85	6.46	67.31	32.69
1921	68.40	7.93	76.33	23.67
1923	66.28	8.51	74.79	25.21
1925	63.59	13.79	77.38	22.61
1927	59.03	18.80	77.83	22.17
1929	71.79	12.28	84.07	15.93
1931	81.16	8.15	89.31	10.69
1933	87.54	6.66	94.20	5.80
1935	90.01	7.33	97.34	2.66

Figures compiled from: Alfred D. Chandler, Jr., *Giant Enterprise: Ford, General Motors, and the Automobile Industry* (New York: Harcourt, Brace and World, 1964), p. 3. The inclusion of Chrysler is from 1925.

the contours of mass production helped determine the specific tasks for which workers were employed, as well as the work rules and work atmosphere in which they worked. Detroit's growth as an auto-associated city placed many auto workers within a specific urban and labor relations context that gave shape to workers' lives both on and off the job. The industry's history provided a setting of change, success, and growth—a setting within which auto workers lived a complex pattern of experiences characterized by hope and despair, acceptance and rebellion.

Chapter Two

The Auto Workers

They came from Mississippi and Arkansas, from Poland and Italy, from Indiana and West Virginia, and from the heart of Detroit itself. They were white, black, foreign, native, young, old, male, and female. But in the main, they were young and male, limited in industrial skills and eager for a good paying job. Auto workers were a diverse lot, and their diversity is as crucial to understanding the nonunion years of auto history as their common working circumstances. A few capsule biographies may help give individual form to the aggregate statistics to follow.

Andrew Montgomery was born on a farm in Jonesboro, Arkansas. He lived and worked on the farm as a child; as a young man, he worked in a paper box factory in Jonesboro, went on to drive a truck, work in an Arkansas factory compressing cotton, be a fireman, a watchman, and a night engineer for a West Memphis power company. In 1926, he was nineteen and a newcomer to Pontiac, Michigan, were he joined the assembly line at the Pontiac Motor Company, putting on splash aprons and hood shields and beginning to move around the factory to various parts of the process of assembling an automobile from polishing metal to installing oil pumps. Finally heading for the big city, he rode a freight train to Detroit, arrived with six dollars in his pocket, and headed for another auto job.[1]

Everett Francis was born in 1901 in Jay County, Indiana. His father worked in the oil fields, and the family moved around Indiana and Ohio until, when young Everett was ten years old, his parents separated and he was placed in a county children's home for five years. As a teenager, he moved to Detroit to live with his mother. He was seventeen years old when he started to work at the Dodge plant in Hamtramck. It was his first job. He left Dodge and worked for a while in small machine shop; by 1923, he was back in the auto industry working successively for Murray Body, the Budd Manufacturing Company, and Fisher Body in Flint, working mainly in the paint and trim shops. He was an avid newspaper reader. In 1930, he participated in a short strike at Fisher Body, and in 1933, he helped to form an American Federation of Labor federal local.[2]

Bud Simons grew up in southern Indiana, the son of a tenant farmer, and he moved to South Bend in 1924. Before starting work in the auto industry he had worked on a farm, in a furniture factory, on the railroad, in telegraph construction, as a structural steel erector, and as a plasterer. In the auto industry, he was a disc grinder, torch solderer, and worked the body shops, working as an auto garage mechanic as a sideline. He played a vital role in the Flint sit-down strike of 1937.[3]

Fred Haggard was born in Liberty, Missouri, and worked on the railroads and in the candy business before starting at Fisher Body in Pontiac in 1926. His railroad experience led him into a Railroad Brotherhood union. In the auto industry, he was a metal finisher, worked in the paint shop, and worked a punch press in the machine shop. An early union advocate, he was blackballed in 1929 for union activity.[4]

Stanley Nowak was born in Poland in 1903. He came to the United States with his family when he was ten and lived in Chicago where his father and brother worked in the stockyards and were involved in a strike that left a vivid impression on the boy. He first worked in the clothing industry where he became a member of the Amalgamated Clothing Workers. He began work in the auto industry under the inauspicious conditions of the depression in 1932, in the parts shop.[5]

Nick Di Gaetano was born in southern Italy and came to the United States in 1909 at age fifteen. He worked around in nickel plating plants and went to Chrysler Corporation in 1928 as a metal polisher. A lifelong interest in politics and a commitment to social change led him into the Italian Socialist Federation, the Industrial Workers of the World, and even into the metal polishers union of the American Federation of Labor.[6]

Shelton Tappes, a black man, was born in Omaha, Nebraska, in 1911. A bright youth, he earned a scholarship to the University of Nebraska, which he attended for one year. In 1927, he moved to Saginaw, Michigan, where his father worked in the foundry at Chevrolet. The following year, young Shelton moved to Detroit and began his own career in the auto industry at the Briggs Mack Avenue plant. He worked as a molder, a spray painter, and in wet sanding; he later took an active role in the young United Automobile Workers.[7]

Another black auto worker, Joseph Billups, was born in Billups, Mississippi, in 1893. After farming in Mississippi, at age eighteen, he headed for New York where he worked at the New York Central Roundhouse. After a few years, he tried life in Mississippi again, but found he "wasn't able to stay there. The people didn't want me there—they said I had been away and would spoil the rest of the people, telling them about the North. So I left there and came north, to Detroit." In Detroit, he worked in several foundries before getting a job at Ford in Highland Park. His commitment to racial equality and working-class justice led him to the Industrial Workers of the World, the Communist Party, and the Auto Workers Union.[8]

Finally, Hodges Mason, another black auto worker, came from Atlanta, Georgia, to Detroit after working as a hotel porter, a roofer, and a warehouseman in the South. He began work in the auto industry in 1928, in the typical place for black men, the foundry. In 1944, he was elected president of the United Auto Workers local at Bohn Aluminum.[9]

Before the big productive upsurge that began in 1908, the auto industry employed mainly native-born Americans from the Midwest with a scattering of British and German craftsmen as well. While craftsmen's skills were still valued in automobile manufacture, skilled workers left the declining carriage and wagon manufacturing companies and moved into the auto plants. The bodies of early automobiles were not so different from carriages, and the same skills could serve both industries. Painters, carpenters, and turners flowed into auto factories. Michigan furniture workers applied their skills as upholsterers and woodworkers to the making of automobiles. Machinists and metal craftsmen from the Great Lakes-area machine shops moved into the auto shops. Builders of marine engines took jobs as builders of automobile engines. Common laborers from the farms, small towns, and declining mining areas of the Great Lakes region also hastened to the new auto factories.

The rapid expansion of automobile production after 1908, coupled with changes in the productive process that eliminated the need for many skilled machinists and craftsmen, meant that the industry needed and was available to more and different kinds of workers. For a few years after 1908, Detroit industrialists perceived a labor shortage in the city and competed intensely with each other. Through competitive advertising, they sought to steal workers away from one company and into another. To combat the destructive chaos of competition for labor, automobile industry leaders joined forces to form the Employers' Association of Detroit. As the Employers' Association saw it,

> The modest little liner had become almost obsolete, and column after column of flaring display advertisements appeared, each trying to outbid the other in its noisy call for help. Hardly had a good man been established in one shop before he was attracted by a call from another, and as soon as he had landed there new attractions were offered in some other plant. Every Monday, following the big Sunday editions, department foremen were at their wits' ends in replenishing their ranks which had been despoiled by neighboring establishments.[10]

The auto industrialists agreed that they could do more to secure their labor needs through cooperation than they could by outbidding each other for labor. They pledged to stop their competitive advertising and instead work together to attract a larger pool of workers to Detroit. To this end, the Employers' Association organized a coordinated campaign using copious advertisements and corps of agents to spread the word throughout Michigan and its surrounding states that jobs were plentiful and desirable in Detroit. In 1910, Employers' Association newspaper advertisements appeared in more than 190 cities outside of Detroit and netted an estimated 20,000 workers new to the city during the year.[11]

Many of these workers were relatively transient members of the auto industrial work force. Unlike their predecessors, they possessed few craft or industrial skills. They came to the cities and automotive jobs when labor was scarce and returned to the farms when bad years came. An auto worker at the Norwood, Ohio General Motors plant explained that rural workers could always "go back home and live off of Mom and Dad and off of the land; we didn't have anything in the city." Many hoped to acquire in the auto factories a bankroll which they could then take elsewhere and did not look on themselves as permanent industrial workers. They saw the auto industry as a place to acquire the funds to do what they really wanted—establish a small business or farm. Looking at the limited opportunities for capital accumulation offered by small town jobs, they saw the auto industry as hope for a new future. A letter from one auto worker's wife to Mrs. Henry Ford chronicled a familiar history. "Work was scarce in our hometown and what work he could get did not pay only enough for a bare living. . . . So my husband went to Detroit to look for work."[12]

But native midwesterners were only part of the solution to the labor needs of the auto industry. Coincidental with expansion in the industry and with the development of productive techniques that stressed willingness to work more than specific abilities and skills, immigrant workers from southern and eastern Europe flocked to Detroit in numbers that caused one contemporary observer to deem them an "immigrant invasion." Many of the immigrants saw themselves as no more permanent than midwestern farm workers. This peasant proletariat sought to make a living and accumulate enough to move on, but the high wages of the auto industry, its growing need for workers, their own swelling ranks, and World War I combined to make many immigrants permanent residents and permanent auto workers.[13]

The Employers' Association courted the immigrants in the same way they did the midwesterners. By 1912, the Employers' Association of Detroit joined with the Detroit Board of Commerce to sponsor an immigration commissioner at Ellis Island empowered to provide transportation costs to newly arrived immigrants willing to locate in Detroit. Agents sought out arriving immigrants and immigrant communities in other cities to attract workers to Detroit. Once the immigrant stream deposited enough members of any particular ethnic community in Detroit, that mass and the community it fostered attracted friends, relatives, and fellow countrypeople. The immigrants already there became their own best advertisement for Detroit and its auto factories.[14]

As the labor shortage eased, Henry Ford added another brick to the auto industry edifice that made auto jobs sought after and prized. With his January 1914 announcement of his intention to pay his workers $5 per day, high wages became a new lure, adding to the number of jobs to keep workers moving within the orbit of the auto manufacturers. While at first it was Ford alone, by the 1920s, high wages were established as a dominant feature of the auto industry's ability to attract and hold industrial workers. The magic of the Ford promise was so great that the number of workers answering the call far exceeded Ford's needs and created a genuine oversupply of workers that seriously alarmed the small group of organized workers in Detroit. In December 1914, the *Detroit Labor News*, the organ of the Detroit Federation of Labor, expressed its concern that,

The five-dollar-a-day advertisement which Detroit got has made
this city the mecca for tens of thousands of wage workers who have
found life hard in other cities. They come and they come to this
city only to find many who were here before them, many of them
long years before the automobile industry was even thought of, out
of work.[15]

At various times during 1914, the *Detroit Labor News* advised workers
to stay out of Detroit and not be misled into thinking that a surplus
of jobs existed when the surplus was actually in workers, not jobs.[16]

The third and final group of workers in the auto industry labor
force came into the industry as a result of the conditions created
by World War I. As the fighting in Europe cut off the flow of foreign
workers to the United States, Detroit began to attract increasing
numbers of southerners, both white and black, looking to fill jobs
in the auto industry. Agents sent south by the auto companies, as
well as by the Detroit Employers' Association, began to attract
workers from the deep South and the border states. Labor recruiters
were paid according to the number of men they could supply; this
system led to an oversupply of workers when the war and the
immediate postwar boom ended.[17]

Thus, auto workers as a population can be divided into three
main groups: white, native-born workers; black, native-born workers;
and foreign-born workers. To do so ignores certain important distinctions. Native-born whites include both northerners and southerners, rural and city backgrounds, skilled and unskilled workers.
Foreign-born workers puts second generation ethnic workers into the
white native-born category, whereas they are truly an intermediate
group and probably more closely identified with their parent's ethnicity than with native-born Americans. Nonetheless, the three-group
categorization is useful, providing a way of studying the auto workers
that detects certain time periods with a preponderance of certain
kinds of workers. Table II–1 provides the statistics for these three
groups for 1920 and 1930. Statistics later in the chapter for Detroit
and for the Ford Motor Company provide a longer timeline.

Before 1910, the new workers were native-born whites, new to
the industry but not to the country or the region; from 1910 to
1920, the new workers were foreign-born immigrants, new both to
industrial life and to the country; from 1920 to 1930, the new workers
were native-born blacks, new to the industry and the region. Thus,
the presence of distinctive newcomers in particular decades provides

TABLE II-1
Auto Workers' National Origin and Race, 1920–1930

Year	Total	Native-Born White	Percentage	Foreign-Born White	Percentage	Black	Percentage
1920	204,505	122,817	60.6	73,362	35.9	8,156	4.0
1930	285,674	176,639	61.4	86,435	30.3	19,705	6.9
1930 (Detroit)	93,159	38,083	40.8	40,340	43.3	13,032	13.9

Figures for operatives and laborers in: U.S. Department of Commerce, Bureau of the Census, *Fourteenth Census of the United States, 1920, Population*, IV (Washington: U.S. Government Printing Office, 1923), pp. 346–349; *Fifteenth Census of the United States, 1930, Population*, IV, pp. 27–29, 803.

one focal point for auto worker history while the continuity of native-born white workers provides another.

Despite the interruption in new immigration World War I caused, the immigrant population continued to be a large portion of the auto worker population into the 1920s; but the number of recently arrived immigrants was cut drastically during and after the war. The information on immigrant workers is most complete for the Ford Motor Company. In 1914, Ford reported to the *New York Times* that 70.7% of his 12,880 workers were foreign born. The five largest nationality groups employed were Poles, Russians, Rumanians, Italians, and Austro-Hungarians. The *New York Times* report combined with Ford's 1917 and 1920 records provide the ethnic backgrounds tabulated in Table II–2.

One way of estimating demographic changes in the Detroit auto worker population is to examine Detroit's general population statistics. These figures reveal a population undergoing clear changes in ethnic and racial composition. Table II–3 summarizes the important trends in race and ethnicity from 1910 to 1930. White Detroiters of foreign stock (foreign born or at least one foreign born parent) comprised 74% of the city's population in 1910; in 1920, they were 85%; by 1930, they were 55.6%. At the same time that an overall decline occurred in the foreign population from 1910 to 1930, an increase in the black population occurred from 1.2% in 1910 to 7.7% in 1930. These shifts are all in the same direction as those shown in Table II–1 for United States auto factory operatives and laborers. Within the foreign stock population, a shift can be detected from 1910 to 1930 in the specific ethnic background toward a heavier representation of the newer immigrant groups from Poland, Austria, Russia, and Italy surpassing the older groups from Britain, Ireland, and Germany.[18] These statistics are presented in Table II–4.

Whereas old immigrants made up 75% of the Detroit population of foreign stock in 1910, they were only 52.4% in 1930. Thus, the proportion of predominantly southern and eastern Europeans in the foreign-stock population increased from 25% in 1910 to 47.6% in 1930. This shift would have been even more pronounced within the auto factories, since old immigrants were more likely to be skilled workers or moving out of the working class and less likely to be working in auto plants.

This heavy influx of non-English speaking workers to the United States stimulated a nationwide response in the form of programs to "Americanize" the immigrants and make them decent citizens. Detroit was no exception to the national desire to make good, English-

TABLE II-2
Ethnic Origins of Ford Workers, 1914, 1917, and 1920

Ethnicity	1914 Total	1914 Percentage	1917 Total	1917 Percentage	1920 Total	1920 Percentage
American	3,773	29.3	16,457	40.2	30,251	52.9
English	380	3.0	1,159	2.8	1,401	2.5
German	606	4.7	1,360	3.3	–	–
Polish	2,677	20.8	7,525	18.4	6,117	10.7
Austrian	388	3.0	–	–	1,814	3.2
Russian	2,016	15.7	1,160	2.8	1,181	2.1
Rumanian	750	5.8	1,750	4.3	–	–
Italian	690	5.4	1,954	4.8	2,409	4.2
Canadian	226	1.8	1,809	4.4	2,312	4.0
Jewish*	–	–	1,437	3.5	–	–
Black	–	–	–	–	1,675	2.9
Other**	1,374	10.7	6,292	15.4	10,000	17.5
TOTAL	12,880	100.0	40,903	100.0	57,160	100.0

*It was probably Ford policy not to hire Jews unless they were needed to fill a labor shortage. "At that time there was a general policy against hiring Jews. It was all verbal. It came from Martin and Sorensen. I never heard Ford say that, but we knew it was he who did not want them in the shop." (The Reminiscences of W. C. Klann, p. 143, Oral History Section, FMCA.)

**"Other" is a very mixed category with no single nationality having more than 800 members.

1914 figures in: "Automobile Trade Notes", *New York Times*, November 15, 1914. Total figure from Allen Nevins, *Ford: The Times, The Man, The Company* (New York: Scribners, 1954), p. 648. American figure is my calculation, subtracting foreign-born from total; 1917 figures in: accession 572 box 27, FMCA; 1920 figures in: J. Herkel, Employment Department, to F. Dolson, September 16, 1920, accession 284, box 10, FMCA.

TABLE II-3
Detroit Population, 1910–1930

		1910		1920		1930	
		Population	Percentage	Population	Percentage	Population	Percentage
Total population		465,766	100.0	993,678	100.0	1,568,662	100.0
Total white Foreign stock		344,820	74.0	638,068	85.0	908,605	55.6
Total white Foreign born		156,565	33.6	289,297	29.1	399,281	25.7
Total white native		303,361	65.1	662,768	66.7	1,040,860	66.5
Total black		5,741	1.2	40,838	4.1	120,066	7.7
MAJOR ETHNIC GROUPS							
England	Nativity	9,038	1.9	17,195	1.8	56,966	3.6
	stock	20,115	4.4	37,897	3.8	57,452	4.9
Scotland	Nativity	3,320	.7	6,933	.7		
	stock	6,872	1.5	13,676	1.4	36,323	2.3
Germany	Nativity	44,675	10.0	30,238	3.0	32,716	2.1
	stock	124,531	32.1	134,232	13.4	126,715	8.1
Poland	Nativity			56,624	5.7	66,113	4.2
	stock	43,000	9.3	88,624	8.9	171,804	11.0

Austria	Nativity	14,160	2.9	10,674	1.1	5,898	.5
	stock	11,796	2.6	28,069	2.8	14,889	1.0
Russia	Nativity	18,644	4.0	27,278	2.7	21,781	1.4
	stock	12,339	2.7	55,879	5.6	45,823	2.9
Rumania	Nativity	313	.1	4,668	.5	7,576	.5
	stock	444	.1	6,277	.6	13,254	.9
Italy	Nativity	5,724	1.2	16,205	1.6	28,581	1.8
	stock	8,478	1.8	29,971	2.3	61,968	5.3
Canada	Nativity	42,814	9.9	59,702	6.0	94,284	6.0
	stock	77,001	16.4	120,109	12.0	174,620	11.2

Figures from: U.S. Department of Commerce Bureau of the Census, *Abstract of the Thirteenth Census of the United States, 1910* (Washington: U.S. Government Printing Office), pp. 95, 210; *Abstract of the Fourteenth Census of the United States, 1920*, pp. 108–109, 312–315; *Abstract of the Fifteenth Census of the United States, 1930*, pp. 98–99, 150–151; Albert Mayer, "A Study of the Foreign-Born Population of Detroit 1870–1950" (Department of Sociology and Anthropology, Wayne University, 1951), pp. 16, 18, 20. (Census is *nativity* and Mayer is *stock*.)

TABLE II–4
Percentage of Detroit Foreign Stock and Foreign-Born Belonging to Old and New Immigrant Groups*

Year	Percentage of Foreign Stock		Percentage of Foreign Born	
	Old	New	Old	New
1910	75.0	25.0	61.5	38.5
1920	57.1	42.9	45.8	54.2
1930	52.4	47.6	52.2	47.8

*Old immigrant groups include those from: England, Scotland, Ireland, Norway, Sweden, Denmark, Netherlands, Belgium, France, Germany, and Canada. New immigrant groups include those from: Poland, Czechoslovakia, Austria, Hungary, Yugoslavia, Russia, Lithuania, Finland, Rumania, Greece, Italy, Palestine and Syria, and Mexico.

Figures in this table summarize those in Table II–3 and additional ethnic groups from Albert Mayer, "A Study of the Foreign-Born Population of Detroit 1870–1950" (Department of Sociology and Anthropology, Wayne University, 1951), pp. 16, 18, 20.

speaking citizens with northern European habits, out of its immigrant population. Here, the desire of auto manufacturers to produce factory-disciplined workers and of city fathers to create law-abiding citizens knowing in the ways of American democracy merged in the Americanization campaign. In a report prepared for the Detroit Board of Commerce, Raymond Cole indicated his perception of the dangers of leaving the immigrant population uneducated in American ways.

> The immigrant races in Detroit have in many cases formed colonies taking, like an invading army, section after section of the city exclusively for themselves. They have been allowed to settle according to racial lines and come in contact with the least successful class of Americans. In these districts—cities within a city—many of the old foreign customs are still observed and the traditions and prejudices of centuries are perpetuated.[19]

The Detroit Board of Commerce launched a campaign to establish night schools for immigrants where they could learn English, principles of American government, and good citizenship and to pressure immigants to apply for citizenship as quickly as possible.[20]

Finding in 1914 and 1915 that 61% of all the unemployed applying to the Employers' Association's Labor Bureau could not speak English, the Board of Commerce prepared for a massive effort to promote the English language. Not only should it provide night schools for the city's foreign population, but it should also encourage the auto companies to establish their own schools and Americanization programs, bringing pressure to bear on their employees either to cooperate or risk losing their jobs. The Board of Commerce recommended that Detroit employers inform job applicants that, "There is no place in our factory, in Detroit, or in this country, for men who are not trying to learn our language, and become good, useful citizens."[21]

The auto companies brought pressures to bear on their employees to participate in the Americanization campaigns. Some companies made attending night school compulsory; others required employees to attend company-sponsored schools after work hours. The Reo Motor Car Company made its employees sign a statement of good intentions, stating that they wanted to become American citizens, adopt American customs, and obey American laws. Packard announced in 1916 that, although it would hire workers who were not American citizens, it would limit "promotions to positions of importance . . . to those who are native born or naturalized American citizens, or to those of foreign birth who have filed with our Government their first papers applying for citizenship." Attendance at the Ford English School was compulsory for employees who wanted to keep their jobs. Lessons consisted of instruction in the English language, which was also designed to impart training in good health habits, factory safety, obedience to rules, American government, and the way to apply for citizenship papers. As late as 1927, one investigator found that at least 50% of all auto manufacturers required that their employees have first citizenship papers or naturalization papers as conditions of employment.[22]

One might suppose that employers would have thought it an advantage to have a work force divided by language. There is little evidence of such thinking in the auto industry at this time. Perhaps the threat of united worker organization seemed so slight that employers saw no need for special advantages.

Employers could stress Americanization and still hold certain jobs for native-born workers and others for foreigners. Widely held beliefs about racial and ethnic suitability for certain kinds of work made such distinctions likely and many native workers insisted on it also. One of Ford's workers objected to being assigned to "the pick and shovel crew." Asserting he was "not above it" and "no slacker when it comes to work," his objection was to the indignity of finding himself in a "crew of Italians and other Foreign races . . . the lone white man." "My record," he complained, ". . . is one hundred percent good. I have had no quarrel with anyone, only I surely feel that I am entitled to something better."[23]

As long as the industry offered few distinctions based on skill, education, or workmanship; ethnic background, skin color, and regional origin were likely to become distinguishing marks. World War I exacerbated this tendency. As government and industry propaganda alike urged workers to look out for slackers and saboteurs, to be suspicious of the patriotism of the foreign born, and even expect treachery; native workers had their worst prejudices confirmed and encouraged. After the war, resentment lingered and took the form of feeling that auto jobs ought to be reserved for the native born, sometimes even the natives of a particular city. One worker complained of his layoff in a letter to the Hudson Motor Company:

> I have always been a patriotic American citizen, working for my Country in any emergency. I went to Madrid, Spain, at the time of the Spanish-American War, and did my "bit" during the recent war. Among the watchmen who were not relieved from duty is one who is a German, who has been in America only a few years. Another watchman is a man who until recently lived in Chicago; there is another watchman, a former shoemaker, from some place in Illinois. I was born and raised in Detroit and lived there practically all my life. It is indeed a great disappointment to me to be laid off at this time, and I feel under the circumstances, if the matter is called to your personal attention, you may make an effort to right what appears to me to be an injustice.[24]

Rather than divide their employees further, employers used Americanization to educate into industrial work habits and factory discipline workers whose previous experience was preindustrial. The material used to teach workers to read English was usually a story illustrating the importance of arriving on time, following orders, keeping clean, and working hard. In an era when even English-speaking school children learned to read through moralistic precepts and patriotic sayings, it is not surprising that the method was transposed to factory workers. Why teach English alone, if it could also establish the association that certain work habits went along with being a good American.[25]

Examining the nationalities present in one of Ford's English classes in 1916 provides another indication of the ethnic makeup of the auto plants. One class of 518 was comprised of 163 Poles, 134

Russians, 46 Austrians, 28 Italians, 23 Hungarians, 20 Germans, 16 Rumanians, 13 Jews, 11 Bohemians, and other small groups making a total of 28 different nationalities in the class.[26]

That the Ford Motor Company took English training seriously is indicated by the pride it took in the growing competence of its employees in the English language. In just three years, between 1914 and 1917, the percentage of English-speaking employees rose from 59% to 88%. Ford also published testimonials to the importance of English designed to encourage others to learn and to demonstrate the language mastery, not to mention proper attitudes, of English School graduates. One graduate, identified only as a *Servian*, testified dutifully:

> School is a very good thing for our brethern [*sic*] because learning is always useful and instructive. I want to continue because without a knowledge of the English language I am handicapped. I want to become a citizen of the United States. Simply because I cannot talk English, I am often looked down upon; because when I go into an English store downtown, I cannot tell the clerk what I want. There are so many ways in which a knowledge of the English language would be helpful to me, and I appreciate what the Company is doing for me along this line.[27]

Considerable ceremony was attached to the Ford English School graduation. Some years, employees gathered in front of the Detroit City Hall on Americanization Day and joined in singing *America*. In 1918, a graduation ceremony featured a pageant in which foreign workers walked into a large pot where they were stirred by Ford teachers and emerged "Americans." Some of this no doubt represented wartime patriotic activity. Such patriotism, however, had longer aims and effects than the winning of World War I. To a significant extent, it served to delineate a proper industrial patriotism and work ethic, equating factory discipline with good citizenship.[28]

By the second half of the 1920s, employers' interest in Americanization lessened considerably. The number of non-English-speaking employees diminished, as did wartime interest in national security and national chauvinism. The need to train a preindustrial immigrant work force into the discipline of the factory lessened as immigration was curtailed. Southern blacks and whites could not be taught discipline as part of an English lesson, nor could they be manipulated by citizenship. By the mid-1920s, Henry Ford could comment,

Of course we prefer employees of American citizenship, as they usually are more loyal and more stable, and have a tendency to establish permanent homes. But we do not discriminate against non-citizens, as a rule feeling that the job of training or conducting a citizenship school, in order that they might become naturalized belongs to other authorities.[29]

The newcomers of World War I and the 1920s were a much smaller proportion of the auto industry work force than the immigrant workers had been. Nationwide, the number of black auto workers grew from .5% in 1910, to 4% in 1920, to 7% in 1930. In Detroit, however, 14% of all auto workers were black by 1930. Their experience was in some ways similar to the immigrant one, but it also had unique aspects.[30]

Black southerners were encouraged to fill the labor shortage created by World War I and the passage of restrictive immigration legislation in the 1920s in much the same way that earlier rural migrants had been induced to move to the Motor City. Employment agencies and automobile companies distributed advertisements with glowing accounts of conditions and wages in northern factories. Bus companies helped distribute leaflets urging blacks to use their services to take them to a better life. In addition, a burgeoning northern black press extolled the virtues of the North as the land of opportunity and freedom. The *Chicago Defender* was especially active in persuading southern blacks to migrate north, caustically observing, "To die from the bite of frost's far more glorious than at the hands of a mob."[31]

The Detroit Urban League was also active in recruiting black auto workers. The Urban League opened its doors in Detroit in 1916 and from the beginning served the function of an employment agency. Cooperation between the Urban League and the Detroit Employers' Association was very close. Until 1930, the salary of the Urban League's industrial secretary was paid by the Employers' Association, and the Urban League reciprocated by sending black workers to the Employers' Association's Labor Bureau to be placed in jobs. The Urban League also cooperated in the Employers' Association's campaign to bring black labor north by issuing public appeals, sending black agents to circulate in the South, and stationing an agent in Cincinnati to advise blacks arriving in that city to continue on to Detroit. Besides aiding in recruitment, the Urban League served the interests of the Employers' Association by instructing black workers in acceptable work habits, from proper clothing to suitable docility and antiunionism. Typical of the advice given black workers in factories during World War I is the following explanation, printed on a card and intended for factory bulletin boards, of "Why He Failed." It demonstrates that the lessons of "Americanization" could be taught also in an already American context.

> He did not report on time; He watched the clock; He loafed when the boss was not looking; He stayed out with the boys all night; He said, "I forgot;" He did not show up on Monday, and He wanted a holiday every Saturday; He lied when asked for the truth.[32]

One of the best sources of information about black Detroiters is a study commissioned by the Mayor's Inter-Racial Committee in 1925 and based on extensive interviews with members of 1,000 black households. This study found that the majority of blacks came to Detroit from western Georgia, western Alabama, and Tennessee. They had an average of six years of schooling obtained in the sporadic educational schedules of southern black schools. Although 9% had no schooling at all, another 8% had at least some high school. Most had worked as farmhands or unskilled laborers before coming north, and many had never before seen the inside of a factory, to say nothing of the work discipline of a company that ran by the clock with a rigid set of rules governing behavior on the job. The majority reported that they came to the North for its industrial opportunity and the chance to improve their financial situations.[33]

From the beginning, black workers were assigned to the lowest-skilled jobs in the auto industry. They were hired for jobs that had the lowest pay scales, required the greatest physical exertion, had the highest accident rates, and the largest number of health hazards. Some black workers were put in paint departments as sprayers and sanders or in maintenance departments as janitors. Shelton Tappes discovered that "wet sanding was the kind of work other workers would prefer not to do, if they didn't have to. It was extremely wet; you were vulnerable for colds, pneumonia, and all that sort of thing." A great many black workers were employed in foundry departments. Auto workers considered the foundry to be the most undesirable work place in the whole factory because of its noise, heat, and filth. Many plant managers expressed a belief in the superior ability of black workers to withstand extreme heat and to display superior stamina on particularly exhausting and difficult jobs. Black workers understood, however, that their main qualification for foundry work was the color of their skin. Finding themselves in the foundry was often their first disillusioning experience with northern equality. One black worker described his reactions after being told the only job openings were in the foundry and then seeing white workers hired for polishing and carpentry jobs.

> As I looked around, [the foundry], all the men were dirty and greasy and smoked up. They were beyond recognition. There were only three or four whites. These were Polish. Negroes told me later they were the only ones able to stand the work. Their faces looked exactly like Negro faces. They were so matted and covered with oil and dirt that no skin showed. My friend and I went home discussing how it was that they could say everyone was free with equal rights up North. There was no one in the foundry but Negroes. We didn't believe those men wanted to be in the foundry.[34]

The situation at the Ford Motor Company, particularly at the River Rouge plant in Dearborn, was somewhat different. Here a greater precentage of blacks found more desirable jobs, a few even becoming supervisors and, the most sought after and respected auto job, tool and die makers. "So far as I know," commented Willis Ward, a college-educated black athlete who worked for Ford as a personnel man for black workers, "there was nowhere on this planet that a colored man could aspire to and become a tool and die maker excepting Ford Motor Company." Although much was made at the time of the uniqueness of Ford, the bulk of black workers, between 60% and 70%, even at River Rouge, worked in the foundry. At Ford, there was only a greater possibility that a black worker might acquire skill and training and be promoted to skilled and supervisory positions. The River Rouge plant was the only one in the entire auto industry to employ blacks in all manufacturing operations, including the final assembly line. Admitting blacks into a few skilled positions at Ford was backed up by admitting a few black workers to the Ford Trade School, the Apprentice School, and the Ford Training School. The numbers were insignificant, but these schools provided practically the only places in Detroit where blacks could be trained as skilled workers.[35]

The black workers' experience at Ford was of more than passing significance since the River Rouge plant employed 10,000 black workers by the mid-1920s, 10% of its entire work force, more than one-half of all black auto workers in the country and about three-fourths of those in Detroit. One black pastor noted that any Ford layoffs for retooling would result in a decided decline in the collection receipts. Ford used several black churches and their ministers as employment agencies, hiring workers who came with a letter of recommendation from certain clergymen. In return, Ford provided contributions of coal to heat the churches during the winter.[36]

While immigrant workers entered the Ford work force at the height of Ford's paternalistic period, before World War I, black workers came into the Ford Motor Company just as its personnel policies were becoming more harsh and impersonal. Black workers in the South had heard of Ford as the benevolent employer who first paid his workers $5 a day, and Ford continued to reap some good feelings on that score in spite of the fact that by the 1920s his wage scale was no higher than the other major auto companies and his personnel policies had become decidedly repressive.[37]

The exceptional treatment of blacks by Ford was more a matter of number of hires than of exalted job classifications. A few unusual persons did manage to rise out of the usual black job categories but many, many more did not. A more realistic expression of the Ford Motor Company's attitudes toward black workers is the following circumlocutory reply to a 1920 charge of discriminaton:

> There are times when we have to pick certain kinds of men for certain kinds of jobs; for instance, our harder jobs call for a different calibre of men than do our so-called easier and cleaner jobs, etc., and it is possible that at such times different classes of people, if they feel so inclined, can imagine that they are being discriminated against.[38]

Besides discrimination in the type of jobs to which they were admitted, blacks faced some discriminaton in wages. Although there was little outright discrimination in different pay for the same job classification, changing jobs slightly and giving them different names or breaking up a work process somewhat differently for blacks and whites was easy to do; these differences were then used to justify paying blacks a lower wage. Wage differentials between black and white workers, however, were primarily a function of discrimination with respect to job categories. Black workers were simply concentrated in the lower-paying categories. This could make a difference that amounted to black workers receiving 80% to 90% of the annual wages whites received. Nevertheless, while black earnings in the auto industry were lower than whites', they were higher there than in any other industry.[39]

Another indication of the systematic relegation of blacks to unskilled jobs is seen in the racial policy of the Wilbur Wright Trade School. Wilbur Wright was the only public school in Detroit where students spent some of their schooltime working and being trained in factories. Up until 1937, Wilbur Wright refused to admit blacks on the grounds that the factories with which it cooperated in its training program would never accept black skilled workers. Thus, blacks found themselves in a position of being refused skilled jobs for lack of training and being refused training since employers would not hire blacks for skilled jobs.[40]

Employers justified maintaining blacks in the worst jobs and segregating them from white workers on the grounds of preventing racial tension. According to Frank Hadas, a Ford engineer,

> You could have them on some dirty, rough job where there wouldn't be many whites to complain against them. But if you tried to mix them in the assembly lines or anyplace else where whites predominated and hung their coats touching those of the whites you know, 'that nigger is poison'; you couldn't do that.

Hadas continued his justification of separate and inferior job assignments for black workers with his impressions of how southern white workers responded to attempts at integration. "Goddamn, I don't want that black SOB to sit on my toilet seat. You know what? I've got to hang my coat along side of his over there. I've got to handle tools that a nigger handled."[41]

Some of these attitudes must, in fact, have been present on the part of white workers. The Ku Klux Klan was growing in Detroit in the early 1920s, and it had members in Detroit auto factories. Sporadic outbursts of fighting between black and white workers in auto plants were clear indications of racial tension. Many sources of friction between white and black workers existed, but in spite of employers' stated apprehensions, none of them created the serious disturbances encountered in some other industries. Employers interviewed in 1925 all agreed that black-white fights were no more frequent than clashes between white workers of different ethnic groups and none of these conflicts were considered major personnel problems.[42]

Primary to understanding the lack of serious outbreaks of on-the-job violence is the fact that blacks were not brought into the auto industry to serve as strike breakers. They were brought into an expanding industry where jobs were relatively plentiful and where the threat of unionization was so slight that management was not seriously concerned with actively pitting workers against each other. A few brief attempts were made to choose white southerners as foremen for black workers and, for a while, Ford tried to use competing black and white crews to increase production. These experiments were quickly abandoned, however, and the usual pattern was one of relatively segregated groups working in different parts of the factory.[43]

Auto workers, thus, were a diverse lot, and many workers felt that diversity acutely. In positive form, identity was established by national, racial, and regional loyalties. In negative form, claims to superiority were founded on group membership. The question arises then, with all their diversity, to what extent these auto workers comprised a working class conscious of its collectivity. Examining a single industry, which took many preindustrial workers into its factories and changed some skilled industrial workers into deskilled ones, can provide a miniature view of the process whereby a working class is developed. If "class happens," in E. P. Thompson's definition, "when some men, as a result of common experiences . . . feel and articulate the identity of their interests as between themselves, and as against other men whose interests are different from (and usually opposed to) theirs," then it seems that the first one-third of the twentieth century created those conditions of common experience in the auto industry through which its workers became part of a working class out of their separate ethnic, racial, and regional identities. That attainment of a unified identity as industrial workers was never easy, often partial, and its accomplishment did not mean that ethnic, racial, and regional identities were eliminated. But it was a necessary step for industrial unionism to be possible or meaningful. In that process, the most important shared experience was that of work itself.[44]

Chapter Three

Auto Work

The work life of auto workers underwent startling changes between 1900 and 1933 as the nature of the work changed through the development of mass production, machine tool technology, and assembly line techniques. Work which had involved considerable exercise of skill and autonomy gave way to work almost entirely lacking in individual satisfaction.

Early automobile manufacturing was primarily assembling component parts already manufactured elsewhere, but in this assembly process, a small group of men would put together an entire car. Two or three men worked on assembling a single car with several cars being built simultaneously by different teams spread around the assembly room. At Ford's Mack Avenue plant in 1903, "There was no system whatsoever on this assembling job. . . . Most of the assembly process was done by hand." Another Ford employee remembered:

> All we did was put the wheels on and put the body on. The body, as near as I can remember, was brought on a hand truck, and they picked it up and put it on. The fellows could lift a car body easy enough. After the car was assembled, one fellow would take hold of the rear end and one of the front end, and they'd lift the whole thing up! The cars were assembled on the spot. They would bring the chassis and the motor and body to one place. I would say there would be ten or fifteen spots for assembling, and there would be just one or two men for each assembly, as near as I can remember. Probably someone gave them help; putting on a body needed two fellows. After they were assembled, they were driven out.[1]

By 1912, the final assembling process had become more systematized, but, at Buick, it still involved a stationary chassis to which other parts were brought and added.

> This Buick chassis room was in a large brick building; it must have been 70 feet wide and about 600 feet long. The roof was supported on wooden posts; there was a forest of these; they were nowhere more than twenty feet apart. In long rows were structures the height of a workbench. On these the chassis of each new Buick would be put together. Then other men would bring the axles and fix them on; others would hang the springs. Then the gang of workmen would go to another table and resume; painters would go to work on the chassis.[2]

As the auto manufacturers began to produce more and more automobile components themselves instead of contracting them out to machine shops and other specialized shops, the same technique used in assembling the finished car was transferred to assembling its component parts: motors, bodies, and the like. One man or a team of men worked around a stationary part until it was completed or another man took over to execute a specialized operation. For example, castings for the motor would be put on a table and a group of men worked on them to attach their various fittings. A variation in this procedure involved moving parts from station to station until complete. At Ford, the engine block was passed by hand from one work station to another to have various operations performed on it.[3]

The first step toward more efficient mass production was arranging the car's construction in an orderly, progressive sequence, allowing a worker, even without a continuously moving line, to specialize in certain operations, either moving from car to car or having the car rolled on dollies to his station. Throughout, the process of developing progressive sequence also depended on the perfecting of individual machines designed to execute specific tasks and make the worker more of a machine tender than a craftsman.[4]

Arranging work in a progressive sequence was well under way in most auto plants before 1910. As early as 1901 at Oldsmobile, auto frames were rolled along by means of a wooden platform with casters underneath. Workers found parts bins at appropriate points along the path of the wheeled platform. At the Cole Motor Car Company, the automobile began as a frame that was pushed along the assembly line on two wooden dollies of eight wheels each. The completed chassis at Chrysler, by 1912, was lifted off the table by a chain hoist, placed upon a track on the floor and pushed by hand while "two men put the fenders on, others in turn added a gas tank, and finally the chassis got its body." At Ford's Piquette plant, by 1908,

> The assembling of the car was on a form of progressive assembly line at Piquette. It was not powered in any way. It was all done by hand. The first unit that came along was the frame, and the first thing that happened there was, we made what you might call a buggy. We attached the front axle and the rear axle and put the wheels on. Now it was ready, so it would roll by pushing it. Then we would push it along from station to station. We would drop in the motor and the torque tubes, and you practically had a complete chassis. It was ready then for the body which was placed on the chassis at the end of the line which practically completed the job after the radiator and hood were assembled. . . . In a sense we had an assembly line. The same people would be assigned to the same job at each operation. We would have a team to hook up the transmission to the motor and another team to put the torque tubes in, and then another team to push it along and put in the radiator, etc.[5]

Just before the moving assembly line was introduced, several shops at Ford included many elements of a moving line without the motive power to move elements along smoothly and evenly. Machines were placed as close together as feasible. The traditional means of grouping machines was to place like machines together, lathes with lathes, power drills with power drills, and so forth. Instead, around 1906 at Ford, "We didn't group our machines by type at all. They were pretty much grouped to accommodate the article they were working on." For instance, in the case of the Ford machine shop, a babbitting furnace was placed between machines in making connecting rods. At Highland Park, motor, transmission, and axles were built by men performing single operations that combined to make a finished product. As the chassis moved from station to station (rolled on its own wheels once they were attached, before that on dollies), stockpiles of parts were found along the floor where they were needed and constantly replenished by stockmen. The chassis moved along and was worked on progressively; but it did not move smoothly and the line's speed was under the workers' control. As a worker or group of workers finished an operation, the chassis continued down the line. The line did not, however, move steadily beneath the worker's hand to remind him of the need for speed. The foreman's voice might do this, but the worker still maintained a measure of control.[6]

Even without a continuously moving assembly line, however, management could exert considerable control over pace and procedure. Roy Chapin of Hudson understood the way "modern production" transferred control of the work process to managers.

> Our Hudson plant was one of those that began early to follow this principle. Instead of putting the motor casting on a bench, and having a single group of men assemble its parts as they walked around it and wasted countless motions, it was placed on a traveling carrier running on a track. It moved along slowly and as it moved different groups of men walked along with it. Each group had its own particular work to perform and at a designated point each group left it and another one took up the work. Every man's job was standardized. Each man had certain prescribed things to do and was required to do them within a designated number of minutes. The speed of the traveling bench was regulated by experiments so that the men were not driven but worked at their normal maximum capacity and at the same time maintained constantly our standard of quality.[7]

Once the sequence of operations was placed in its most efficient organization, introducing a continuously moving assembly line was possible. The final ingredient was developing overhead conveyors meshed with the operation of the line to feed parts as the line went along. At Ford, the final assembly line was the last (and most spectacular) sequence to come under continuous motion. In the summer of 1913, Ford conducted several experiments. Time studies showed that it took an average of twelve and one-half man hours of labor to produce each chassis. Introducing a crude assembly line brought a striking reduction in man hours per chassis to five hours and fifty minutes; refining the process reduced the time to one hour and thirty-three minutes. Throughout the rest of 1913 and 1914, the Ford Motor Company worked out the exact timing to mesh its various lines with overhead conveyors, thereby creating a truly smooth operation that could produce 1,200 automobiles per day. In the process, lines also were placed waist high to eliminate bending over, lessen fatigue, and increase worker efficiency.[8]

The process of developing an increasingly sophisticated technology for the auto industry took place simultaneously on several levels. On one level, it meant the grand advance from custom production to mass production involving a system of highly synchronized assembly lines. On another level, it meant continually improving machines and tools, and replacing one skilled craftsman with a semiskilled or unskilled worker doing the same job faster and more uniformly with the aid of a machine. Assembly speed depended on how sophisticated the machines along the line were, especially the feeder lines that brought parts to the main assembly process. Eliminating hand fabrication of metal parts was crucial to the industry's ability to increase its production rate. The new techniques and machines were numerous, but a few examples will convey the nature of the changes taking place. By 1911, a machine had been invented for painting wheels which handled six rows of wheels at one time; painting, drying, varnishing, and inspecting 2,000 wheels each day. A machine for drilling holes in the cylinder block drilled forty-five holes from four different angles in ninety seconds, eliminating the need to remove the casting to turn it around and upside down. The advent of spot welding during World War I enabled one man to operate a spot welding machine, thereby doing the work of eight hand riveters. Painters, too, found new machinery eliminating the need for skill and judgment. With a paint gun, any worker could "walk in and take the gun and paint an automobile probably with one week's teaching. . . . He did not require any skills." By 1928, even the proud stripers who painted the narrow gold band around the auto body and had once been "quite confident that nobody could ever invent a machine that would take their place," found themselves displaced by a machine that could do the work of ten men.[9]

Changes in auto body construction were slow and gradual, wooden bodies being used as late as 1925. But the invasion of metal started early, and with it came more advanced machine techniques requiring even fewer of the skills left over from carriage making. Wooden bodies needed many coats of paint and varnish, had to be sanded before painting, and generally could not take enamel because of the high temperatures needed. After each coat of paint, the paint needed a long time to dry. Such painting procedures had been standard in producing carriages, but auto makers soon created new ones. Around 1908, manufacturers started using wooden frames combined with pressed steel panels for bodies (before that they had tried aluminum panels). The woodworkers would build the body and smooth out the bumps so that metal finishers would have a smooth surface onto which they would nail the metal panels. In some body shops, a small crew "would build a complete body in the wood, finish it and then the metal finisher, maybe a couple of them, would finish the complete body. It was slow production." Finally, in the mid-1920s, the all-metal body became standard, and it could be run through an enameling oven. Throughout this process, painters, originally highly skilled, lost their positions to a variety of technological advances.[10]

The interior of the car, the upholstery, seating, trim, and so on, also yielded slowly to more advanced techniques. Many trimmers came to the auto factories from previous jobs in furniture factories where hand skills had been important. Much hand work was involved as is apparent from this worker's account:

> At that time we piled the hair. There were tufted headlinings in the car. The buttons were drawn down and tied. Of course, the hair was piled before the button was drawn down. On tufted headlinings it was pasted around the edges and then tacked in on the headlining. The quarter panels were all tufted. The window lifts at that time were straps with a piece of broad lace that covered one side of it. It was sewed with buttonhole stitches. There were holes where you could lower your windows or keep it at a certain place.[11]

The constant improvement in machines and their increasing precision was a vital ingredient in the new mass production techniques, and had a particularly direct effect upon the machinists. In the early years of auto production, machinists were skilled production workers. They worked with machines that they understood, maintained, and modified as the need arose when the parts they produced were modified by the car designers. Some of their work consisted of hand finishing parts that their machines produced in rough form. Early machine shops included workers who could start with a blueprint and emerge with a finished part. In the auto industry skill structure, the early machinists occupied a position between the tool makers, whose work was more varied and challenging and required greater technical skill and inventiveness, and the laborers, whose work was limited to lifting, carrying, and the simplest mechanical operations. The increasing sophistication of the machines used in the auto industry and the practice of creating new machines for new parts rather than modifying the old ones and making do had the effect of reducing, and in many cases eliminating, the need for the machinist's skills.

Wyndham Mortimer, who operated a radial drill at White Motors in the 1920s, understood the changing position of machine operators. His job of drilling various sized holes in transmission housings was "simple, since it was all jig and fixture work requiring no layout of any kind. In other words, the precision was built into the jig or the fixtures." Machine maintenance was separated from operation and made into a special department, eliminating the need for the machine operator to make repairs. In addition, machines were crowded together to facilitate flow, leaving the worker with no space to spare and underscoring the fact that his work was routine, needing no extra space to move in for working out problems or hand-finishing parts. Thus, mass production techniques not only eliminated the craftsmen's skills dating back to preindustrial or nonmechanized modes of production, but also eliminated machine-related skills associated with an earlier stage of industrialization. As Stephen Meyer has shown, the development of a sophisticated machine tool technology was crucial to the auto industrialists' ability to control production and transform it into fully developed modern mass production.[12]

Managers were well aware that machinists had undergone a striking transition. A well-known 1919 description of Ford's new production techniques commented directly on the change in machinists' status.

> As to machinists, old-time, all-round men, perish the thought! The Ford Company has no use for experience, in the working ranks, anyway. It desires and prefers machine tool operators who have nothing to unlearn, who have no theories of correct surface speeds for metal finishing, and will simply do what they are told to do, over and over again, from bell-time to bell-time.[13]

Another early student of the auto industry, R. R. Lutz, writing in 1916, understood the most important influence of the auto industry on techniques of production in all industries to be defining modernity in terms of the abandonment of older traditions rooted in the metal trades.

> As they scrapped their last-year models, so they scrapped many a cherished shop tradition, and the influence of the industry on general manufacturing methods has been only a degree less revolutionary than the changes it has brought about in street and road transportation.[14]

In 1910, nearly three-fourths of all jobs in the auto shops were classified as skilled work. By 1924, skilled workers were estimated to comprise 5% to 10% of the work force in the auto shops, where they constituted a respected and envied aristocracy of tool makers, experimental room hands, and draftsmen. This massive shift in the nature of work in the auto factories entailed a significant change in the lives of the workers involved. It did not mean unemployment, for a constantly expanding industry was able to maintain its skilled workers on the payroll, but it did mean a totally different kind of work experience in which skill and training lost meaning.[15]

The following statistics provide an idea of the kinds of changes taking place in auto factory jobs. A 1917 count of occupations and trades at the Ford Motor Company found machine hands to be by far the largest groups, comprising 32% of those employed. The next largest single category, about 10%, comprises assemblers. A 1924 investigation of auto industry work yielded the following divisions: machine tenders, 25% to 49%; assemblers, 10% to 15%; skilled workers, 5% to 10%; inspectors and testers, 5%; helpers, 15%; and laborers, 10% to 15%. In 1923, Henry Ford estimated the amount of training necessary for employment in his plants. A significant 43% of the jobs needed only one day of training; 36% could be learned within one week; 6% in one to two weeks; 14% in one month to one year; and a mere 1% (tool makers and die sinkers) took up to six years' training.[16]

Of the jobs remaining in the 1920s, one that still demanded considerably more skill than most was that of the metal finishers. "It took me about a month to learn the metal finishing operation," estimated John Anderson, arriving at Seaman Body in 1926. "We used a soldering iron, several heavy files, finishing hammers, and emery cloth. It required skill to use a soldering iron so that a minimum of finishing was needed; then one had to learn how to use a file to make the solder and metal perfectly smooth." By 1929, working at Chrysler's Kercheval plant, Anderson found metal finishing "had changed considerably since I began finishing at Seaman Body. Soldering had become a separate trade and a power tool, the disc grinder, was used to do most of the work." Not only had the required skill declined and the job been broken down into specialties, but the disc grinder made a "hard, dirty job" out of the previously skilled one of hand filing. "As we worked, our disc grinders threw a stream of lead particles in the face of our partners. It was impossible to avoid it." In spite of the remaining pockets of skilled work, many of them associated with body making, 79% of all jobs took no more than one week to learn in 1923, a complete reversal of the 75% skilled jobs in 1910.[17]

The developing technology of the automobile industry tended to blur the distinctions between highly skilled craftsmen needing training and experience and unskilled labor depending primarily upon physical strength and endurance. Where new techniques eliminated exhausting physical labor—door hanging, for example, had been a very heavy job—workers found little quarrel with them. They were aware, however, that new techniques might make their work physically easier, but did nothing about tension and speed; they "eliminate the hardship . . . but not the speed." The majority of new auto workers required neither skill nor excessive strength. Rather, they needed dexterity, alertness, and stamina to keep at a repetitive job as a "deskilled specialist," a machine tender or assembler throughout the working day.[18]

The following auto worker's recollection of his father, who was a trimmer for Cadillac, summarizes much of the process of increasing elimination of skill in the industry. In it, one can sense the father's pride in his craft and his sadness at the loss of the opportunity to exercise his trade, a sadness echoed by his son.

> I remember seeing him one time in the factory and he wore a leather apron which was filled with all types of needles, round and semicurved and long and short and thick and thin, and he had thread in his pocket. And I remember he used to say that he would take a bolt of cloth and some springs, some mohair and tacks and a hammer and his needles and go into a car and trim it from one end to another. . . . He had a half dozen pairs of shears and he used to have yellow chalk that had a string around it and it used to hang from a cord around his neck and he would stick it in his pocket. My father would draw the patterns out for the cushions and the various other pieces of upholstery that was necessary for the trimming of the automobile. Then came the automatic cutters or machine cutters and the scissors got rusty around the house. We kids used to use them for all sorts of things. I remember one finished up as a hedge cutter. Then came sewing machines and my father no longer sewed. Then came men who just tied springs together, and my father was no longer in spring tying. Gradually he lost all of the components of his trade. . . .[19]

The son remembered the experience of witnessing his father's progressive deskilling as humiliating. "This was a lamentable thing for a child to see his father's job, the source of income, the security of the family, taken away, as it were, piece by piece, to have your father reduced to the status of other men in the neighborhood who were just plain ditch-diggers."[20]

Workers in many different industries have undergone the transition from skilled craftsmen to semiskilled or unskilled workers. It is always a sad and difficult process for workers, and is frequently accompanied by great militancy on the part of those workers whose skills are being displaced. That this did not occur in the auto industry may be due to the fact that while skills were displaced, jobs were not and unemployment did not result. Overall employment in the industry increased by 353% from 1909 to 1919 and by 30% from 1919 to 1929. Different skills became obsolete at different times, and any single, small group of workers found it difficult to protest effectively. The very newness of the auto industry and the rapidity with which mass production became associated with it meant that only a relatively small number of workers had experienced the nineteenth century traditional work process where pace and method of work were largely under the workers' control. The changes in productive process that minimized skill in the industry were accompanied by an expansion in hiring of workers whose background was not in the skilled trades but in agricultural labor or heavy unskilled labor of other industries, such as steel. The massive hiring of immigrant workers in the period before World War I greatly diluted the ranks of those who were experiencing a loss of skill, a degradation of the work process, with those who were experiencing the need to adjust to factory discipline and control but whose personal economic status was rising.[21]

R. R. Lutz's 1916 observations on the new auto workers are again instructive. "They are not artisans reduced to a lower economic level by specialization, but chiefly semiskilled workers to whom specialization has afforded the means of reaching a higher industrial and economic status." To conclude that auto workers passively accepted a productive process characterized by specialization, little skill, and management control would be wrong. Chapter Six documents the workers' response. It was a response, however, that was primarily indirect and certainly tempered by the attractiveness of auto industry wages.[22]

Those actual craftsmen who did witness the great productive changes in the auto industry were represented by a great variety of trade unions, where they were represented at all, and these unions had never been strong within the auto industry. A man who was a member of the painters' or the metal polishers' union might have found this membership helpful in previous employment, but within the auto industry, such unions were virtually powerless groups. The extreme antiunion atmosphere of Detroit and the auto industry, along with the uselessness of organization along craft lines, made it difficult for those workers who did belong to craft unions to use these unions effectively in the developing auto industry.

The fifteen years from 1910 to 1925, therefore, were ones of rapid technological change in which auto workers had to adjust to a continual loss of place for skill in the industry. Scholars analyzing the labor process in capitalist industry have sometimes seen the progressive deskilling of jobs as synonymous with the degradation of labor. There is no question that deskilling characterized the development of the automobile industry during its successful emergence as a "giant enterprise." The question concerns how that deskilling was experienced by the workers themselves, whether as progress, or loss, or something else entirely. No single answer to this question is possible. Those workers for whom deskilling was experienced as degradation (the previously quoted Cadillac trimmer as an example) were those who personally lost the need for their particular skills and saw their pride in workmanship diminished as machines took over their jobs and their own autonomy was diminished by a division of skills and increased management planning. For these auto workers, degradation was very real, diminishing their pride and status and undoubtedly contributed to making them among the most militant and union conscious of their fellows. Such workers comprised a minority of the auto industry work force. Much more common was the experience of the auto worker for whom machine tending replaced simple, heavy labor or the semivariegation of farm work. Not only could such workers make more money as automobile workers, but they also experienced their work itself as more modern and sometimes identified with the skill of their machines and indeed with their own skill in running them. Their discontent, and it was profound, was not so much with work that had been deskilled as with the working conditions over which they had little control and that demanded of them speed, accuracy, and obedience to managerially imposed rules.[23]

By the 1920s, then, the new pattern of work in the auto industry was clear, and most workers had to make different kinds of adjustments—to monotony, speed, and tension—rather than loss of skill. The repetitive, monotonous nature of auto factory work was probably the most commonly noticed aspect of factory life mentioned by visitors, and it seemed to symbolize the new factory. Although visitors and journalists often deplored the monotony of the work, determining exactly how workers themselves reacted to monotony is difficult.

Their response was complicated, as it could not be a simple choice between monotonous, repetitive tasks and challenging, interesting work. No such choice was offered. Workers were occasionally offered the chance to change tasks and to rotate jobs. To this choice they often said "No," expressing a preference for staying with the same job. Employers reported, "We ran into people that did not want to get off monotonous jobs. We ran into more of those than the others." Employers often assumed that workers' reluctance to change jobs signified contentment. "Their work on the assembly line was easy. It became a sort of routine. They were able to do their work easily, and there was nothing ever very laborious about that." Henry Ford concluded, "I have not been able to discover that repetitive labor injures a man in any way. . . . We shift men whenever they ask to be shifted and we should like regularly to change them—that would be entirely feasible if only the men would have it that way."[24]

Basically, workers were only offered the chance to change from one dull, repetitive job to another. The slight advantages offered by such a plan were evidently outweighed by the disadvantages and by the feeling that shifting might represent being "pushed around." Henry Ford was undoubtedly more perceptive than he realized when he commented that workers "do not like changes which they do not themselves suggest." In plants which paid for piecework (and Ford was the only important exception to the piecework rule), some monetary loss might be involved until the new job became as routine as the old. But even where no loss of wages was involved, men often refused the change. Here, it seems that men wanted to retain familiar surroundings, friends with whom they might occasionally talk, and, perhaps most of all, the chance to free themselves from a task by knowing it so well that they did not have to give it all their attention. Workers appreciated the chance to remove themselves mentally from the job, to let their minds wander, to gain some small personal space in the middle of the factory. In fact, much of the complaining that was heard about monotony from workers was not so much about monotony alone, but against those jobs that coupled monotony with a constant need for attention to the task.[25]

This discussion is not intended to suggest that workers preferred dull, monotonous tasks to more challenging ones, but given the choices available to them—switching from one repetitive job to another or sticking with the same one—workers often preferred to keep to a familiar routine. In the summers of 1925 and 1926, a small group of Yale Divinity School students took jobs in the automobile industry with a specific interest in examining the effects of auto industry work and practices upon the humanity of the workers. One of the students, employed at Ford's River Rouge plant, had heard stories of previous attempts to shift workers to different jobs according to some regular schedule and was told by company representatives that the workers rejected the plan. This student had no difficulty in analyzing why workers might reject the reform of change.

> The men on the fast production line, which is repetitive work of the worst kind, did not care to change to other jobs on the line because they also were repetitive. They were used to one job and what was the use of changing. How could one use his brain by changing from one repetitive job to another.[26]

Additional support for this thesis comes from interviews with auto workers conducted in 1949 by Charles Walker and Robert Guest. The interviewers found that workers were motivated to change jobs by a desire to escape repetitive tasks; where escape was possible, workers wanted to take it. Inspection, material handling, and repair work rated high: workers could exercise more independence with these jobs than with most production jobs. In ranking the most disliked characteristics of their work, first place went to mechanical pacing, then repetitiveness and minimum skill, all of which were job characteristics of the 1920s; and one can reasonably assume that they were no more liked in the 1920s than they were in 1949. Eli Chinoy's 1955 study of automobile workers concluded that the workers' expressed preference for a gas station or farm rather than the factory was a desire for variety and autonomy.[27]

> In both small business and farming, workers see an opportunity to gain what they rarely achieve in the factory, a rich and full sense of self. The variety of tasks and the individual control of the tempo at which one works in a business or on a farm contrast favorably in the workers' eyes with routine factory jobs.[28]

In the 1920s, workers complained especially about the tension of their work, the pace of the line, the inability to exert any control over pace, the impossibility of making a mistake without having it affect everybody else. All of these mass-production features were soon concentrated around the concept of the *speed-up*. When organization finally came to automobile workers, speed-up was one of the chief organizing issues. This tension of the line was noted even before 1920. Samuel Marquis, the director of the Ford Sociological

Department in 1918, worried that "a good many men break down mentally and physically." Noting that foremen were equally suscep- tible to such breakdowns, he attributed the problem to "the sense of responsibility and the continuous application to one line of work." During the 1920s, tension and speed came to symbolize auto work even for many who had never seen the inside of an auto factory.[29] The grinding effect of such tension was expressed by one Ford worker who observed:

> The weight of a tack in the hands of an upholsterer is insignificant, . . . but if you have to drive eight tacks in every Ford cushion that goes by your station, within a certain time, and know that if you fail to do it you are going to tie up the entire platform, and you continue to do this for four years, you are going to break under the strain.[30]

The enormous changes which took place in the type of the work performed inside auto factories made possible the production of large numbers of precisely identical vehicles, efficiently constructed, and equipped with price tags that much of the public could afford. But mass production did not just mean the ability to exert standardized control over the product being made; it also meant greatly increased control over the workers and the means they employed to carry out their assigned tasks. This is apparent, primarily, in the great changes that mass production created in the skill structure of the auto industry. By the 1920s, the great variety of skills represented in the early auto factories had been eliminated in favor of a much more uniform skill level in the work force so that approximately 80% of the workers shared a similar level of skill required for their jobs. This shrinking of the skill scale lent itself to a similar contraction of wage differentials, increasing speed and efficiency of operations, and greatly increasing productivity. It also tended to remove from positions of power in the industry's work force those skilled workers who traditionally in labor history have been some of the most militant and, because of their irreplaceable skills, powerful members of the work force.[31] The system, in its completed states, was one in which rapid pace of work and simplicity of skills led to low production costs, even when workers' wages were above average.

In January 1914, Henry Ford startled the world with his an- nouncement that he intended to pay his workers $5 per day. The experiments, which meshed the final assembly line and its feeder lines with overhead conveyors, were operating at full speed throughout 1913 and 1914 at Ford, ushering in a fairly well-developed system of assembly line mass production. The $5 day was only appropriate to the new modes of work and the new levelling of skills they entailed. Where it meant doubling the wages of many common laborers, it also symbolized the degradation of skill in lessening the distance in wages between skilled and unskilled workers. This fact was not lost on Ford's skilled workers who complained bitterly that a floor sweeper could now make almost as much money as they could. Some toolmakers even left Ford, moving to other auto companies where they earned less money but where there was no confusion between their pay and that of a floor sweeper.[32]

Skilled workers generally adhered to fairly rigid ideas about what constituted a fair day's work. Eliminating skilled workers had the effect of eliminating those standards and opened the opportunity for new standards to be created by management. The school of scientific management applauded the productive changes taking place in the auto industry and gave them a theoretical articulation in theories of management control over the work process. In 1911, Frederick Taylor published his *The Principles of Scientific Management*, in which he summarized his ideas about a theory of management which he had developed in the steel industry and which was complementary to the new theories of production taking hold in the automobile industry. Taylor's system called for analyzing jobs into their component units and subdividing work into units of least motion and waste in order to remove control over the labor process from the hands and brains of workers and place it firmly in the brains and coercive controls of managers. All of the important changes which had developed in the auto industry around new methods of production, lessened skill requirements, opportunity for greatly increased speed, and a more uniform wage structure could be systematized in the ideas of scientific management. Taylor's ideas were known to Detroit auto executives, although they apparently had little influence upon the industry-leading changes occurring at the Ford Motor Company. Taylor made a strong impression on Henry B. Joy, president of Packard, when he lectured at the Packard plant in 1909. In 1914, Taylor again spoke in Detroit before a large audience— including superintendents and foremen from most of Detroit's major companies—and was told that Detroit industrialists had anticipated many of his ideas.[33]

The principles of scientific management, in their insistence that the work process should come under the tight control of management, had already been partially accomplished in the auto industry by eliminating skills and introducing numerous new machines that could be tended with efficiency and about which no tradition of proper use existed. The main thrust of scientific management was to take control over the labor process out of the workers' hands and into management's hands, who not only directed laborers to attend to business and keep up the pace, but also, and even more importantly, told them in minute detail how to do the job. Eliminating the workers' need to make decisions about their work and giving all decision-making power to management was part and parcel of the elimination of skill.[34]

All in all, auto factory work by 1933 was characterized by far less skill and autonomy than it had been in 1905 and by far more speed and tension. Control over speed, variety of tasks performed, how to do a specific job, and problem solving had moved from the workers to the managers and the machines. In 1905, Ford Motor Company workers might know Henry Ford personally, take an interest in developing auto design, and offer suggestions for improvement. In 1932, in the words of one worker, "A man checks 'is brains and 'is freedom at the door when he goes to work at Ford's."[35]

Chapter Four

Conditions on the Job

From the beginning, the automobile industry paid its workers comparatively decent wages. It could not compete with the craft shops employing organized workers, but, as the industry developed, its wage rates compared favorably with other major industries hiring predominantly semiskilled workers. Generally, from 1899 on, the auto industry maintained an edge—sometimes a substantial edge—in wages paid over the average wage for all industries combined. By 1914, the auto industry ranked seventh in average annual wages received by its employees; by 1919 it was fifth; and by 1925, first, and it remained one of the better paying industries even into the Great Depression of the 1930s, ranking second in 1931, first in 1935, and second in 1937. Table IV-1 presents the average annual wages of workers in the motor vehicle industry for selected years from 1899 to 1933. The average *annual* wage is the best indicator of income since seasonality and insecurity of employment make *hourly* and *weekly* averages difficult to interpret.[1]

With the significant exception of the Ford Motor Company, most automobile workers were paid by piecework, which was tied to the theory that the more money a worker could earn the harder he would work. Skilled workers had traditionally operated on a different basis, acting out standard notions about what represented adequate output. Unskilled workers had traditionally been thought to be incapable of working very hard without constant driving and bullying. The theory of incentives, applied to unskilled workers, assumed that their level of output depended more on rewards than on driving and need only be tied to wages to result in a great increase in productivity. Roy Chapin, president of the Hudson Motor Car Company, stated, "The day of the oath and the lash is gone"; the

TABLE IV-1
Average Annual Wages of Workers in the Motor Vehicle Industry, 1899–1933 (in Dollars)

Year	Average Annual Wage
1899	$ 589
1904	594
1909	643
1914	802
1919	1,431
1921	1,498
1923	1,630
1925	1,675
1927	1,659
1929	1,638
1931	1,228
1933	1,035

Figures from: U.S. Congress, House, Federal Trade Commission, *Report on Motor Vehicle Industry,* House Document No. 468, 76th Congress, 1st Session, 1939, p. 8.

new system depended upon "proper incentive." Frederick Taylor and his scientific management school had already begun revising the traditional notion of the fair day's work to one more suitable to unskilled labor and modern conceptions of efficiency. Taylor insisted on management's need to control the pace at which goods were produced and labor expended. To determine the proper pace, Taylor recommended a careful analysis of each job to reduce it to its basic components, combined with incentive wages based on the number of pieces produced or tasks accomplished.[2]

For American industrialists, then, piecework was a device to extract as high a production rate as possible from the workers without undue cost to the company. It also made workers pay for downtime caused by machinery breakdown, since they could not produce during those times. The auto industry employed time study men to set the original rates whenever a new operation was introduced into the productive process. Although time-study men were supposed to be objective practitioners of science, they were not immune to pressure; they clearly knew what the production office wanted—higher output per manhour. They sometimes erred in the direction of unreasonable expectations for high production. Workers protested that rates were set based on the performance of "speed merchants. . . . When they worked on a long enough set rate then they [management] moved them off to some other job while the other fellows had to meet these standards." It was standard practice in the automobile industry, and in other industries, to change rates once the workers had worked themselves up to a fairly high standard of pay.[3]

Although Taylor himself disapproved of rate changing, workers found that if they worked hard to increase their earnings, the company was likely to establish a new piecework rate to reduce their earnings, while still maintaining a high production. Often this process was repeated until the company felt that the rates were set as high as the workers' capacity for speed. When workers protested, new rates were set under the guise of some change in productive technique, but this change was often insignificant. These practices on the part of the companies gave rise to worker practices to defend their wages and keep their speed low. Workers frequently attempted to deceive the time-study men. Once a rate was set, the workers often agreed informally on what production should be and informed any new-comers of their agreed-upon pace. Thus, they tried to keep their earnings as high as they thought they could without making them so high that the company would revise its rates.[4]

Individual piecework had its inconveniences for the companies. It was expensive to administer, involving extensive paperwork and counting each worker's production. It also produced considerable dissatisfaction among those men who simply could not keep up with the pace of the fastest, and highest paid, workers. As pieceworker Tracy Doll remembered the system at Hudson, "The slow man, the man who was not as adaptable, could not keep up so he was creating a considerable amount of turmoil because the fast man made more money and, of course, he was working himself to death but the slower man was always dissatisfied." Individual piecework was also incompatible with the increasing use of the moving assembly line, where to some extent the speed of the line determined the production expected.[5]

Responding to these disadvantages associated with individual piecework, many companies swithched to a group piecework, or bonus, system, where a group of workers or a whole department were paid according to the production of the entire group rather than that of the individual worker. This system produced several advantages for the company. Auto executives were aware of the resentment caused by the practice of rate cutting. Group incentive plans offered the benefit of being too complex and difficult for workers to interpret. Rates could be set in such a way that each increment of production produced a smaller and smaller increment in pay, in effect cutting the rate without having to announce it as such.[6]

Most important, group piecework made the men take over the foreman's call to "hurry up," exerting pressure on the slower men to keep up so as not to lessen the group's wages. "If one man slowed down," Tracy Doll recalled,

> he was slowing down the livelihood of all the people. So the other guys went over and jumped onto him and said 'hurry up, get moving.' This was the idea. Now they got the men stretched out to where they could not stretch any longer and we have got the fast men carrying the slow men and all of them getting wages based on a percentage of their day rates.[7]

Sometimes, faster workers helped the slower ones along. But if one worker was consistently unable to keep up the pace workers might ask the foreman to shift him to another department. There were instances of workers fighting outside the plant, faster workers beating up slower ones to persuade them to work faster and keep pay rates high. Concomitantly, the foremen were motivated to push the men hard, since their pay was based on their departments' output.[8]

Group piecework also made the workers "pay" for training new men, since their wages usually decreased the longer a new man took to become competent and increase speed. Thus, the workers were forced to assume much of the cost of high turnover. Workers felt dissatisfied with group piecework because they could never predict the amount of their paychecks. With individual piecework, workers could count their production, and many felt they had a check on the honesty of the company. Once piecework extended to a large group or a whole department, bookkeeping fell entirely to the company; workers often felt they were being cheated, but they had no way to prove exactly what their pay checks should be. One investigator of the industry in the mid–1920s at Packard found the bonus system "in such disrepute" that he could find ". . . no man who believed that working harder whould raise it. . . . The men of years unanimously said that we would get the bonus if they wanted us to have some, if not, we received none." A company spy at Dodge reported the bonus system to be the source of much worker dissatisfaction in 1931. As long as piecework rates prevailed, workers were disadvantaged in asserting any control over the speed of their work. While they could band together in work groups to restrict production to what they could produce at a reasonable pace, they did so more as a protest against company rate cutting than as a direct attempt to control production schedules. Auto workers' main argument was that the system did not work; greater effort did not produce commensurately greater rewards. In that context, they attempted to strike a balance, pulling along the slower workers and holding back the fastest ones to achieve a pace that would maximize wages while minimizing effort. It was no mean task, and involved a constant battle.[9]

The hours worked by auto workers were about standard for their time. The ten-hour day, common in the beginning, was supplanted by the nine-hour day by 1915. While Ford shifted to an eight-hour day and three shifts in 1914, most other auto plants remaind on the nine-hour plan; as late as 1925 they averaged a fifty-hour week. Of all auto workers in 1925, 48% averaged a fifty-hour week (the single largest group), while 23.7% averaged a forty-eight-hour week. The only breaks were for lunch or machinery breakdowns, and these were not paid breaks. Overtime was common; in 1912, the Ford Motor Company limited overtime so that no worker could work more than twelve hours in any twenty-four. Usually workers were expected to work overtime for as long as the company required and to do so at the regualr pay rates. A common grievance of the 1920s concerned the failure of the auto companies to pay extra for overtime. For most workers, the work day was longer than the official eight or nine hours of a normal work day. A worker at Ford in the summers of 1925 and 1926 reported the Ford worker who spent an official eight-hour day on the job usually arrived ten to thirty minutes before work began and left five to fifteen minutes after work ended. He was expected to get his tools from the crib and be at his place ready for work when the shift began; clean-up was usually on his own time. He had to wait in line to punch the time card. Taking a fifteen- or twenty-minute lunch break and approximately one hour travelling to and from the factory, a work day would amount to nine and one-half or ten hours.[10]

The fifteen-minute lunch was often more of an ordeal than a break, and it became the subject of bitter humor among workers. Many workers purchased their lunch from a concession wagon with a fairly standard menu. In the 1920s, 15¢ bought three sandwiches; a piece of pie and a piece of cake; an apple, banana, or orange; and coffee, tea, or milk. Opinion varied as to the quality of the food, some workers referring to the lunch wagon as the "ptomaine wagon" and claiming that 15¢ purchased a "damn big pile o' sawdust" and "some wonderful water that hasn't seen milk for a month." There was general agreement that fifteen minutes was an inadequate lunch break, as a Ford worker commented, "To transfer this to the stomach in fifteen minutes without choking, and still have time to wipe the crumbs from one's mouth before the production bell sounds again, is an exact science made possible only by the application of Ford production principles." Of course, the fifteen-minute lunch of the 1920s was some advance over the ten-minute lunch break of the pre-World War I period, a ten minutes during which most workers ate at their machines. Charlie Chaplin knew what he mocked in *Modern Times* when he had the company test out a feeding machine that would allow workers to keep working throughout the lunch period, while the machine fed them.[11]

To have a lunch break at all was to have a job, at least. For unskilled or semiskilled workers, the process of getting a job was often haphazard, especially in the early days of the industry. Most hiring was done by foremen who secured the workers they needed to run their departments. They usually cared little for experience and skill and more for stamina, strength, and ability to maintain the pace. Big men had an initial advantage; they stood out and looked like they could do the work. Many workers moved back and forth quite freely from one company to another, always looking for better working conditions and pay and, at least, finding a little variety in changing jobs. Around 1910, several companies began to set up hiring offices that removed the function of hiring from the foremen and put it into a central office from which the foremen requisitioned the men they needed. Foremen were allowed to fire long after they lost their power to hire, a practice much hated by workers. Although Ford removed the foreman's firing power—if not his power to harass—as part of the general reforms of 1913 and 1914, of which the $5 day was also a part, many companies continued the practice even into the 1930s.[12]

In general, men who wanted jobs gathered early in the morning and applied to the hiring manager. Finding a job meant waiting in line, sometimes even when the company could have dismissed most of the line because they knew they needed only a specific skill. The employment office showed little concern for workers' comfort or dignity. They used the hiring process to establish who was boss, insisting that new hires start immediately, even near the end of shifts, and turning away those found unsuitable with rough comments. Workers developed a variety of tactics to cope with the frustration of waiting. They reported what they knew of which companies were hiring and what kind of men they wanted. They held each others places in line so they could break the monotony or get in out of the cold. They inquired of those being turned away to find out what job classifications were being hired on that day and then proclaimed themselves qualified. If a worker claimed a skill, he was sometimes tested by the hiring department, but often workers claimed experience and skill they did not have and their deceptions were not uncovered. Stan Coulthard's story is typical. He heard that Chrysler was hiring millers and went to apply.

> I didn't know what a milling machine was; in fact I'd never worked in a machine shop before. I was taken on in the morning and told to report for the night shift the same day. As soon as I got in I was asked where were my tools? I lied by saying that I'd had no time to go home to get them. I got to the milling machine and didn't even know how to switch it on. I mucked about for a while pretending to be busy until the foreman had gone. Then I told the feller next to me that I'd just got in from Boston, that I didn't know one end of the machine from the other, that I needed a job and could he help me? He said he came from Boston too and showed me what to do. After a while he said that the stock I was making was scrap, that there was some good stuff in a pan behind me and to let on that I'd produced it. When the foreman came round to check and he passed it alright! I went on like that for two or three days until I'd got the hang of things. They got it out of my hide before I'd finished so I had no qualms about cheating them whatsoever.[13]

Irregularity of employment was a common complaint among auto workers, especially in the 1920s. Men might wait long hours and be told to go home. Or they might work a few days and be laid off. Or it could be weeks of steady overtime and then nothing. "How many days are you going to work this week?" was the standard question from the auto worker's wife; and the worst of it was that he had no way of knowing. One worker-investigator described his work at Chrysler in 1926 and 1927 as follows:

> We came all set for work this A.M. and two minutes after we started we were informed that it was all off because they were short

of bodies or of steering wheels. It is so hard to get authentic information. Of course just the assembly line is laid off. Monday worked all day and Tuesday quit at three. This was Wednesday. Thursday came ready to work and were informed that we were off until Monday. Steering wheels and self-starters were wrong all along the line. Thus we get a 5 day vacation although we did waste sleep and time and carfare getting to work Wednesday and Thursday with no result. But after this lapse of 5 days they worked 3 days overtime. Monday we worked til 8:30 with the usual three quarters of an hour for lunch plus thirty minutes for supper. The other two days we had no time for supper but could eat while we worked after buying available food from company lunch wagons.[14]

Seniority had no bearing on layoffs; therefore, predicting how much employment workers would have during a year was difficult. "You were at the will of the supervisor. In layoffs, you had no seniority as to coming back or any security from the time that you hired out. On many occasions you would come in and they would run out of stock as soon as you got in the plant and the foreman would tell you to go home." Whenever possible workers tried to set a little money aside for the lean days, since finding another job during layoffs was sometimes difficult.[15]

With no seniority, the foreman could exert considerable pressure on the men to do him favors in order to retain their jobs when layoffs occurred. Workers complained about foremen asking them to work on their houses on Saturday, cut their lawns, buy liquor from their stills during Prohibition, make regular dollar contributions, and even contribute their wives for sexual favors. While some of these complaints suggest legends, foremen did make personal demands and the system provided no process whereby workers' complaints could be heard. "I would see the people come in the shop and the ones that took the foreman out and bought him drinks or had a party for him were the ones that would stay on regardless of seniority and regardless of ability." And from another worker, "Every single payday certain men, who did not have too much on the ball and wanted to stay in the shop, just peeled off two dollars and gave it to the boss so that he had a little spending money that weekend. That is how they hung onto their jobs." Foremen were known to favor their relatives and friends at other workers' expense, laying off workers in the summer to make space for high school students in their own families or putting special friends in on weekends. "Numerous times I have had the foreman to bring his brother-in-law in and tell me to break him in on the job. As soon as you would get him broken in, they would bring you in a slip, lay you off, and leave him working." Henry Ford's wife, Clara, to whom aggrieved workers often brought their stories, received many a pitiful letter from wives of laid-off workers, unemployed in favor of the foreman's relatives.[16]

Besides a problem of general irregularity and unpredictability of employment, auto workers were also plagued by seasonal unemployment caused by the practice of bringing out a new model each year. In the early days, seasonal buying was tied to the logic of roads being closed and unpassable in the winter. Big sale times were the fall, when the new models came out, and the spring, when the weather restored roads to drivable condition. Since dealers did not want to stock more cars than they could sell, production slowed around October and picked up again early in the year, to slow again in late spring and early summer. This resulted in many workers being able to depend on employment for only six to eight months out of the year, spending the other four to six months on an involuntary "starvation vacation." For those auto workers who made up the "suitcase brigade" of rural workers who returned home when laid off, this seasonality became part of a regularly patterned work year. For those committed to living permanently in an auto city, off-seasons were difficult indeed. Automobiles are large, bulky items that cannot be stored economically in large quantities. Neither the dealers nor the manufacturers wanted to keep assembled cars on stock, and production was geared accordingly. As long as a ready supply of auto workers remained, companies didn't have to worry about permanently losing their workers during slack times and lay offs. Whatever jobs they might pick up outside the auto industry were not likely to hold them. As soon as the auto plants started rehiring, "the big money in the factory" brought the workers "back to the plant again." Seasonality continued to be a problem for workers up until the Great Depression of the 1930s, although industry executives discussed various schemes to regulate work. "We had seasonal layoffs lasting from three to five to six months at that time. If you could not get a job, you would come around to find out how your working status was coming along. There would be hundreds of people standing out in the winter."[17]

One of the most unpleasant features of auto factory life was the pettiness of factory work rules. In general, these included rules against smoking, talking, sitting down, as well as strict adherence to time-keeping (for example, washing hands for lunch *after* punching out but having tools ready *before* the starting bell rang). Such rules could govern behavior outside the factory walls as well. At Ford, using alcoholic beverages was frowned upon and Packard prohibited smoking on the sidewalks outside the factory. Of course, all of these rules were often honored in the breach, but it was the foreman's job to see that they were adhered to and they increased his capacity for petty tyranny.

The rule against talking was in effect in both Ford and General Motors plants in the 1920s and workers feared for their jobs if they broke it. Even where no rules prohibited talking, conversation was almost impossible because of the general din of the factory and the need to pay close attention to one's work. One journalist reported, during the post-World War I speed-up, "no speech among the men" because "they haven't time for it. Each is keyed every moment to the necessity of keeping pace with the relentless onward march of the conveyor. . . ." During the heyday of Harry Bennett at Ford, servicemen regularly monitored the toilets to check on the men using them, another practice recorded by Chaplin in *Modern Times*. Without any organized collective representation it was impossible for workers to challenge petty rules except by individual acts of defiance that could result in dismissal or fines. To be safe, resentment had to be repressed; employers allowed no challenge to or discussion of their decisions.[18]

The 1919 Packard training manual for foremen, in attempting to moderate foreman practices, gives a good picture of what conditions were like in most auto factories. In general, plants creating high-quality, luxury cars such as the Packard tended to be somewhat more liberal in their treatment of employees. The Packard manual warned foremen against the use of "rough methods, such as loud and boisterous talking, cursing, threats of dismissal or any other attempt to intimidate the workman," stressing instead that the foreman should appeal to the employee's "sense of honor." At the same time, however, the foreman's own worth was measured by his ability to maintain discipline and by his department's production record. Foremen, then, were likely to use whatever methods they thought necessary to maintain high production without incurring a high turnover rate.[19]

Auto workers particulary resented the constant pressure for speed. Sometimes this pressure could push workers to the breaking point; sometimes it relaxed a little; but the pressure to avoid ever letting up was incessant. Before the continuously moving assembly line was widely used, speed-up generally took the form of the foreman yelling at the men. "We used to drive our men pretty hard in those days," reminisced W. C. Klann, a Ford production supervisor. "It was nothing to call a man a dirty name and tell him to keep on going. . . . We used to have every man learn how to say 'hurry up.' It was *putch-putch* in Polish; *presto*, Italian; *mach schnell*, German; and *hurry up* in English. That was all a fellow knew, just drive, drive, drive."[20]

With the increasing use of power driven assembly lines, speed-up could be effected by turning up the speed of the line. After the introduction of the $5 day at Ford, the production manager was told to get twice the work from the men since they were getting twice the pay. "You wouldn't tell them to go faster. You would just turn up the speed of the conveyor to go faster, that's all, until they kicked that it was going too fast and they couldn't do it. Then we would drop it back a notch." In general, World War I was a time of increasing speed requirements as was the period from the depression of 1921 into the mid-1920s. Speed pressure increased again in the 1930s during the depression. The tension produced by speed combined with the tension resulting from careful attention to monotonous work led to frequent cases of chronic nervousness (even off the job), inability to relax, and insomnia. A participant in the wave of strikes in 1933 complained:

> When the line would be speeding up, the pusher would keep after me, urging me to work harder and faster. Sometimes he would help me slightly and then go on to the next man. This was happening on the job when I went to Ford's four years ago, and it is worse today. The speed-up is so great that a man cannot go to the toilet, physical needs are not met, nervous results occur, and I am at present suffering pain as a result of the high tension I have been working under. I could not leave the line when I needed to. If I had left it, then I would have been fired.[21]

Making a major beginning with Ford's $5 day, and especially after World War I, the automobile companies participated in the national wave of reforms intended to rationalize industry and make it more efficient. The grandfather of company-initiated reform plans was the Ford Motor Company's package of labor practices introduced in January 1914, generally known as the $5 day, or in Ford literature, as the profit-sharing plan. This plan involved rationalizing the Ford employment and wage structure by greatly reducing the number of job categories, regularizing pay scales, reducing the foreman's power of dismissal, and raising the pay of certain classes of employees to

$5 per day after a six-month probationary period during which they proved themselves eligible. Those workers eligible for the $5 wage were married men who could demonstrate that they lived with, and took good care of, their families; single men a least twenty-two years old, who could demonstrate thrifty habits; and men younger than twenty-two who were the sole support of some next of kin or blood relative. Women who supported relatives and had thrifty habits were admitted to the plan in 1916 after protest by some feminist leaders. Most of these women workers were young single women, as Ford disapproved of hiring married women if their husbands were employed. During the two years that women workers were excluded from the $5 day, stories circulated in Detroit of women who disguised themselves as men when applying for employment.[22]

The whole program was supervised by a newly created Sociological Department empowered to judge a worker's eligibility for the wage by visiting his home, talking with his relatives, overseeing his living conditions and habits, and offering advice as to money management, housekeeping, and family relations. Many of the activities of the Sociological Department were seen as teaching foreign workers to adapt to American ways. Ford was particularly concerned that workers be discouraged from the practice of taking in boarders and encouraged workers to buy homes for single families. In addition to investigating workers' eligibility for the $5 wage, Sociological Department members visited the homes of workers who were absent from work to determine their reasons and offer help where the reasons were legitimate.[23]

There was considerable difference of opinions as to whether Ford workers resented the interest taken in their personal lives by the Sociological Department. Most probably simply thought of the visits of the investigators as hurdles to be leaped as best as possible, considering Ford's practices more eccentric than offensive. Some professed to find the company's concern beneficial, although usually to someone else. The man who did not drink thought the drinker was benefitted by Ford's prohibition against alcohol. As a clerk in the Employment Office saw it, "instead of spending his money in a saloon, the employee was bringing his money home to his wife and children for the simple reason that he knew very well that the social worker would catch up to him on the next trip, and he wouldn't know when that would be. It kept the men in line." Drinking men, no doubt, had a different opinion, although their standards of living and that of their families may well have improved under the Sociological Department's solicitous eye. Some workers did complain that the system subjected them to "humiliating experiences" and interfered with their personal freedom. Samuel S. Marquis, who succeeded John Lee as director of the Sociological Department, conceded that personal liberty was violated but argued that those individual liberties had consisted of "getting drunk and beating up one's wife, abusing one's family, and wasting one's money," liberties a man could well do without. No doubt, it was a patronizing system, although consistent with general social work practices of the day. In Ford's mind, the justification was simple. A well-regulated home life made for a well-regulated work life. If home happiness cost additional wages, he was willing to pay. but he was also going to make sure that he got his money's worth.[24]

The immediate effect of the Ford announcement was to double the salary of many Ford workers and produce a crowd of 15,000 job-seekers at the gates who were eventually dispersed with fire hoses. The more far-reaching result was a sharp drop in the turnover and absenteeism rates of Ford workers and an increase in worker efficiency and morale. One observer thought that "such problems as keeping good workers and securing good will in work, have almost been automatically settled by the increased wages." A Ford worker recalled,

> when the $5 day came into effect, it gave a greater incentive to the employees, and I personally can recall taking even more interest in my work than previously. I felt that Mr. Ford was doing something to help us and I wanted to show my appreciation by doing better than ever.[26]

That Ford jobs were coveted for a few years after 1914 seems undeniable and can be explained by higher wages alone. Ford jobs were sufficiently desirable to result in numerous bribes to foremen and employment office personnel and, even in the 1920s, promises to purchase a Ford car if employed. At the same time, workers were kept to a stiff pace of work. In the words of Ford's production manager, "Ford was one of the worse [sic] shops for driving the men. I have been an s.o.b. with everybody in town." Still, for many years after 1914 Ford's reputation as an employer benefitted from the $5 day. By 1920, the other auto companies were paying wages competitive with Ford's, but being first conferred its privileges.[27]

By 1920, the activities of the Sociological Department had greatly diminished and concentrated on emergencies. If a worker died, the Sociological Department might find employment for a family member. The program had never been popular with the production men, however, who thought it coddled the workers and rewarded them for virtuous living rather than speed and high productivity. The post-World War I push to cut costs combined with Ford's declining interest in the project to kill it. With the death of paternalism working conditions at Ford grew progressively more harsh, reaching a peak of brutality that began in 1927 when Harry Bennett dominated personnel policy. Bennett hired a force of gangsters, fighters, and ex-convicts (the Ford Service Department) who patrolled the factory, spied on workers, and disciplined them in harsh and arbitrary fashion.[28]

Although the 1920s' policy of harsh labor practices and speed-up resulted in Ford acquiring a local reputation as a hard place to work, Ford's reputation outside the Detroit area remained favorable. As late as 1940, a *Fortune* survey conducted among workers found that almost 74% considered Ford among those Americans "helpful to labor." All in all, the $5 day was a great success for the Ford Motor Company, summed up by Charles Sorenson's comment, that, "with it all, the company made more cars and greater earnings than ever before."[29]

Henry Ford was not the only auto manufacturer who enjoyed a reputation for paternalism, although at Ford's, paternalism certainly found more systematic expression than anywhere else. Tom White and his son, Walter, of the White Motor Company were both known as benevolent employers, as was Ransom Olds of Oldsmobile. Packard and Hudson both had reputations for providing superior working conditions supposedly connected to requirements for producing a superior car. Both Hudson and Dodge had welfare departments that investigated hardship in workers' families, gave advice, and made referrals to other social agencies. The Dodge brothers were remembered with special fondness for taking a personal interest in their employees. John Dodge's concern for his workers was recounted by a foundry worker. During an exceedingly hot summer evening, Dodge arrived at the factory in formal dress on his way to a party. Upon being informed that four men fainted from the heat, "Dodge insisted on being shown where this was happening." Taken to the place where hot castings were shaken out of the molding sand, he demanded a "pig snout" (respirator), and in full dress and tails, he started shaking out castings. After twenty minutes he was covered with black soot from head to feet, his clothes ruined. "I couldn't do that all day myself. How can you expect anyone else to do it? Get the Engineering Department down here and tell them to stay with it until this is a fit place to work."[30]

In some auto factories, paternalism created conditions superior to much of American industry, but it did nothing to alter the nature of the work. Automobile workers were granted certain reforms emanating from the top at the same time that their control over the work process was destroyed. The two went together, for just as scientific management and mass production created a situation where control over the productive process resided entirely in management's hands, paternalism was a system of human relations where justice and reward originated in a benevolent management rather than in the workers' ability to secure justice for themselves. Packard taught its foremen that "a small increase coming unsolicited is just as gratifying to the workman, if not more so, than is double the increase which he had to fight for." As long as fighting for it meant individually wheedling a superior into a small raise, the Packard philosophy probably held true. But it carried with it a terrible insecurity, for it meant depending passively on the goodness of the employer and trusting that right would prevail. The paternalistic employer assumed the right to exact unquestioning loyalty since anything else would be unreasonable in the face of true benevolence. "Packard rules of conduct," as the Packard Motor Car Company saw it, "are not to be arbitrated. They are reasonable and just. They await no one's approval for their enforcement. Having been established, there is but one course for each of us: that is the path of implicit obedience."[31]

The era in which personal paternalism was strongest in the automobile industry ended with World War I. After the war, a more impersonal corporate liberal approach to labor relations came to dominate the industry, fading in the depression and turning to harsh discipline and spying as labor unionism finally became a serious possibility. The corporate reforms of the 1920s approached combatting high turnover, unions, and low morale through bonuses, savings and investment plans, insurance, training schools, and housing and recreation programs. All such plans had the creation of a more loyal and company-oriented work force as an aim.[32]

The earliest bonus plans were directed toward managers and office workers more than toward production workers, but by 1908, Ford had a bonus plan for production workers based on length of employment. Employees of one to two years received 5% of their yearly salaries; those of two to three years, 7.5%; and those with more than three years, 10%. That this bonus plan does not seem to have been sufficient to keep worker turnover at a low rate is indicated by the turnover rates that Ford was trying to combat in 1914. He introduced, instead, a plan of higher wages, a much more successful plan in winning worker loyalty to Ford. [33]

Generally, employees had access to various forms of bonuses, investment in company stock, or savings plans offered at different times by various companies. Of these, the savings plans were probably the most important in reaching substantial numbers of workers. Savings plans were generally conceived of as providing retirement incomes since few companies had pension plans. Studebaker did initiate a pension program around World War I whereby employees earning less that $3,000 could retire at age sixty on a pension equalling 25% of their average pay for the past five years. Savings plans were particularly popular during the 1920s. As might be expected, after 1929 they tended to fade away, since companies no longer needed them and workers could not afford them. Ford's savings plan allowed workers to invest up to one-third of their paychecks in savings certificates of $100, $500, or $1,000 upon which the company guaranteed a 6% return with higher returns at the directors' discretion. Actual returns were often as high as 12% to 16%.[34]

At General Motors, starting in 1919, workers could save up to 10% of their wages, on which the company paid 6% interest. In addition, General Motors contributed to an investment fund, matching dollar for dollar (50¢ for each $1 after 1922) saved in the savings fund, with these dollars then being invested for the workers in General Motors common stock. Payments to the savings fund might be applied toward purchasing a home without losing benefits from the investment fund. Since leaving the company meant losing the benefits of both funds, there was an inducement for workers to stay in General Motors employ.[35]

Packard and Lincoln both offered their workers favorable terms for purchasing preferred stock, Packard contributing $10 per share and Lincoln selling stock at 20% less than par to employees of at least one year. Yearly bonus plans were also paid, usually at the year's end and varying according to the length of time an employee had worked for the company. General Motors, starting in 1918, paid bonuses in stock to all workers based on longevity. By 1922, however, employees making less than $5,000 were excluded. In January 1920 at Ford, workers making $6 per day and hired before October 1, 1919, received a bonus of $50 while those hired before October 1914, received $270.[36]

The welfare reforms of the 1920s also included insurance plans that provided benefits to workers' families in case of death or permanent disability. The most extensive of these plans was General

Motors'. Starting in December 1926, all General Motors employees could insure themselves for $1,000 after three months on the job, with part of the costs being paid by the company. Some earlier plans had been much more erratic, depending on the annual feelings of the board of directors as to the value of life insurance. Some plans were used punitively; Studebaker introduced a plan in 1915 to insure its workers, but the benefits were cancelled for workers who protested hours or wages.[37]

For a time both General Motors and Ford participated in projects to build houses which their employees could buy or sometimes rent. For a brief period around 1917, Ford even considered building an extensive housing complex divided into areas to house different ethnic groups each with its own community center, school, and stores. This project never fully materialized, but Ford did create housing for some of his workers at the Dearborn tractor plant. Many Ford workers made a lengthy commute from Detroit homes to Dearborn, which made the construction of houses in Dearborn particularly desirable. Ford established the Dearborn Realty and Construction Company in 1919, constructing 250 houses using many prefabricated building materials. Ford hoped his houses would not only be a model of company developed housing but also of efficient and sound housing construction in general.[38]

These houses stand today as a tribute to an intelligent paternalism (although a limited tribute in the number of workers actually housed), and as a model of Henry Ford's conception of how his workers ought to live. Although the homes were similar in construction, six models were available. All included a living room, dining room, kitchen, three bedrooms, bathroom and porch. They were intended to be sturdy, comfortable, and within the means of a Ford worker. In addition, for workers thinking of buying other houses, the Ford Legal Department appraised the properties and gave legal advice.[39]

General Motors' Modern Housing Corporation built homes for its employees in Flint, Pontiac, and Janesville, all auto cities where rapid population growth had created serious housing shortages. Workers could buy these houses at the company's cost, purchasing them through long-term monthly payment plans. By the end of 1929, 35,000 General Motors employees had purchased houses through the Modern Housing Corporation.[40]

Several auto companies ran a variety of training schools for skilled workers, foremen, and managers, often touted as providing the opportunity for poor but industrious boys to better themselves. Most of these programs originated in the industry's need for a reliable corps of skilled workers. By 1910, Henry and Wilfred Leland of Cadillac had a plan whereby selected young workers were put through a two-year training program in which they learned to run machinery in all Cadillac departments and acquired training in all the plant procedures.

The Employers' Association of Detroit was successful in persuading the city to establish a technical high school that, in effect, served the auto industy. In 1916, Oldsmobile started the REO Apprentice School for Boys. The Henry Ford Trade School, opened in 1916, trained high school boys who spent one week in the classroom and two weeks in the shop. They were paid for their work in the shop, but at greatly reduced rates, which led to charges by workers in the 1920s that Ford was using underage labor at low rates of pay to take jobs away form men with families and keep wages low in general. In addition, young men aged twenty to twenty-five could attend the Ford Apprentice School, which concentrated on producing tool and die makers. General Motors operated the Flint Institute of Technology, later renamed the General Motors Institute of Technology, primarily to train managers, but also included training in scarce skills. Like Ford, General Motors advertised its school as an opportunity to escape poverty and low status and to find rewards for hard work and initiative. A General Motors brochure proclaimed,

> These are your days of opportunity. Every man is the director of his own destiny. Within your own being you have the ability for greater tasks, larger responsibilities, a wider field of effort, with the resultant increased return. To achieve this larger success, however, you must develop these latent possibilities within you. Your spare time affords the opportunity. Are you using it to the best advantage? Remember, 'the Trained Man wins.'[41]

As the techniques of automobile production became increasingly mechanized and sophisticated, the health and accident hazards increased, and along with them, company campaigns to create as much safety as was compatible with high production and contemporary standards of acceptable accident and disease rates. Jobs associated with painting and metal finishing carried the most severe health problems in the auto industry. Lead poisoning, silicosis, and other lung problems led the list of job-related diseases. Men operating milling machines found themselves "spitting up rust and blood" although management calmly assured them that "iron dust did not cause severe or serious lung conditions." Lead poisoning could result from the cloud of paint fog in which most painters worked in the 1920s. Paint sprayed at a high velocity created a misty atmosphere and made it virtually impossible to avoid the danger of lead poisoning over time. When workers in Ford's paint department tried to solve the ventilation problem by opening windows, they also brought in dust which settled on the wet paint causing the company to lock the windows. Although "accidents happened to the locked windows," a more permanent solution awaited the improved ventilating systems of the 1930s. But paint was not the only source of lead poisoning. Even in the mid-1930s, when ventilation was somewhat better, auto workers contacted lead poisoning from work as metal finishers. The solder used had a high proportion of lead to block tin. Solder was smeared over joints when car panels were welded together, then ground off. Also, lead was used to fill in depressions in metal panels and then ground smooth. The grinding process sent pulverized lead into the air surrounding the grinders.[42]

Respiratory problems, lung irritations, and skin irritations and infections were other common problems of auto workers. Metal polishers who buffed chrome suffered from sneezing, nose bleeds, and skin ulcers. Polishers chewed tobacco to help keep their throats free from metal dust. Polishers also suffered from a skin irritation due to brass particles working into the skin. The ensuing itching and scratching often led to infection and, among especially sensitive men, the necessity to look for other jobs. Other skin problems came from exposure to the cutting fluid that constantly flowed over tools and products in the machine shops. This fluid, used to reduce the heat of friction and aid the cutting edge of the tool, contained oil to prevent rust. Its danger came from the cutting fluid's tendency to pick up and multiply bacteria causing a skin infection called *oil dermatitis*. In the 1920s, approximately 30% of all machine operators were affected.[43]

Foundry workers suffered from severe heat, lack of ventilation, and problems encountered in handling hot materials. During the shake out and knock out operations, as hot, dried sand was knocked from the casting, it flew through the air and landed on the faces and arms of the men leaving pockmarks to attest to their occupation. In the summertime, heat was a problem everywhere, sometimes requiring departments to close. Some employers attempted to refresh workers by circulating a bucket filled with raw oatmeal mixed with lemon juice and water, a mixture thought to prevent heat prostration.[44]

Many companies maintained some sort of clinic or first aid station at the plant for workers who became ill on the job. The clinic also helped ascertain the extent of damage in accident cases for protection against later compensation claims. Often there were extensive precautions against using the clinic for malingering, as in Ford's 1916 directive:

> Foremen to be instructed to issue passes to the Doctor's Office but when a man leaves his department with a pass, clerk to ring his time card with the understanding that the man goes to the doctor's office on his own time. If the illness be feigned, the doctor to lay the man off, using his judgment as to the length or period of vacation needed. If the case be worthy of attention and bonafide, the man to return to the department to be given credit for time consumed in going for attention.[45]

Employers were also concerned about getting men back to work as soon as possible. In 1919, Hudson's first aid station dispensed medicines and drugs to employees, in the words of a company spokesman, "for the purpose of keeping the men at their work, so that production may necessarily not be retarded."[46]

The automobile industry's safety record was generally good compared to other major industries of the time. Throughout much of the 1920s, the auto industry ranked as the third or fourth safest in accident frequency. Ford was particularly concerned with safety and at both the Highland Park plant and the River Rouge plant ranked first among all auto companies in its safety record and sometimes first among all companies. The kinds of accidents suffered were typical of industrial accidents of the day. Regardless of the relatively good safety record of the auto industry, being an auto worker meant a constant danger of injury or illness. A lapse in attention, letting one's mind wander to counter the monotony of the job, failing to heed warning noises because of the general din of the plant all could lead to an accident that might mean a nasty cut carrying the danger of infection, the loss of a finger or hand, or even death.[47]

Before the widespread adoption of the assembly line, most accidents occurred to machine workers. As assembly lines became more common and complex, assembly line related accidents also increased. Getting caught in belts or between car chassis, or being run over by small shop trucks added to the general danger created by noise, monotony, and closely spaced machines. Machine operation continued to carry dangers in spite of the various safety devices added to machines. In 1917, Packard inaugurated a safety campaign after finding that an average 24% of its workers suffered accidents during the year. By 1919, the Packard accident rate was reduced to 10%. By 1925 and 1926, accident rates for the industry as a whole were reduced to 3.2%.[48]

The most common cause of permanent disability in the early 1920s was loss of fingers or parts of fingers. One worker explained,

> I was a shaper hand in the mill for twelve years. I was very proud of the fact that when they ended the wooden construction on the bodies and it was necessary to transfer to other departments that had increased production, I left the wood mill after twelve years with all five fingers, which was an unusual thing at that time.[49]

A safety expert figured that a punch press operator, manufacturing 300 pieces per hour, put his hand and fingers into "the danger zone at the point of operation 5,000 times per day or 1,500,000 per year."[50]

Between 1925 and 1931, lacerations were by far the chief accidents suffered in auto plants followed by injury to eyes, then contusions, puncture wounds, and burns. For example, in October 1925, at a time when almost 57,000 workers were employed there, Ford's River Rouge plant hospital treated 28,416 cases of lacerations or abrasions; 4,480 new cases of eye injuries; 2,443 contusion cases; 1,925 puncture wounds; and 1,213 burn cases. In October 1931, the figures for 61,000 employees were: 8,755 lacerations; 5,183 eye injuries; 717 contusions; 539 puncture wounds; and 619 burns. The 1931 figures represent a considerable improvement, attesting to some success in implementing safety practices; nevertheless, during 1931, sixteen Ford workers died from accidents at work. In 1935, when Erskine Caldwell published his observations on life in Depression America, he named Detroit "the eight-finger city."[51]

Sometimes spectacular accidents occurred, similar in scope to the kinds of disasters often associated with earlier factory conditions or with mining. In April 1927, failure to ground the metal nozzles on the paint sprayers at the Briggs Harper Avenue Detroit plant led to an explosion followed by a fire. Highly flammable chemicals used in mixing auto body lacquer ignited in the third floor paint department, and the fire quickly spread throughout the five-story building. In all, twenty-one workers were burned to death and many more permanently injured, many because their clothes were saturated with paint mixture and instantly went up in flames. Although the Michigan

Department of Labor and Industry termed the tragedy "an act of Providence," auto workers tended to agree with the conclusion of the *Auto Workers News* that the Briggs Company had been negligent in failing to provide an adequate ventilation system to remove flammable fumes released in lacquering bodies.[52]

Serious management-sponsored safety campaigns began around World War I in most auto plants. Before then, Ford had probably been the most safety conscious and also the most concerned with cleanliness, a closely related problem. As early as 1906, a Ford operative, employed to report on workers' attitudes, recommended cleaning the assembly room floor that was covered with a quarter inch of grease in which some workers had to lie. Ford's Safety and Health Department, organized in 1914, published monthly departmentalized accident reports so that foremen were publicly identified with their departments' accidents. Packard did the same. Ford used red paint on all crushing and cutting parts of machines to alert workers to danger. It also used warning bells, signs, and safety locks.[53]

Employers insisted that factory safety was, first and foremost, the workers' concern and that workers—not employers—should make sure appropriate care and precautions were taken. A General Motors safety pamphlet from 1926 was typical in its advice. "Most accidents," it asserted, "are caused by CARELESSNESS OR THOUGHT-LESSNESS. . . . Remember that a careful worker is the best safety device." Many employers complained that workers failed to use the safety devices available to them. They either neglected to wear safety goggles, failed to check safety devices, or deliberately disengaged safety devices. "Our foreigners understand when it is payday; they know where the toilets are; they know how to shirk their work; but when you tell them about some unsafe practice, they claim they do not understand." Apart from the employers' desire to blame accidents on the workers, workers displayed some real lack of cooperation due partly to the fact that some safety devices slowed workers, made their work more difficult and less efficient. For workers paid by piecework, this was often enough to encourage self-destructive behavior. Sometimes, the line's speed counteracted the time needed to work safely, and safety practices became impossible.[54]

Workers reported to the committee investigating the 1933 Briggs strike, that they often removed the safety devices from their machines in order to increase speed. When working at high speed, workers' goggles quickly became damaged and needed to be changed frequently, something workers found "no time to do." Goggles were also inconvenient to put on and off for short jobs, and many were tempted to take a chance without goggles. In addition they fogged up and trapped sweat; companies rarely worked to perfect goggles so they could be worn with comfort and efficiency. Workers in Packard's spray paint department were issued little aluminum respirators to wear but few did. When asked why, one worker replied, "Hell, we'd choke to death with one of them on." Typically, workers saw such devices as just one more inconvenience forced upon them by the company. Apart from reasons connected to earnings and speed requirements, workers who came to factories from the farms or the mines were used to danger and high accident rates and considered them a simple fact of life which they had little expectation of changing.[55]

Workmen's compensation for accidents was erratic. The main principle was the injured worker's constant vigilance and legal knowledge if he hoped to receive any compensation. In general, the worker's difficulties with job-related illness and accidents were his own problem. Companies even kept a blacklist in the 1930s of men suffering from lead poisoning. Often, workers who were injured were transferred to other jobs to demonstrate that they were capable of earning a wage and thus not in need of compensation. One worker complained that a Chevrolet plant in Toledo always kept the job of elevator operator vacant in order to transfer injured workers to the post. "The company in this way does not have to carry such a high rate of compensation insurance, while at the same time they make the workers feel that the company is good to them." Before World War I, Ford instituted a policy of hiring handicapped workers found in the Detroit community. In the 1920s, looking outside the Ford "family" to find handicapped workers in need of jobs was no longer necessary because, ". . . we had enough of our own Company liabilities to take care of. . . . It helped the employee and the Company. The Company didn't have to pay Workmen's Compensation because the man was employed."[56]

Another problem was that after two years, workmen's compensation suits were no longer admissible, so workers were sometimes told they would be taken care of, given jobs for two years, and then dismissed at the end of two years after being transferred to a job they could not handle. In addition, the companies could often charge the worker with contributory negligence, thereby being absolved of responsibility. In general, the burden of proof lay with the worker, usually legally unsophisticated with no organizational backing or money to carry on law suits.[57]

Industry spokesmen, and celebrants of the American industrial system in general, proclaimed the 1920s a New Era, an era characterized by a prosperity to be shared by workers and industrialists alike, an era whose prosperity was based on efficiency, intelligent management, an advanced technology, and workers whose skills lay more in accepting discipline than in exercising craft. The "new" in the new Era stressed cooperation between labor and management since both stood to gain from the shared profits of an efficiently run corporation. Labor conflict was inefficient, an old-fashioned way of resolving differences to be replaced by a reasonable spirit of cooperation that could be seen by both sides as enlightened self-interest. Capitalists, in effect, would restrain their greed; workers, their pride.

Corporate reformers of the 1920s were proud of an entire benefits package for workers that included more than merely wages. Bonuses, savings and investment plans, insurance, training schools, housing, and recreation programs all found a place in the auto industry with the aim of creating a more loyal and company-oriented work force. They combatted high turnover, unions, and low morale through plans that depended upon continued employment with the same company for their effectiveness. While these benefits may have produced some small measure of increased security to workers, their most important benefit was to employers in helping them develop a more stable work force. The real problems of insecurity faced by auto workers were caused by seasonal layoffs, arbitrary treatment in firing, unpredictability of employment, and the ever-present threat of sickness or injury, and none of the welfare measures of the 1920s did much to alleviate them. While the surrounding paraphenalia of company welfare in the 1920s may have been of little importance to most auto workers, the overall promise of a secure and decent standard of living was most important.

American industry's attempt to practice a welfare capitalism through the 1920s, as David Brody has reminded us, was based not merely on a desire to increase efficiency through controlling workers, but also on an idea that employers should accept responsibility for their employees' welfare. In one auto industry observer's formulation:

> Higher standards of living, shorter hours of labor, a further development of art and a greater degree of leisure are possible and near at hand as fast as man enslaves the machine for his welfare. But the success of the machine must not only be measured by the goods it creates. We must see to it that those who build and operate

it share in a greater happiness because of this master giant now in our midst.[58]

To the extent that auto employers created wages, hours, and safety policies that compared favorably with other major industries, the auto industry was a major practitioner of a paternalistic welfare capitalism. A major ingredient of welfare capitalism was missing in the auto industry, however, and that ingredient was employee representation. While a few auto companies, the White Motor Company being the most prominent, did have representation plans, most did not. That they did not is an indication both that they felt their workers sufficiently content not to need such additional reforms and that they saw that such plans were risky. The most vulnerable spot in the auto industry was the work it had to offer and the immediate conditions surrounding that work. Speed-up, tension, monotony, and small room for individual accomplishment or pride were submerged by the industry's ability to provide other compensations. Employers did not want to encourage any discussion of work itself; here they felt their control must remain absolute. It remained for the Great Depression to remove the industry's ability to offer its superior compensations, deal a death blow to welfare capitalism, and create conditions where workers took matters into their own hands.

Chapter Five

Quality of Life Outside the Factory

Sometimes it seemed that auto workers inhabited two separate worlds: they worked in factories and they lived at home. The division between life and work is a defining feature of modern industrial society. Auto employers of the 1920s saw factory work providing a decent standard of living that freed workers from insecurity and poverty, thereby justifiying itself beyond any questions about the lack of intrinsic satisfaction in that work. Auto workers were more aware of the complex ways in which working and living communities interacted.[1]

The two worlds of work and home, separate and distinct though they seemed, were intricately bound. At home, workers experienced the human ties of family and community and often, within the family, some of the authority and command that were denied them at work. At home, many workers lived in a world of racial and ethnic communality, in a culture which, while adapting to urban conditions, was familiar, reassuring, and preserved communal values. Workers took some of these values with them when they moved from home to factory. But even more pervasive were the ways in which work could dominate the rest of life. Life's material conditions were limited by the amount of money and degree of security that work could provide. The kind of recreational opportunities that existed were bound by the factory settings in urban areas. The strict demarcation between home and factory, between work time and "spare" time, were determined by the ordering of the day and the week around the factory whistle and the factory time clock. Most of all, the way a man felt about himself, his sense of physical and

71

psychological well-being were tied to the monotonous, determined, tension-filled nature of auto work itself.

Auto workers lived in a variety of circumstances. Contemporary observers seemed most concerned with housing as an indication of overall standard of living. Indeed, housing provides the home life analog of the factory for work life. Even workers earning similar wages might inhabit widely differing abodes. Some had inside plumbing, some did not; some took in boarders, some lived only with their families; some were boarders, others rented or owned their own homes; some kept farm animals and garden plots, others lived entirely on store-bought produce.

In 1914, the Ford Motor Company made its first investigations of the home conditions of its employees, ranking 47% of workers' homes good, 31% fair, and 22% poor. Conditions that could eliminate a home from the "good" category included the presence of boarders, dirt, unhealthy diet, and what was considered an "excessive expenditure on foreign relatives." By 1917, the Sociological Department ranked 88% of workers' homes good, 10% fair, and 2% poor. Canadian and English workers had the highest percentage of "good" homes, 97% and 96%, respectively; while Italian and Rumanian workers' homes were rated lowest with 75% and 76% "good" ratings.[2]

Ford expected foreign workers to adhere to standards of "American" living that must have seemed capricious. The Ford Motor Company complained that it had to educate its foreign workers as to the proper use of bathtubs (for baths, not the storage of coal) and to impress upon them the impropriety of keeping chickens in the house. The company saw such customs as un-American and, by association, almost immoral. "You know, when we found people keeping chickens in the house and carrying their coal in the bathtub and things of that kind, we knew they were not fit citizens. I think that the Ford profit-sharing plan made real citizens out of our employees, out of the type that never would have been otherwise." Ford had an effective weapon in his struggle to make "real citizens" of his workers. The $5 wage went only to those who complied with his standards. By 1917, the Sociological Department considered that at least 67% of the workers in each ethnic group employed at Ford had good habits. But the requests, particularly those against animals, must have seemed strange to former peasants trying to supplement their incomes with a few chickens. Thrifty habits won approval only if they fit "American" urban standards.[3]

Another common practice deplored by Ford and others concerned with Americanization was taking in boarders. Ford regarded male boarders as a moral problem, tempting wives and daughters into sexual lapses and endangering family solidarity. "Employees," warned a Ford publication called *Helpful Hints*, "should not sacrifice their family rights, pleasures, and comforts, by filling the house with roomers and boarders, nor endanger their children's morals or welfare by allowing them to associate with people about whom they know little or nothing." Ford Sociological Department investigators were instructed specifically to discourage workers from having boarders in their homes. The presence of boarders does much toward explaining the fact that ethnic workers found qualifying for the $5 day on the basis of home conditions much more difficult than did native workers.[4]

The practice of taking in boarders was widespread and augmented many workers' incomes. It was a flexible practice—boarders could be taken in when times were bad and space restored to family purposes when times improved. It also provided lodging that brought with it social ties with other workers of the same background and provided the boarders more cheer and companionship than the larger rooming houses of the city. English migrant Stan Coulthard found a home in which to board on his first day in Detroit. "It was like a second home for me. They were English people and very nice. . . . They helped me a lot—told me how to get jobs and find my way around." In addition, taking in boarders provided home employment for workers' wives at a time when few married women worked outside the home. Without the labor of the women of the family, who did the laundry, made the beds, and cooked the meals for their household's boarders, the whole system would have failed. It thus had advantages for both married and single workers, although it could create crowded living conditions.[5]

A 1916 study of ninety-six working-class homes, conducted by the Detroit Board of Health, found bed capacity for 1,974 persons in homes which they judged should have a capacity for only 1,477 persons. In addition, only eleven of the ninety-six homes were judged to have sufficiently sanitary bed conditions and only 19% were in compliance with the plumbing code. In some Detroit houses, beds did double or triple duty, as workers accommodated themselves to the shifts of the auto factories. "The men that worked nights would sleep in there; then the fellows on the day shift would sleep there, and then the ones on the afternoon shift. That bed would never get cooled off; they'd just keep that bed going all the time." If conditions were often crowded for boarders in private homes, they were not necessarily any better in public rooming houses where sanitary standards were often casual and comfort totally absent. One much-travelled worker complained, "I have traveled United States from coast to coast. And redgestered [*sic*] in some of the Rooming Houses in other citys [*sic*]. But I find some of the filthy dirty rotten stinking dumps in Detroit and Detroit is advertised to be a clean city oh yes not much."[6]

If crowded living, especially among foreign workers, was common before World War I, it was more from economic necessity and choice than from a shortage of housing in Detroit. Much of the Ford pressure to obtain better housing before World War I was successful because houses were available and often at a price that enabled workers to buy them. By 1920, however, the situation was quite different and a genuine housing shortage existed to the degree that even Ford was forced to soften his preference for single-family dwellings. Samuel S. Marquis, director of Ford's Sociological Department, reported, "In the old days we would go to a man who was in an undesirable place and say, 'old fellow, you have to get out and get this straightened out,' but now you have got to go to the Board of Health and ask them to let him stay in a condemned house, otherwise he would be on the street." One investigator reported a semibungalow in Highland Park housing four families in three bedrooms. When one renting couple reported to a Ford social worker that two couples and one eleven-year-old girl slept in one bedroom, he responded they should "be thankful that they had a roof over their heads." Detroit had become a boom town; the Board of Health felt pressured by the housing shortage to relax standards and waive provisions of the housing code until such time as "the supply of dwellings for housing this vast majority of our population has been greatly increased. . . ."[7]

A 1919 survey of Detroit's housing needs estimated a shortage of 33,000 dwellings and found 165,000 persons living in improper housing. Around 1920 and 1921, some people lived in tents on the outskirts of Detroit. Flint also had a tent city at its edge. Whereas single boarders had formerly shared some dwellings with a family, now several families might share a house or flat of one or two rooms that had never been meant to house more than one small family at most. From 1923 until 1928, more than 50,000 single homes were built in Detroit, but this was still not enough to provide decent housing for all the city's working class. Scarcity of housing kept rents high, most auto workers paying from 27% to 34% of their incomes for rent. In 1920, the Detroit Board of Commerce asked employers in the Detroit area to respond to a questionnaire about their employees' housing arrangements. The results of this study indicated that 33.6% of all employees owned the houses in which they lived and another 4.2% owned the flats in which they lived. This is a high percentage of home ownership by working people since the 1920 census counted a total of 37.8% of all Detroit families owning homes. Among these employed people, auto workers must have figured large. The additional increase in percentage of Detroit families owning homes from 1920 to 1930 (up to 41.3% from 37.7%) probably also included a sizable portion of working-class home owners. Owning a home meant much as an indicator of success and stability, even when mortgage payments might place an undue strain on the family budget.[8]

Owning a home provided some security and status but it did not free workers from worry. Wyndham Mortimer discovered the joys of home owning in 1923.

> Although I had worked steadily and my income was above average for the kind of work I did, life was still a real struggle. Mortgage payments, taxes, and insurance put a strain on my income. There was little money for anything except the essentials. Like other wage-earners with families, I was a do-it-yourself man. If the house needed repairs or paint, I did it myself. If my shoes needed half-soles, I did it myself. We had gotten rid of the landlord, but were now in the clutches of the mortgage holder.[9]

The preceding discussion of housing must be combined with other measures to provide a composite sense of the standard of living that an auto worker's income could provide. In the immediate postwar period, both the Visiting Housekeepers Association of Detroit and the National Industrial Conference Board prepared budgets of estimated minimum expenditures necessary to provide a "decent" or "fair" standard of living for a Detroit family. These requirements are presented in Tables V-1 and V-2 for a family of five. The expense categories of the two studies are not totally comparable, but both result in an estimated necessary income for a family of five that is greater than the average annual income of an auto worker for the year. In 1919, the average auto worker earned $1,431 with which to purchase the estimated necessities costing $1,702. In 1921, the average auto wage of $1,498 had to cover $1,698 of expenses. Obviously something had to be left out, a condition that the Visiting Housekeepers Association recognized when they suggested that the categories of insurance, health, and savings might be considered optional, a bookkeeping measure that still failed to provide an adequate income but did come closer to balancing the books. While an auto worker with a wife and three children might have some difficulty providing for them, the outlook improved with fewer dependents. In fact, a single man making the 1921 average auto wage of $1,498 might do quite well in as much as his estimated expenses for a minimum fair standard of living came to $912. Thus, although a single man might not be psychologically disposed to do so, saving was possible. And, indeed, we have John Anderson's word that in a fifteen-month period in the mid-1920s, motivated by a desire to attend college, he saved approximately $1,200. The breaking point between sufficient and insufficient income to provide the fair minimum standard of living in 1921 came with the second child. With a wife and one child an auto worker's income still exceeded his estimated expenses of $1,252. But with two children the estimated expenses jumped over average income to $1,527 leaving a $29 gap.[10]

Comprehensive statistics on the family status of auto workers is nonexistent. But, once again, Henry Ford provides some help. A 1917 Ford survey indicated that more than one-half of all Ford

TABLE V–1
Average Annual Cost of Maintaining Decent Minimum Standard of Living in Detroit, Family of Five, 1919

Expenses for:	Amount
Food	$ 557.16
Housing Rent	330.00
Clothing	368.64
Fuel and Light	118.32
House supplies and furniture	92.28
Insurance, health, and savings	164.04
Extras*	72.00
TOTAL	$1,702.44

*Includes carfare, recreation, and so forth.
Source: Visiting Housekeepers Association of Detroit, Minimum Budget for Decent Standard of Living in I. Paul Taylor, *Prosperity in Detroit* (Highland Park, MI: By the Author, 1920), p. 46.

TABLE V-2
Average Annual Cost of Maintaining Fair Minimum Standard of Living in Detroit, Family of Five, 1921

Expenses for:	Amount
Food	$ 535.60
Housing	420.00
Clothing	295.15
Fuel and Light	114.40
Sundries*	332.80
TOTAL	$1,697.95

*Includes carfare; recreation; medical care and sick benefits; insurance, church, and charity; tobacco; candy; toilet articles; and laundry.
Source: National Industrial Conference Board, *The Cost of Living Among Wage Earners, Detroit, Michigan September 1921* (New York: National Industrial Conference Board, 1921).

workers were married and lived in families that included dependent children. Table V-3 provides a breakdown that indicates a work force slightly less than one-third single and slightly more than two-thirds married. If one assumes that the number of dependent children in auto workers' families in 1921 was not too much different from 1917, the table suggests a situation where most auto workers were just able to provide for their families at the minimum rate recommended by the National Industrial Conference Board.[11]

For 1925 and 1929, even more revealing standard of living statistics are available based on interviews with auto workers about their actual expenditures rather than based on estimates of minimum necessary budgets. In 1925, the Visiting Housekeepers Association published information gathered for the purpose of studying black residents of Detroit. Nine of the families studied were headed by auto worker breadwinners, six black and three white. Table V-4 presents the figures and displays a wide range of living standards that could be met with comparable incomes. The average auto worker's income in 1925 was $1,675. Table V-4 provides information on workers whose income was commensurate with the average as well as ones that were considerably above and below that figure. Some of the variation might be explained if missing information

TABLE V–3
Family Status of Ford Workers, 1917

Ethnicity	Percentage Married	Percentage Single	Percentage Widowed	Percentage Divorced	Percentage with Dependent Children	Average Number of Dependent Children
American	67.1	30.3	1.6	1.1	45.5	1.3
Polish	79.7	19.7	.6	.1	69.3	2.3
Italian	62.9	35.7	1.2	.2	53.0	2.2
Canadian	75.8	21.1	2.4	.7	54.6	1.6
Romanian	69.2	27.7	2.8	.3	54.3	1.6
Jewish	69.9	28.7	1.0	.4	56.5	1.9
German	83.2	13.8	2.1	.9	66.8	2.0
Russian	61.6	37.8	.4	.2	49.2	1.7
English	73.3	23.2	2.6	.9	52.3	1.4
OVERALL AVERAGE	70.9	27.0	1.4	0.7	53.6	1.8

Sources: Accession 572, box 27, FMCA.

were provided. Some outspending their auto worker incomes may actually have had other income from boarders or other family members. One worker making less than the average income managed to save, while others making substantially more than the average ended the year in debt. The overall picture nonetheless is one where basic family necessities of food and shelter are met but little is left for other expenditures. The extras of the table include primarily carfare and recreation, one necessary to get a man to work, the other the only true "luxury" on the list.[12]

During the spring of 1929, Henry Ford requested that the International Labor Office provide him with sufficient comparative information to assist in establishing wage scales for his European plants that would provide the European workers with a standard of living comparable to that of his United States employees. Adequate information on exactly what that standard of living included was unavailable; therefore, the Bureau of Labor Statistics agreed to conduct a study of Ford workers in Detroit to acquire detailed information on standard of living. Ford insisted on certain criteria that would define the way a "natural family" lived on a $7 per day wage. Therefore, the following conditions had to be met before a family qualified for the study: During the entire year of 1929, the husband had to have earned approximately $7 per day; he must have worked at least 225 days during the year; the family must have had no important income other than that of the Ford worker (the husband); the family must have consisted of a husband, a wife, and two or three children younger than age sixteen; no boarders, lodgers, or other relatives must have been living with the family; no expenditures could be made on people living outside the family; the family must have lived in a single-family house, flat, or apartment; and families buying homes must have been making payments comparable to the rental value of such a home. These criteria were intended to provide information on the standard of living of a family that Ford considered both typical and desirable. That such a family was far from typical must be stated at the outset. Of the 1,740 married Ford workers earning approximately $7 per day, the investigators had no easy time finding their required 100 families to study. Although the study was reported at the time as an indication of "How Ford's Lowest Paid Workers Live," many workers must have been eliminated from the study because their standards of living were too poor to measure up.[13]

Tables V–5 and V–6 summarize the Ford study. By the 1929, the average auto worker's income was $1,638. The figures in Table

TABLE V-4
1925 Detroit Auto Workers' Budgets*

Income	Estimated Expenses	Family Size	Race	Budget for: Food	Shelter	Clothing	Fuel & Light	Rest**	Extras***	Balance/ Deficit
$1,800	$1,800	5	White	$540	$ 360	$120	$151	$468	$161	Even
$1,560	1,457	5	White	704	180	180	78	255	60	+$93
$1,632	1,387	6	White	633	420	34	50	75	187	+$245
$1,632	1,632	6	Black	449	588	96	80	140	252	Even
$1,596	1,338	7	Black	734	370	72	33	118	111	+$258
$1,590	1,816	8	Black	738	162	60	45	285	526	-$226
$1,376	1,662	10	Black	649	540	48	79	275	60	-$286
$2,412	2,573	3	Black	720	780	144	48	660	221	-$161
$2,244	2,520	4	Black	535	1,200	31	60	564	121	-$276

*The average annual income for auto workers in 1925 was $1,675.

**Includes home furnishings, insurance, health, taxes, and debt payments.

***Includes carfare, recreations, etc.

Figures compiled from data in: Detroit Mayor's Inter-Racial Committee, *The Negro in Detroit* (prepared by Detroit Bureau of Governmental Research, 1926), vol. XII, pp. 47–54.

V-5 translate into certain characteristic patterns of living standards. Most of the families (68%) rented their homes and managed to maintain fairly decent standards for shelter. The average family studied lived either in a separate house or occupied the entire floor of a building. The family lived in four to five rooms plus a bathroom (including an inside toilet and running water). Their rooms usually consisted of two or three bedrooms, living room, and kitchen, which served the multiple functions of food preparation, dining room, and general meeting area for the family. Their diets were judged to be sufficient in quantity and well-balanced nutritionally. Because only a few lived within walking distance of work, most used public transportation. They averaged a distance of 8.2 miles from home to factory. Slightly less than one-half of the 100 families owned an automobile, but only used it to provide regular transportation. The folklore of the day was replete with notions of the American industrial system as one so plentiful that its productive workers could consume the best that that system had to offer—often symbolized in the auto worker who owned a car. The evidence suggests that such an auto worker was more likely an exception than the rule.[14]

While the Ford survey certainly indicates a moderately comfortable standard of living, one that exceeded that available to many other working-class Americans, 44% of these auto workers still spent more than they earned at their auto jobs (see Table V-6). Consequently, 59% made installment plan purchases, which helps to explain how they accumulated the range of household products reported: 80% had sewing machines; 98% electric irons; 21% vacuum cleaners; 49% electric washing machines; 36% radio sets; 45% phonographs; 13% pianos; and 5% telephones.[15]

Table V-7 is a composite of budgets and expenditures from 1919 to 1929, providing only a rough basis of comparison because the categories of expenditures are not uniform from year to year, nor is family size. Most important, the 1919 and 1921 expenditures are estimates of necessary spending to provide a decent standard of living; the 1925 and 1929 figures are actual expenditures. Nonetheless, the gap between recommended or actual expenditures and income was narrowing. The overall picture is one of a modestly increasing standard of living accompanied by a modest indebtedness. It was a standard of living sufficiently desirable to keep most auto workers if not content, at least fairly quiet throughout the 1920s and sufficiently desirable to allow auto employers to present themselves as the representatives of a capitalist system that benefitted its workers not through charity but through the natural working of the system

TABLE V–5
Average Budgets of 100 Ford Workers, 1929*

Expenses for:	Amount	Percent of Income
Food	$ 556.12	32.3
Housing	388.81	22.6
Clothing	210.67	12.2
Fuel and Light	103.20	6.0
Furniture and house furnishings	88.55	5.2
Life insurance	59.16	3.4
Streetcar and bus fares	37.40	2.2
Sickness	64.73	3.8
School	6.41	.4
Cleaning supplies	16.64	1.0
Barber	12.37	.7
Miscellaneous	175.77	10.2
TOTAL	$1,719.83	100.0

*The average income of these Ford workers for the year was $1,711.87, slightly more than the national auto worker average of $1,638.
Source: "Standard of Living of Employees of Ford Motor Company in Detroit," *Monthly Labor Review,* 30 (June 1930).

itself that allowed wages to be high enough to provide comfort and security. The extent to which American workers shared in the profits of the New Era has recently been questioned by Frank Stricker. While Stricker includes auto workers among those minority of blue collar workers who "did well," I argue that his conclusions about all workers generally apply to auto workers as well. "Material living standards," Stricker concludes, "probably did rise in the 1920s; incomes were higher than before the war. But the struggle for economic security, not the struggle to keep up with the Joneses, dominated working-class life in the prosperity decade." In the case of auto workers, what mattered is that they saw themselves winning that struggle for security in the 1920s. That victory might be measured in modest gains, but it was still a genuine victory. All of this suggests

TABLE V-6
Ford Families Living On, Above, and Below Income, 1929

	Number	Average Income	Average Expenditures	Average Difference
Families living on income	19	$1,718.97	1,718.97	.00
Families living above income	44	1,698.28	1,829.01	−130.44
Families living below income	37	1,724.40	1,590.44	133.96
All families	100	1,711.87	1,719.83	−7.96

Source: "Standard of Living of Employees of Ford Motor Company in Detroit," *Monthly Labor Review,* 30 (June 1930).

an informal bargain in which workers traded pride in work and control over the work process for decent wages and an acceptable standard of living. After 1929, this standard of living was to be greatly eroded making the terms of the bargain moot on both sides.[16]

Thus, from around 1915 until 1929, the wages of an auto worker with steady employment could provide an increasingly decent standard of living if he lived without much catering to desires for even small extravagances. Before the 1920s, auto workers barely lived within their means, and many scrimped and did without or found it difficult to support a family. By the mid-1920s (earlier at Ford), auto wages could support a modest but comfortable standard of living for a family. Before World War I, the auto workers most likely to fall through the system and into poverty were immigrant workers; after World War I, black workers took their place as the most vulnerable and insecure category of workers. At all times, however, the auto workers' margin of security was never very wide. Security was difficult to acquire because the margin of difference between auto wages and falling below a decent standard of living was slim. A short period of illness, drinking and absenteeism, or layoff was enough to put most auto workers' families in financial danger. One Ford worker's wife described how life could change. "Up until five months ago my husband was employed at the Ford factory and we were very comfortable, when he started to drink and has been at it ever since. He has not brought a cent home in nearly two months now and all our savings are gone."[17]

The records of Detroit's United Community Services provide a revealing look at the fragility of the auto workers' security. Auto workers were not immune from needing welfare services. Often they

TABLE V–7
Standard of Living Detroit Auto Workers, 1919–1929

	1919	1921	1925	1929
Food	$ 557.16	$ 535.60	$ 633.56	$ 556.12
Housing	330.00	420.00	511.11	388.81
Clothing	368.64	295.15	87.22	210.67
Fuel and Light	118.32	114.40	69.33	103.20
House supplies and furniture	92.28	—	—	105.19
Insurance, health, and savings	164.04	—	—	123.89
Extras and sundries and other *	72.00	332.80	504.34	231.95
TOTAL	$1,702.44	$1,697.95	$1,805.56	$1,719.83
Auto income national average	1,431.00	1,498.00	1,675.00	1,638.00
Difference	$−271.44	$−199.95	$−130.56	$ −81.83

* Includes carfare, recreation, and so forth.
Source: Composite of statistics and sources from Tables V-1, V-2, V-4, V-5.

were referred to the United Community Services by factory welfare offices who found their circumstances inappropriate for company help. By far, illnesses and accidents were the most common instances that brought an auto worker to public assistance. Tuberculosis was often the villain. If the auto worker himself became ill, his illness meant unemployment, loss of income, rapid depletion of any savings, and dependence upon public services and other family members for survival. If illness struck another member of an auto worker's family, the results could be the same. Hospital bills could be staggering. If the wife became ill and unable to care for the children, workers had no resources other than public assistance. Public help often meant losing the children if the mother or father were deemed unfit to care for them. An Armenian worker at Ford in 1915, after periodic bouts of unemployment, finally became eligible for the $5 day. His wife, however, attempted suicide (not without reason, it should be mentioned, since he had deserted her and their five children earlier when she was in the hospital), and the social worker put the five children (ages ten, six, four, two, and one) into boarding houses. The father wanted them back, had difficulty understanding the welfare agency's authority over his family, and kept attempting to remove them from their new homes to return to his. An Armenian minister was enlisted to explain to the father that he must leave the children in the homes provided.[18]

Most of the auto workers who sought aid from the United Community Services before 1920 were foreign born and frequently categorized in the case records under the heading "Americanization incomplete." Of fifty-six auto worker families found in the case records before 1920, thirty-eight found themselves needing aid because of an illness or accident in the family. In another seven cases, the unemployment was not related to illness. As long as nothing went wrong (no sickness, no accidents, no drinking, no desertion, no layoffs, no seasonal unemployment) auto workers before 1920 could generally get by. But the multiplicity and normality of the things that could go wrong clearly indicated that most auto workers, especially those not yet integrated to urban living, had little cause to feel secure by merely having an auto industry job, not even if it happened to be one of the much-coveted $5 per day jobs. In some instances, even the case workers could find no explanation for the family's difficulty other than the all-encompassing "income insufficient."[19]

During the 1920s, when previously arrived immigrant workers acquired more security, black workers often took their places seeking welfare services. Various conditions could render a black auto worker's income insufficient for his support and that of his family. Note, for example, the case of one black family receiving aid from the Department of Public Welfare in 1926. The man, his wife, and children, came to Detroit in 1919 with experience as a worker in a southern plow factory. By 1926, his family consisted of eight children, the oldest fourteen and the youngest not quite one year old. The father found immediate employment in 1919 at the Kelsey Wheel Company and was soon earning $40 per week until the spring of 1920 when he was laid off for one and one-half years. This was presumably a recession-connected layoff, one shared in by many new workers in the industry. When he returned to work late in 1921, hourly wages were cut from 75¢ to 60¢ leaving him with an average weekly wage between $30 and $35. From 1922 to 1926, he suffered from periodic layoffs ranging from two weeks to three months and in 1926 averaged two to three days of work per week. Although the family had begun purchasing a home in 1919, they lost the house when the man became unemployed in 1921 and had not been able to begin buying again. In 1926, they lived in a five-room plus bath house for which they paid $45 a month rent. They had no roomers or boarders, and the investigators from the city welfare department found the house in good condition and in a good locality. Their housing then was comparable to that of some of the better-housed auto workers in the city but in order to maintain themselves in decent circumstances they also needed help from the city, help for which the man did unpaid work for the city in return. From 1920 to 1926, the Welfare Department sporadically provided grocery orders and milk tickets. They were exactly the kind of family of which the department approved, "self-respecting, good type of family, children clean and well-kept"; the father was an experienced factory worker; but still they found living on the uncertain income of auto employment impossible.[20]

Another Welfare Department case was of a black Ford worker who came to Detroit in 1918 and was laid off in 1922 and had been unable to find steady employment in the auto industry or anywhere else since. The department found his wife and six children (ranging in age from two months to nine years) living in six rooms in a "dilapidated and unsanitary" house for which they paid $24 per month rent. The husband's whereabouts were unknown but he was thought to be in the city and his wife believed he would return to the family if he could find secure employment. These cases are similar to those of pre-World War I immigrant workers and suggest a repetitive pattern as new groups of workers moved into the auto industry. Insecurity and discrimination were greatest for the newest arrivals who fit into categories defined by prejudice.[21]

Both immigrants and blacks comprised particular communities within auto cities. A look at their separate community existence is necessary to provide an overall sense of the auto workers' home life. The Poles, as the largest ethnic group in the auto industry, provide an example of the urban life of people who had been largely rural in Poland. In Detroit, many Poles lived in the separate municipality of Hamtramck, with an 80% Polish population by 1915. Hamtramck had much of the ambiance of the village in spite of its location, surrounded by the city of Detroit. In the second decade of the twentieth century, Hamtramck was an attractive enclave. Its neat lawns, small well-cared-for cottages, and air of hard-working respectability spoke strong communal values. By the 1920s, Hamtramck had already lost much of its attractiveness. Detroit's housing shortage set in, and small single-family homes now housed two or three families. About one-third of the houses still had outdoor plumbing in the early 1920s.[22]

The Polish family structure was patriarchal and tight even under New World conditions where many women eventually worked outside the home as domestics in hotels, restaurants, and other homes. Hamtramck was very much a family city. Unlike Detroit, where young adults were the most highly concentrated age group, in Hamtramck young children abounded. In 1920, more than 20% of Hamtramck's population consisted of children younger than five years old, giving Hamtramck the highest concentration of people younger than five years old in the United States.[23]

Hamtramck was a thoroughly working-class city. Those Polish businessmen and professionals who did live in Hamtramck had followed the Polish auto workers and were there to earn their living from providing services for the working-class majority. The many Polish associations, such as the Polish Falcons and the Alliance of Poles in America, that arose to furnish recreational opportunities and promote ethnic pride were also working-class associations. They provided a cultural milieu that was both ethnic and working class, but they did not foster working-class organizations along union or political lines. Their members were predominantly workers and their families, but their approach was to foster an ethnic solidarity that gave leadership to the much smaller number of small businessmen, professionals, and, especially, to the priests.[24]

Before World War I, the Polish ethnic associations were concerned especially with the home country. The Polish National Alliance and the Polish Falcons were primarily interested in creating pressure for Polish unification and independence. During the 1920s, associations designed to foster unity among Poles in the United States and to promote their interests became the dominant groups. The Alliance of Poles in America held a variety of social activities for Polish families and provided insurance benefits in case of illness or death. The Polish American Veterans Club sponsored social gatherings, parties, dances, and emphasized the Americanization of Poles. The most powerful and important of the Polish associations in the 1920s were within the Roman Catholic Church. The Church provided the clearest continuous tie with the past, supported traditional family values, and encouraged the continuation of the Polish language and culture amidst the pressure for Americanization. The Polish Roman Catholic Union was suspicious of all drives for assimilation, viewing them as threats to the power of the Polish clergy. Hence, they countered outside agencies with those of their own, offering insurance and aid to the needy for death, unemployment, or illness. So jealous were the Polish clergy of their prerogatives that they effectively prevented the Dodge brothers from sponsoring the construction of a YMCA building in Hamtramck. The lot which was to have housed the YMCA became a parking lot and the Church maintained its dominance over the social and cultural activities of Hamtramck.[25]

Black workers also found and created special living conditions different from both the native white workers and the white ethnic communities. Before World War I, the influx of black workers into the auto industry and Detroit was very slight. While segregated living patterns certainly existed, these patterns were to become more rigid and strictly enforced as a result of World War I. Even as early as 1910, almost 85% of Detroit's black population were concentrated in only four near east side wards. The increase of black workers during World War I, coincided with the developing housing shortage in Detroit and was sufficient to lead to discrimination against blacks, strictly segregated residential areas and social facilities.[26]

The World War I housing shortage was exacerbated for black workers by the growing racial segregation. Black workers were subjected to severe overcrowding, housing unfit for residential use, and in some cases total inability to find any housing at all. One report made in 1919 found

> not a single vacant house or tenement in the several Negro sections of this city. The majority of Negroes are living under such crowded conditions that three or four families in an apartment is the rule rather than the exception. Seventy-five percent of the negro homes have so many lodgers that they are really hotels. Stables, garages and cellars have been converted into homes for Negroes. The pool-rooms and gambling clubs are beginning to charge for the privilege of sleeping on pool-room tables overnight.[27]

Other men were found renting sleeping space in cars while some with money to spare slept in parks. Thus, some migrants confronted the ironic situation of earning much better wages than they ever had before, but were still unable to rent decent lodgings. In 1920, black workers were found "living in shacks unfit for human habitation and paying for them excessive rents."[28]

The average size of black Detroit households dropped between 1919 and 1925 from 8.83 people to 6.57 people, and this decline is accounted for almost entirely by a drop in the number of lodgers per household, an indication that the amount of doubling up had slacked off to some degree. Nevertheless, the 1925 investigation of the Motor City's black population found one not atypical case of a Ford worker who was the head of a family of three with five lodgers. In his home, four adults slept in a seven foot by nine foot room.[29]

That housing that did become available to blacks during the 1920s tended to be in areas of the city previously inhabited by earlier immigrant groups who owned their own homes and were able to exact very high rents for them, allowing them to move out to other areas and build new homes in new subdivisions where restrictive covenants were the rule. New housing went mostly to white workers, while black ones paid unusually high rents (approximately 33% of their incomes as compared with 27% for whites) for very crowded housing in older parts of the city. By the late 1920s, a small neighborhood of black-owned homes was located on the west side of Detroit where perhaps 15% to 20% of the black population of the city lived in their own homes. Much more typical were the crowded east side black neighborhoods which led the Mayor's Interracial Committee to report in 1926 that "sanitary dwellings at a reasonable rent" were still "the exception."[30]

Detroit investigators found in 1925 that black auto workers lived under a variety of conditions ranging from extremely bad to reasonably comfortable. One two-family dwelling housed several Ford workers who travelled two hours and twenty minutes to get to the River Rouge plant. While a small black community was located on the outskirts of Dearborn, named Inkster, many black workers at River Rouge lived in Detroit and often travelled considerable distances to get to work. These Ford workers lived in a house without a bathroom with one outside toilet for the two-family dwelling. Another Ford employee was found living in a tar paper house papered with scrap paper inside. Rooms were partitioned off with drapes and quilts. The house's only source of heat was the kitchen stove, and it had no electricity.[31]

By the mid-1920s more than one-half of the black families surveyed still took in lodgers. This was both a financial aid for black families and a service for single black men since no reasonably priced workingmen's clubs or hotels were available for black workers in Detroit in the mid-1920s. Almost 50% of the families shared houses with at least one other family; 33% housed other relatives. Although considerable crowding remained, tenement-apartment living was not the source of the crowding. Most of the older housing in Detroit into which black workers moved was of the detached type; 84% lived in either single or two-family dwellings and almost all lived in wooden houses. This was urban housing which bore much resemblance to rural housing. Still in 1925, 30% had no indoor bathrooms.[32]

In the 1920s, more racial tension surrounded residential patterns and competition for housing and residential areas than surrounded jobs. Detroit experienced a race riot in 1925 occasioned by a black physician's attempt to move into a white working-class neighborhood. Tension over housing was undoubtedly aggravated by the housing shortage, a scarcity not found in the job market. In addition, white workers had more control over housing patterns than they did over employment practices, and they exercised that control to create sharp distinctions among residential areas.[33]

The standard of living of white and black auto workers probably diverged the most at housing. Although incomes were roughly comparable, sufficient decent housing for black Detroiters simply did not exist at any price. The importance of housing both in helping to alleviate at home the harshness of industrial life and in providing a source of self-esteem was great. Here the differing experience of black and immigrant workers was also greatest. Immigrant workers were discriminated against in job classifications, forced to attend Americanization classes, and had their homes inspected by Ford investigators. The problems of crowding and taking in lodgers were part of the immigrant experience also, but far greater numbers of immigrants than of black workers eventually were able to purchase their own homes. Probably the single most important measure of success in America for the European immigrant population was homeownership. In fact, by 1920 Detroiters who were first and second generation immigrants were more often homeowners than were Detroiters of native stock.[34]

The city offered very little in the way of organized recreational programs for black workers, although a few settlement houses welcomed black families and the St. Antoine district, one of the poorest black residential areas, had the "colored" YMCA. The YMCA offered the usual athletic program of swimming, volleyball, basketball, boxing, and even tennis. But in spite of such occasional secular attempts to provide a social life to Detroit's black workers, the most important social institutions by far were the black churches.

Churches served the vital role of trying both to integrate rural blacks into the urban atmosphere and to cement and develop a sense of racial community and solidarity. At the heart of the churches' appeal were warmly remembered religious experiences and communities in their southern homes that migrants hoped to recapture in Detroit. In addition, the churches served as all around social centers hosting suppers, lectures, recitals, debates, plays, picnics, athletic events, and sewing and cooking clubs. One major black church even boasted a full-scale gymnasium. Where blacks did not always find doors open to them elsewhere in Detroit, they found in their churches a seldom-closed arena for communal life. A 1925 survey of Detroit black families found that church entertainments came second only to motion pictures in general popularity. Sunday services were also extremely popular and the leading black churches filled early on Sunday and turned away hundreds of worshippers for lack of space. Counting the established churches alone, church members comprised 55% of the entire black population of Detroit in 1925, not including the many members of storefront churches that mushroomed in the early years of the migration. The 1925 study concluded that for black workers facing the additional difficulties of a segregated city, the black church "takes the place of the theater, the dance halls, and similar amusement places, and fills the vacancy created by the failure of the public and commercial places of recreation and amusement to give him a cordial welcome."[35]

Leisure was a concept that New Era business welfarism promised its workers as part of the well-rounded life opening to American workers. For many auto workers, working ten hours a day, spending an additional two on the streetcar, and exhausting themselves at work, it may have seemed like a cruel joke. And yet Sunday always came, and for the young and very healthy even sleep seemed sometimes unnecessary if greater attractions beckoned elsewhere. Auto workers' recreational habits were much like those of other urban workers of the Midwest. Before World War I, they tended to be noncommercial; during the 1920s, they were decidedly more commercial. A 1914 poll of more than 1,250 male Ford workers revealed the following recreational preferences. Outdoor sports, especially football and cricket, led the list as the favorite of 452 men; then came walking, 227; cycling, 178; bowling, 157; gardening, 82; reading 63; homelife, 35; music, 32; and none, 30. Daily newspapers were consumed with avid interest as was neighborhood news.[36]

By the 1920s, commercial recreational facilities (such as movie theaters, burlesque and vaudeville shows, dance halls, and pool halls) had become more popular. They were patronized as gathering places to exchange news and gossip in addition to the specific entertainment offered. The 1929 Ford study revealed that 86% of the families spent some money on motion pictures. In addition, 2% reported expenditures for plays and concerts, 48% for magazines, 7% for books,

9% for excursions, 7% for vacations outside the city, and 1% for music lessons. Every family spent some money on newspapers. Houses of prostitution also flourished, and some observers thought they served as much as social centers for men to get together as they served a sexual function. "To many male newcomers the house of prostitution furnishes a social center to which he has ready access and where he receives a cordial welcome." Prohibition era speakeasies also served as social clubs, and the comeraderie of the drinking group was much prized. For Clayton Fountain, prohibition liquor shared with fellow workers was a welcome release at the end of a long day. "We tore around all night in automobiles, speeding from one blind pig to another, banging away on ukeleles and singing such tunes as *Me and the Man in the Moon* at the top of our voices."[37]

Some auto companies sponsored recreational programs, especially around World War I when labor was in demand and rapid city growth left workers without organized recreational facilities. Packard sponsored a Recreation league that provided athletic equipment for a variety of sports. The Packard Senior League limited its membership to men of at least five years employment with the company and provided pins, moonlight boat rides, and other outings along with speeches on company loyalty. In Kenosha, Wisconsin, Nash supported a recreational organization called the Kenosha Club, which promoted both athletic events and social gatherings. General Motors, particularly in Flint, had the most elaborate recreational program. Its Industrial Mutual Association, with the motto "Somewhere to go in Flint," provided a gymnasium, bowling alleys, billiard tables, card rooms, and a dance hall. It also sponsored an extensive intramural sports program open to all Flint residents. Company-sponsored sports programs were sufficiently popular in the 1920s to persuade the Auto Workers Union to "combat the bosses' sport organizations" and urge workers instead to support the Labor Sports Union.[38]

Ultimately, a worker's life away from the factory was not an independent existence, responsive only to its own rhythms and opportunities. By the late 1920s, workers increasingly reported feeling so fatigued after work that most of their off-hours were spent sleeping. Workers' wives frequently lamented that their husbands were too tired to be sexual partners. Black auto worker Charles Denby reported a "man would sit a half hour after work too tired to change clothes and go home." The auto worker asleep on the streetcar was a common staple of Detroit folklore of the 1920s.[39]

Coming down in a Woodward car this morning, a toiler was on one of the side seats. His legs were spread out, his arms hung out loosely, his head hung on his chest. He was sound asleep. The Ford workman's badge pinned to his cap, his clothes and the marks of toil on his hands showed where he had come from.[40]

The possibility of recreation compensating for the unpleasantness of work was increasingly offset by the way work could dominate all of life. In the words of a Ford employee interviewed in 1933, "I do absolutely nothing in the evening. I get so dumb working in there, I even forget how to use the English language. All the things which annoy me at the plant come out at home and it is not fair to the folks."[41]

Chapter Six

Auto Workers Respond to Their Work

The early years of auto worker history seemed to represent a break with the past. Here a new invention was produced in factories whose efficiency and marvelous machinery rapidly came to symbolize a new industrial order and whose workers seemed to have abandoned older traditions of trade unionism. For many Americans, ordinary folk and industrialists alike, the automobile assembly line came to define modern industry and its practices, a definition that did not include unionism or its attendant conflict; instead, it substituted a vision of the modern industrial world in which workers and industrialists saw their interests as one. In such a world, trade unions were merely old-fashioned anachronisms. The auto industry seemed perfectly designed to present the case since union power was almost nonexistent anywhere in the industry throughout its first three and one-half decades and only very occasionally did that situation threaten to change. Freedom from major union activity was used by industry spokesmen to argue that auto workers were basically content and readily accepted their work and its conditions. But unions are not the only means workers have developed to express their opinions about their work and its conditions nor are they the only means by which workers have ever attempted to exert some control over their working lives. When one looks beyond the mere existence or nonexistence of unions in the auto industry, one discovers workers whose behavior was not nearly so docile or passive or accepting as their employers liked to contend.[1]

Employers often made their case around the much-discussed issue of monotony. They cited their workers' lack of enthusiasm for shifting to different jobs within the factory as an indication that workers did not find monotonous work onerous, in fact preferring it to the opportunity to change. We have seen that workers understood they were being offered a meaningless choice that would not, in fact, allow them to escape monotony. On their own, however, workers made a similar choice, fundamentally just as meaningless if escape from monotonous work is the measure of meaning, but having the appeal of being self-initiated. They quit their jobs at one auto factory and went to work at another.[2]

Traditionally, high turnover was a problem for auto manufacturers and a release for workers who could maintain a sense af autonomy and freedom in frequent changes of jobs. As long as the industry was expanding and hiring practices remained relatively casual, workers could move from one company to another with considerable ease. Basically, they simply walked out of one on Thursday or Friday and into another on Monday, often without bothering to quit formally. The auto companies referred to "five-day men," that is, workers absent for five days without explanation or notice, who were then dropped from the payroll. Most workers leaving one company for another fell into the category of "five-day men." In 1913, Ford hired 52,445 men to maintain a constant labor force of only 13,632. Of that number, only 8,490 were fired during the year, while 50,448 (nearly as many as the total hired for that year) left voluntarily. In 1918, 26,572 workers entered Ford's Highland Park plant and 24,349 left, about one-half as "five-day men." By 1919, the rate of voluntary quits at Ford was considerably less but still very high. More than one-third of those workers dropped from the Ford payroll fell into the "ten days absence without notice" category. In 1919, Packard reported its heaviest turnover was among workers who had been on the job for less than one month. A worker who made it through the first month of employment was then likely to stay another four or five months when another high turnover point occurred, a pattern which Packard tried to eradicate by granting a small raise at the end of six months' employment.[3]

While the auto industry's rationalization measures of the 1920s helped to decrease labor turnover, relatively high turnover remained characteristic of auto plant life. As late as 1928, the auto industry had the highest quit rate of any Michigan industry, 5.2% of the payroll quitting every month. Seen from the viewpoint of the auto manufacturers, labor turnover represented a nuisance, although a nuisance they were capable of handling in an industry in which few jobs demanded extensive training. From the workers' viewpoint, changing jobs represented a kind of small individual frontier, a way of leaving personal disagreements with foremen, specific work rules, paychecks, and job routines behind, even if the new ones differed only slightly. A few cents per hour more in pay opened the possibility of material advancement and was enough inducement, especially for the young and single, to move on. Without pension plans, chances for advancement, or job security, workers had little incentive besides friendship and familiarity to remain loyal to any one company.[4]

A casual attitude toward attendance on the job was also characteristic of the preunion auto work force. "We have a large number of men in our employ who work only enough days per week to enable them to earn enough to live on—in lots of cases working every other day, making the total number of days worked, three per week," the Ford Motor Company complained in 1916. "These men are well aware of the fact that their record cannot be pulled as a quit unless they have been absent five consecutive days."[5]

Another way in which workers expressed their attitude to their work was in a general carelessness or outright abuse toward tools and materials of production. This was particularly important in an industry which minimized skill and in which many workers had little sense of tradition or pride in tools or the product they produced. Carelessness toward tools and materials meant that the auto companies suffered in several ways. They replaced tools frequently, spent money on devising especially durable and sturdy tools, eliminated substandard products (scrap), and instituted an elaborate inspection and supervision system to reduce the abuse of tools and the creation of scrap.[6]

One of the most persistent instructions to foremen at Packard was constantly to guard against the tendency of workers to abuse tools and use them nonselectively. "We find that the jobsetters and workmen have very little respect for tools. They use a steel hammer or wrench or anything they may get to pound with and abuse them in every way possible until one is scarcely able to identify them." Packard made many of its own tools in an effort to create tools that would be as indestructible as possible. But tools alone were not the entire problem; companies also had to deal with a large scrap pile which they struggled to reduce through better supervision and more foolproof production methods.

> The class of labor which we are getting today requires better and more persistent instruction and supervision. Many of these workmen have never before seen the inside of a machine shop, and unless

we all get busy and make them more thoroughly acquainted with their jobs we may expect more scrap than ever before. This close supervision is especially needed with respect to the use of poor tools. Through the operators' ignorance many tools are rendered unfit for use and yet they continue to use them, producing nothing but scrap.[7]

In addition, companies suffered loss from theft by workers. Tools, parts, and even tires regularly disappeared from auto factories, another indication that while workers were unorganized and relatively quiescent, they should not be considered content or loyal or having a strong personal identification with the companies for which they worked.[8]

Besides these individual means of resistance to the factory, workers acted cooperatively when they were slow and clumsy when observed by time-study men and when they established their own production rates and tried to keep maverick workers from exceeding them. Foremen often collaborated with their men in attempting to have times expected for job completion set as high as possible since that gave the foremen more leeway to compile a high efficiency record for their departments. Packard found it necessary to warn foremen that failure to give time-study men "proper support" would result in disciplinary measures. In general, workers exerted as much control as they could over the pace of production by limiting their piecework output to an agreed-upon level that struck a balance between exertion, wages, and the danger of company changes in rates if earnings became too high. New workers would soon be informed of a proper day's average, sometimes by the foreman himself, and workers who had been around would usually make it their first question when on a new job.[9]

Workers could have varying motives for restricting output, although fear of rate cutting by the company was certainly the most common. Stanley Mathewson's 1931 study of output restriction in American industry cited numerous examples from the automobile industry. For instance, workers on a transmission assembly line set for themselves an agreed-upon number of units for each shift. A group of machine tool workers set their quota not to exceed earnings of 72¢ per hour. Workers on an hourly wage sometimes limited their production if they thought their wages were too low, in effect adjusting the wages by working fewer hours than they were physically on the job. A gang of electrical maintenance men agreed to work effectively for five hours of a nine-hour shift since they were paid less than they thought they should be. Maintenance workers had an advantage over line workers in employing this technique since their work made it necessary for them to move about the factory and it was difficult for the managers to know exactly how much time each job should take.[10]

Fear of layoffs could also impel workers to limit output if they thought the company was waiting for a limited stockpile to be produced. Sometimes workers could adjust their rates to even them out by creating a bank of parts produced in excess of a day's quota that could be saved to be included in another day's total. Responding to a management directive that production for the second part of the shift must equal production for the first part, Chevrolet camshaft department workers agreed to produce 124 shafts per shift. The pickup man took only sixty-two shafts at lunch time and another sixty-two at the end of the shift. Any extras were saved from the morning to add to the afternoon and counter the natural tendency to work harder early in the shift. Cylinder grinders at Continental Motors in Detroit limited production to twelve six-cylinder blocks in a nine-hour shift. Those few who broke the agreement and exceeded the limit were called "hungry bastards" and the other cylinder grinders had ways of bringing them around. "They were ostracized; no one would talk with them. Every time one of them went for a drink of water or to the washroom, the belts on his machine were cut, the grinding wheel was smashed, his personal tools were damaged, the word RAT was chalked on his machine in block letters." The auto companies were not totally unaware of these worker practices, nor did they fail to see that they arose largely from the company practice of changing rates. In fact, they occasionally encouraged a temporary burst of speed by guaranteeing that speed would bring no rate cuts. This could produce a dramatic rise in production.[11]

Restriction of output was more than simple protection against rate cutting. It allowed workers some control over their work practices and production pace. It also provided a kind of measure of status whereby experienced hands could feel their superiority over new ones and all could come to see the benefits of working together to limit output wherever possible. Company rate-cutting practices combined with line determination of pace created a moral universe where an ethic of unceasing hard work and constant pushing oneself made little sense. Pride could not be found in workmanship or even in simple unremitting diligence: the system rewarded neither. But some measure of pride could be restored by trying to beat the system.

Walter Ulrich, a student who observed the auto industry from a worker's job, noted these distinctions. Finding himself shocked at first by what he saw as an unethical attitude on the part of workers that stressed doing as little as possible to "get by," Ulrich soon found himself falling into the same pattern and able to "stall around myself occasionally and really enjoy it." His comments, written in 1929, are particularly incisive.

> This developing of a 'get-by' attitude is almost inevitable because a man does not need to be a hard worker to win the approval of his fellow workers. In fact I found the opposite to be true. The old workers disapprove and curse the new man who comes in and works 'as if he were on a farm'—unless he has to, as is the case on many line jobs.[12]

Restriction of output was, then, an assertion of the ethics of a workers' culture that recognized values of solidarity to one's fellows and a reasonable balance between effort and reward above those of making every possible penny or meeting company standards for best worker. Workers could do little to affect basic job definitions or skill levels, but they could have some effect upon pace and tension, and they humanized the work environment by adding a level of comeraderie based on besting the company that may have taken over for older forms of comeraderie based on shared skills and greater control over the labor process.[13]

Auto workers did not limit their collective activity to restriction of output; they also engaged in direct collective activity against their employers in the form of walkouts. These walkouts often lasted less than a day and were usually defensive in nature, but they were a clear and direct defiance of employer domination. Those strikes and walkouts that occurred outside of any union context were often collective only in the sense that a certain group of workers walked out at the same time. There was often no collective bargaining with the company and workers either found new jobs elsewhere or straggled back to their old jobs, negotiating individual terms of readmittance. In 1906, core makers at Leland and Faulconer struck to increase their wages and maintain their union. "The management," commented Michigan's Bureau of Labor and Industrial Statistics, "found very little difficulty in filling the places of the strikers." Another example of this type of walkout occurred at the Hupp Motor Company in 1911 when a department of forty men walked off the job in the morning only to be replaced by twenty-eight workers from the Employers' Association Labor Bureau by the afternoon. Two days later, ten of the strikers were rehired, and the department was once more fully manned. In another case, the Seaman Body Company announced a cut in the piecework rate for doorhangers in 1926. John Anderson described the reaction:

> When the men were notified of this most of them refused to work. They didn't walk out but just sat around talking about what ought to be done. There was no union or talk about a union. There was some hostility toward those men who turned in too many pieces and thus brought about the cut in piece rates. Some of us got tired of standing around. We went home at noon and returned the next morning. Most of the men had returned to work at the reduced piecework rate.[14]

A similar walkout occurred at the Briggs body plant in 1929 when the company cut piecework rates on the backs and cushions line. After lunch the workers simply refused to obey the whistle and "sat around on cushions waiting to see what would happen." What happened was a visitation from company brass who threatened to fire the men if they did not start work immediately. The workers were sufficiently angry to let loose with a few comments and threats of their own.

> We told them that the Briggs plant was run by a bunch of rats who did nothing but scheme how to sweat more production out of workers and that we didn't care a damn how many of us they fired; we just weren't going to make any more cushions or backs at the new low rate. . . . Some of the workers threatened to take the bosses outside and beat hell out of them.

This "verbal free-for-all" with "no epithets barred" erupted spontaneously without benefit of a union or any recognized leadership and resulted in a small workers' victory. The old rates were restored and the men went back to work.[15]

Patriotism, too, could spur informal workers' actions. Flint auto workers expressed their displeasure at being expected to work on Armistice Day in 1925 by holding a parade with a drum and some flags through their plant and then to adjacent plants, all of which closed down for a mass rally.[16]

The most common occasion for such walkouts was the announcement of a wage cut or change in piecework rates, which amounted to a wage cut. Usually such walkouts were only department wide and were often a tribute to the company's ability to divide the workers by dealing separately with each department, making wage cuts one at a time and thus limiting the workers' potential for striking back. In addition, craftsmen were represented by separate unions, thereby increasing the factory's divisiveness. A striker in a Fisher Body plant who belonged to an American Federation of Labor woodworkers' union described what happened when his department received a 10% reduction in wages.

> My unit went on strike. The strike lasted for about three weeks and during that time we walked the picket line. But due to the set up under the old craft union, the metal finishers in the body shop, the painters, the trimmers and all the other units continued to work because they did not receive a cut. They hired in people to replace us. Within three weeks' time the plant was running normal. We lost the strike and I was blackballed, fired.[17]

Even where skilled workers were successful in winning demands through a walkout, their victory did not extend beyond their particular skilled group. The painters at Packard protested a wage reduction in 1921 by staging a twelve-week strike. The result was company recognition of the painters' right to collective bargaining through Local 127 of the Auto Workers Union, but the recognition extended to painters only even though the union was open to all auto workers.[18]

When strikes and walkouts did occur they sometimes raised issues other than wages and piecework rates, but only after the workers walked out. The original reason for the walkout was to defend against a company attempt to set workers back. If strikers got as far as composing a list of demands they might include other issues, particularly the desire for job security. Such demands were more likely to be articulated when an appeal had been made to some union for help. Many of the strikes and walkouts of the pre-World War I and the 1920s period occurred without benefit of any union, and even where the Auto Workers Union was called in it did not gain permanent members once the strike ended.[19]

Despite the generally defensive nature of auto walkouts, workers occasionally went on strike with a specific offensive position. In 1910, Lozier Company workers in Plattsburgh, New York, circulated a petition requesting a nine-hour day with the same pay they were receiving for a ten-hour day. The workers agreed beforehand that they would walk out if the company refused their request. After a few days the company announced it would fire all workers failing to report to work the next day. Some of the younger men took their pay and left town while the rest drifted back to work a ten-hour day. A 1919 strike at the Wadsworth Manufacturing Company, a builder of automobile bodies for Ford, demanded recognition of workers' shop committees and worker control over who should be elected to such committttees. The shortlived strike was broken by Ford's cooperation in allowing Ford employees to be used as strike breakers.[20]

Auto industry walkouts before 1933 were an expression of spontaneous worker resistance to total domination by their employers, evidencing capital's inability to exert complete control over the labor process as long as that process involved human workers. But preunion walkouts were usually unsuccessful in having any major effect upon the workers' chief employment grievances. Not only were they unable to gain concessions on the immediate issue that sparked the strike, but even more important, they were also unable to serve as a catalyst for creating a lasting organization to build "for the next time." When, after the initial successes of the United Auto Workers in 1936 and 1937, workers responded with a rash of spontaneous wildcat strikes, no one should have been surprised. Such strikes were not just the result of the pent-up frustration of years of depression and no union; they were also a part of the auto workers' tradition. The difference was that from 1933 on, they had a chance of winning.[21]

Neither absenteeism, turnover, output restriction, nor sporadic walkouts added up to a work force continuously able to defend itself against inhumane work rules, speed-up, or fluctuating and insecure employment. Even less did they mean a work force individually concerned with protecting its dignity and maintaining a line beyond which it would not be pushed but, at the same time, lacking the collective institutions to do so. Such collective institutions are unions and while their absence from the auto industry does not signify worker contentment, that absence does require an explanation.

One factor in the lack of any successful organization in the auto industry was the hostility of the industry leaders and the united opposition to unionization represented by their combined presence in the Employers' Association of Detroit. The Employers' Association was formed in 1902 to spark a drive to make Detroit an open-shop city. By 1910, all the major automobile manufacturers were represented within the organization, meeting together within an automobile division. In the 1920s, the Employers' Association publications proudly carried the message: "Ninety-seven percent of Detroit's work-people pursue their various callings without let or hindrance from organized labor domination." The Employers' Association accomplished its aims in several ways. Its employment bureau supplied strike breakers and was capable of replenishing a striking work force before the strike was one day old. Both before and after World War I, it kept records and compiled lists of labor radicals, especially Industrial Workers of the World and Communist organizers. The names were circulated for employers so they could keep their factories free of troublesome influences. It also bound its member employers to refuse to deal with union representatives whenever possible.[22]

In the 1920s, companies were likely to supplement the Employers' Association agents with elaborate spy forces of their own to keep tabs on their workers and attend radical and union meetings. Such tactics were extremely effective in making workers afraid to show any open interest in unions for fear of losing their jobs. This fear even extended to taking a leaflet from organizers outside the plant.

> People would be standing there handing out these leaflets to organize the auto workers. There would hardly be 10% of the people who would even accept them. A lot of people were afraid to accept them. It was just that same fear that you have heard about. They were walking out with somebody they did not know. They figured he was a stool pigeon and vice versa.[23]

One indication that the auto manufacturers felt secure in the effectiveness of their simple antiunionism was the extreme rarity of company unions in the industry during the 1920s, a period of great popularity for company unions in other industries. The White Motor Company, in keeping with its generally paternalistic procedures, did have a company union, but White was the only auto company of stature to have a company union before 1929. There was no large-scale initiation of company unions until 1934 when auto manufacturers saw them as a way of meeting the collective bargaining provisions of the National Recovery Administration's automobile code.[24]

The united opposition of the auto manufacturers certainly served to make organization difficult, but it can hardly explain the magnitude of the failure, for even without the activity of the Employers' Association labor organizing in the automobile industry had many obstacles. The potential membership of the traditional American Federation of Labor unions was a small proportion of workers in the industry, especially after mass production was widely implemented. Even those skilled and semiskilled workers who did belong to craft unions often were inactive members while they worked in automobile factories. The instability of the work force also made it difficult to organize. The attitude of "just passing through" of many workers who did not expect to remain auto workers for long periods of time made them indifferent to efforts to change. A student worker in noting that some of the men he worked with at Packard did not expect to remain long at their jobs, found they "want to see the world or try it somewhere else." Especially the younger men saw the job as a "temporary makeshift till they can go into [a] grocery business or what not." Many of the auto workers came originally from areas and situations where unions were unknown or uncommon. This was as true of many European immigrants with agricultural backgrounds, as it was of the black and white southerners who came to northern auto factories. It was also true of many young men from midwestern farms.[25]

Perhaps the greatest obstacle to union organization of the automobile industry lay in its earned reputation as a high-wage industry. The pace might be rugged, the work rules rigid and dehumanizing, and the work itself mind-numbing and grueling, but as long as the paycheck was one of the highest in the nation for blue-collar labor, unionization never scored large successes. Even in 1919, the technical journalists of the auto industry, Horace Arnold and Fay Faurote, ascribed to large paychecks the power to make the workmen "absolutely docile." Roy Chapin, president of Hudson, observed to Samuel Crowther, the journalist collaborator of Henry Ford, that the most important aspect of labor relations was "whether the laborer is well-satisfied with the size of his pay envelope." From the initial lure of Henry Ford's 1914 $5 wage through the high-wage period of the 1920s, workers were drawn to auto cities by dreams of making a killing even if only for a few years. Workers around the nation talked of "fabulous wages" in auto. After Clayton Fountain landed his first automobile job at Packard in 1928 he tried to sleep in preparation for his shift. "Each time I closed my eyes, visions of hundred-dollar paychecks danced in front of them. Daydreams full of new suits and Saturday nights with a pocketful of dough to spend in the speakeasies floated through my mind." Black auto worker, Charles Denby, remembered his dreams, nourished in 1920s Tennessee, of what the auto industry could give him:

> We had heard at home that you could make twenty five or thirty dollars a week in the factory. I thought I'd be rich. On the farm

if you had five dollars you'd carry it around for six months. Ten dollars seemed impossible. . . . After a few years in Detroit I would have several thousand dollars. I always planned to send money to my mother and father. I wanted them to build a home like the white people had."

Indeed, $25 to $30 per week wages did exist. They did not spell riches, but for some they did mean feedom from the insecurity of farm tenancy or very low southern factory wages and the possibility of a higher standard of living and a better future for one's children. Where relatively high wages were available to workers with little skill, without the aid of a union struggle, many years and a depression were necessary to convince workers that they must organize.[26]

The auto factories were a new arena for organized labor where many of the rules of the past were invalid. The very work itself, with its annihilation of the need for skill and craft, meant that even those workers who came from a craft union tradition could make little use of that tradition. Auto workers were not bound together by a common craft nor did they share a pride in workmanship. Instead, they were divided into hundreds of job categories, few of which bore any relation to older traditions of craft.

Nor did auto workers share a common history. One group experienced a transition in their work experience from a mode of production which involved small shops, the need for a variety of skills, intimate work groups, and a craftsman's pride in work. For these workers, primarily native Americans from midwestern shops who started to work in the auto industry before 1908, the shift from carriage or machine shops to auto shops involved little noticeable change except perhaps the excitement of working on a product that was a promising new invention. The difficult transition for them came from within the auto industry and was caused by the intro-duction of mass-production methods. Another group of workers, primarily before World War I, made the transition from European peasants to American industrial workers. While some had manufac-turing experience in Europe, many arrived in the United States without industrial experience. Unencumbered with a craft tradition associated with the small shop, they coincided perfectly with the needs of an auto industry shifting into a mass productive mode. Some of these workers came to the auto factories after previous industrial experience in the United States, especially in steel. Their work experience before coming to the auto factories, if they had industrial experience at all, was likely to have been as laborers doing heavy work requiring considerable strength, not as the machine tenders they were most likely to become in the auto industry. Whether or not auto was their first industrial experience, they had to learn a new attitude toward time, precision, and taking orders than had been appropriate previously. During World War I and after, many midwestern and southern farm laborers became auto workers who, like European immigrants, had little or no previous experience with industrial life and work, although they did have the advantage of not having to adjust to another language.

The arrival of culturally distinct groups of workers into the auto industry tended to take place in successive time periods, although midwestern farm laborers were a fairly constant stream throughout the whole period from 1900 to 1930. The great majority of automobile workers during this period came into an industrial situation already established, although the pace of transition to mass production varied from one aspect of automobile construction to another. All of them, the native craftsmen, the Polish immigrants, the southern blacks, the white farm workers from the South and Midwest faced a difficult shift from a previous work pattern and way of life in which their work habits and attitudes toward time were more informal and irregular and, perhaps most important, more under their own control. Nonetheless, for some, auto work seemed an improvement over the past; for others, a decline. Those workers for whom auto work came to mean a loss of skill were consistently the core of the small union movement that did exist in the industry. That such workers were not present in large numbers helps to explain the weak union presence in auto plants.[27]

The ethnic and racial diversity of the auto work force was also a barrier to worker unity in itself. In the years before World War I, when the foreign work force was at its heaviest, organizers were confronted with a situation in which many workers did not speak English and others did so only minimally. Furthermore, eastern and southern European immigrants had found American auto factories' wages sufficient to raise their standards of living. Not only were the immigrants physically separated from the American workers, but they were also separated by language and culture. The Ford Motor Company conducted a study of its discipline cases from 1914 to 1917 and found that 85% were American born or English speaking suggesting that American workers (who after all knew something of the ropes) found fighting back easier than did immigrants. Immigrant workers needed time to develop a sense of what their rights might be in an American factory context. The study also suggests that immigrant workers may have been more eager to please their employers and saw their jobs, deskilled though they were, as a step up rather than as a step away from autonomy and craft.[28]

Racial division was another source of disunity and black workers displayed considerable neutrality even in the 1930s union struggles. The main problem was that black workers felt their interests were not well served either by employers or unions and, in the case of Ford, the employer may have had an edge. Black workers at Ford understood that some white workers objected to their presence and were afraid that a union would mean white workers could deny them jobs. As with the immigrant workers, the existing unions made little effort to win over black workers other than a policy statement that included them as potential members. There were no black members of the Carriage, Wagon and Automobile Workers Union and only a few in the Auto Workers Union in spite of the latter's stated emphasis on winning black workers. Like the rural immigrants, southern blacks had no previous experience with unions. They did, however, have experience in observing white people in organized groups acting against the interests of blacks and were suspicious about joining overwhelmingly white organizations in the name of worker unity.[29]

Thus, many of the trademarks of the auto industry made it a difficult setting for a thriving trade unionism. As a vigorous, expanding industry built around a revolutionary invention that captured the public imagination and approval, the industry had a decided edge over its workers. While the industry continued to grow and thrive, it provided good jobs for little-skilled foreign, black, and white workers who could not find comparable jobs outside the auto industry. Especially for younger workers, even in the 1920s, the auto industry had an aura of excitement and opportunity about it that could be matched nowhere in industrial life. Divisions in the work force combined with high wages might lead either to a cocky individualism or to a quiet apathy, but it was not a combination conducive to the collectivism of industrial unionism.

Chapter Seven

Auto Worker Unions

From the beginning of its history, the automobile industry experienced a small union presence, which was of great importance in preparing auto workers for finally embracing industrial unionism in the 1930s. The Carriage, Wagon and Automobile Workers (CWA); the Industrial Workers of the World (IWW); and the Auto Workers Union (AWU) were never successful in unionizing the industry; indeed, many workers were left unaware of their presence. Nonetheless, the activities of these unions combined with the spontaneous collective activities of the workers themselves to create a ready atmosphere which, mixed with the Great Depression's conditions of economic deprivation and new organizing drives, resulted in the eventual unionizing of the industry.

Before World War I, only two organizations, the Industrial Workers of the World and the Carriage, Wagon and Automobile Workers, attempted to organize automobile workers as automobile workers, rather than as specific groups of skilled workers. The IWW's history in the auto industry was not as significant or newsworthy as it was in the textile or lumber industry, nor did it ever stage a successful free speech fight in Detroit. It did, however, contribute substantially to a 1913 strike that aroused considerable apprehension among auto manufacturers and may have contributed to the introduction of the $5 day. The IWW had maintained a local in Detroit since 1905, but it was not until 1910 that it showed serious interest in attracting auto workers. In 1910, the IWW established a Metal and Machinery Workers' Local No. 16. By 1911, the IWW in Detroit claimed more than 400 members, an increase from only fifty in 1910. By May 1913, 200 auto workers were counted among Detroit's IWW membership.[1]

The years just previous to 1913 were ones of considerable uncertainty and instability for workers. There was concern over length of the working day, fluctuating pay scales, and changing work routines. Most auto plants except Ford operated on a ten hour day. Ford instituted a nine-hour day in 1905, but reverted to a ten-hour day early in 1913. The IWW had done intermittent campaigning for an eight-hour day snce 1911. In a 1912 report, a labor spy for the Employers' Association of Detroit informed that the IWW included within its organization a group of automobile workers and that the American Federation of Labor (AFL) in Detroit was not averse to working with the IWW on specific issues. The Employers' Association of Detroit warned Detroit employers in 1912 that considerable dissatisfaction existed in their factories, stating that there was "more restlessness, more aggression among the workmen in Detroit . . . than there has been for several years past."[2]

In March 1913, IWW national headquarters decided to aid their Detroit local's organizing efforts by sending several organizers to Detroit to give speeches and lead a concerted campaign of agitation at Ford's Highland Park plant. Standard practice for labor organizers who were not themselves part of a local factory work force was to try to speak to the workers when they left the plant for lunch. Capitalizing on Ford's recent return to the ten-hour day, IWW speakers concentrated on the advantages of an eight-hour day for workers. After a few days of speeches and arrests of speakers, Ford ruled that workers must remain inside the plant during lunch periods. According to one Ford worker, Ford followed a carrot and stick policy in dealing with the IWW, on the one hand refusing to let workers attend rallies during lunch and on the other hand promoting IWW members to foremen. As foremen, they were ineligible to belong to the IWW.[3]

When lunchtime speakers were banned at Ford, the IWW shifted its efforts to Studebaker where some members were already employed. Here workers had an immediate grievance resulting from a recent company change in pay practices from a weekly paycheck to a biweekly one. Workers within the plant had already formed committees to negotiate for the return of weekly pay days and the IWW organizers were thus able to speak to a situation already in existence.[4]

In June 1913, workers in three Studebaker plants (6,000 workers in all) went on strike. The strike did not involve skilled workers organized into AFL unions, but it did have the sympathy of the iron molders and metal polishers who also requested the company to agree to the strikers' demands. The strike, which lasted one week and was marked by several clashes between strikers and police, was the first important industrially organized strike in the auto industry and was an exception to the rule that only workers eligible for craft unions could be moved to action. The strike was, therefore, of concern to all auto manufacturers because it suggested the possibility that large numbers of workers could become unionized. While the industry was willing to deal with a few AFL craft unions, especially in a situation where skilled workers were becoming a very small portion of the work force, it was not willing to change the whole picture of labor relations in the industry and see the great majority of workers come under union protection.

The strike occurred during the summer slack season in automobile production when many workers were laid off and looking for jobs. There was little hope that it could last beyond a week and the strikers themselves were hoping to get their old jobs back before they were taken by unemployed workers. One of the national IWW organizers, Matilda Robbins, herself described some of the difficulties of the strike:

> There were some 50,000 or 60,000 auto workers in Detroit at the time. The IWW local did not have the ability, nor even the comprehension, of the magnitude of the job. And the speakers were not organizers with plans and discipline to help tackle the job. The strike dissipated itself. Many years were to elapse before the auto workers would move as a mass toward industrial unionism.[5]

In those many years, the IWW remained a small but vocal group whose members comprised part of the core of committed unionists and radicals in the auto industry. For awhile after 1913, the IWW was visible in Detroit working-class neighborhoods primarily as a source of relief for the unemployed. During 1914 and 1915, the IWW converted a cooperating Unitarian Church into a soup kitchen and overnight shelter known as the IWW Flop. For 10¢, an unemployed worker could secure a pew to sleep on for a week, plus supper and breakfast, wash facilities, and help in locating employment.[6]

IWW's weakness regarding daily organizing and its strength in giving direction to specific strike struggles was particularly noticeable in the auto industry where no AFL union was prepared to move in and reap the benefits of an IWW-led strike. No group was ready to convert strikers into steady union members or to build a continuing organization out of the strike. The Carriage, Wagon and Automobile

Workers Union saw the opportunity created by the IWW's presence and the Studebaker strike and requested an organizer from the AFL. The union argued both the need to defeat the radicalism of the IWW, which it saw as particularly appealing to foreign workers, and the need to take advantage of the enthusiasm for worker unity created in the Studebaker strike to move strikers into the Carriage, Wagon and Automobile Workers. The AFL, however, argued that it could not afford to send an organizer at the time—a decision perhaps colored by growing jurisdictional disputes among its affiliates in the automobile industry.[7]

Although the IWW continued to operate in Detroit, in the 1920s its role became almost exclusively educational. By 1932, it had occasion to rejoice over the growth of its membership to eighty. One student of the auto industry felt in 1933 that the IWW still suffered from its old organizational problems, problems rooted in the philosophy of anarcho-syndicalism. He judged the IWW leaders "fine fellows" but "very poor executives, whose temperament embodies so completely the philosophy of rank and file control that they give no real leadership when it is needed." If the IWW's ability to construct a lasting organization in the auto industry was minimal, its influence was not necessarily correspondingly small since individual members of the IWW in their conversations and presence were one of the few reservoirs of the union idea and helped keep that idea alive through the 1920s. By 1933, the IWW again had a hard-working nucleus active in the Briggs strike.[8]

In 1891, the AFL granted a charter to the International Union of Carriage and Wagon Workers, an industrial union open to all workers in the carriage and wagon building industry. This union, which was to add "automobile" to its name in 1913, was the longest continuing union in the automobile industry before the advent of the Congress of Industrial Organizations (CIO). It was also the most successful attempt to organize the auto workers if success is measured by the size of its membership. Its history is instructive for the insights it provides into the problems of organizing auto workers into an industrial union during the period before and after World War I.[9]

The Carriage, Wagon and Automobile Workers Union was peculiar because it was an industrial union inside the largely craft union organization of the AFL. This presented numerous problems for the union and led to its eventual expulsion from the AFL in 1918. It was also a peculiar union because, in spite of its industrial form of organization, its membership throughout all of its history consisted primarily of skilled workers (painters, trimmers, sheet metal workers, woodworkers, upholsterers) who saw themselves primarily as auto workers and refused to put all of their allegiance into the appropriate craft union for their trade. These workers were visionary enough to understand that the auto industry could only be organized along industrial lines and to see that their position in the industry made them auto workers rather than carpenters or painters. Nevertheless, they were never able to use that vison to draw into their union the great mass of automobile workers who had no traditional association with a trade and who represented the workers who had to be won if the industry were to be unionized.[10]

Table VII–1 presents an estimate of the membership of the Carriage, Wagon and Automobile Workers from 1902 through 1926. By 1910, the Carriage and Wagon Workers' membership had dropped to 1,100 from 5,500 in 1902. This decline in membership reflected raids by craft unions on its membership and the greatly diminished activity of the carriage and wagon industry due to the growth of the automobile industry. As early as 1899, the union had expressed its appreciation of the role of automobile manufacturing in its future:

> Though but few of these vehicles are in use at present, their practicality proves beyond a shadow of a doubt, that they will be the means of throwing the present constructed carriage or wagon on the scrap pile in the very near future. The Carriage and Wagon industry will be completely revolutionized before the dawn of another decade, of this there seems to be no doubt.[11]

The union leaders understood that its only hope of survival, indeed its only reason for existence, was to follow its former members into the automobile industry and attempt to become a union of automobile workers. To this end, the Carriage and Wagon Workers in 1910 petitioned the AFL for jurisdiction over all workers in the automobile industry

The relationship between the Carriage and Wagon Workers and its parent federation, the AFL, had been uneasy for several years. Each year from 1902 to 1905 and again in 1908 the Carriage and Wagon Workers had presented formal complaints to the AFL against raiding of its members by either the painters', blacksmiths', or upholsterers' unions. In 1910, the craft unions claiming jurisdiction over auto workers disagreed as to how the AFL should respond to the Carriage and Wagon Workers request for jurisdiction in the auto

TABLE VII–1
Carriage, Wagon and Automobile Workers
Union Membership, 1902–1926

Year	Number of Members
1902	5,500
1910	1,100
1915	3,000
1919	13,000
1920	40,000 to 45,000
1921	39,000
1926	3,000

Figures compiled from: James O. Morris, *Conflict Within the AFL* (Ithaca, NY: Cornell University Press, 1958), p. 22; Edward Levinson, *Labor on the March* (New York: University Books, 1938), p. 42; Joel John Lowery, "Labor Relations in the Automobile Industry During the Nineteen Twenties," M.A. thesis, Michigan State University, 1958, p. 56; *Proceedings,* Carriage, Wagon and Automobile Workers, 1915; Philip Taft, *Organized Labor in American History* (New York: Harper and Row, 1964), p. 484.

industry. They arrived at a compromise whereby auto workers were to be allowed to have their choice between a craft union and the Carriage and Wagon Workers. This was an unhappy compromise from the beginning. The painters never agreed to it and one year later, in 1911, the blacksmiths demanded that all blacksmith members of the Carriage and Wagon Workers be returned to the blacksmiths' union.

The following year brought another short-lived compromise. As a result of the so-called peace conference of 1912, the AFL gave permission to the Carriage and Wagon Workers to organize the auto factories "without interference from the craft unions." For their part, the craft unions were assured the "right of craft unionists to remain within their respective organizations if they so preferred." Apparently too many workers chose the Carriage and Wagon Workers union, for within a year the blacksmiths charged the Carriage and Wagon Workers with dishonoring the agreement.

In 1913, the AFL national convention acceded to the demand of nine craft unions and ordered the Carriage and Wagon Workers

to stop all efforts to organize workers who came under craft jurisdiction and to release to the craft unions those members who belonged
to their respective trades. In 1914, these same nine unions launched
an unsuccessful campaign to organize auto workers into their respective craft unions. All of this hostile activity from within the
AFL was the beginning of a series of steps which would lead to the
expulsion of the Carriage, Wagon and Automobile Workers Union
from the AFL in 1918. In 1914, the AFL ordered the union to drop
Automobile from its name, which it refused to do. From this point
on, even the previous façade of cooperation was dropped. The
Carriage, Wagon and Automobile Workers continued to insist on
retaining *Automobile* in its title and persisted in organizing automobile workers without regard to the craft jurisdiction of other AFL
unions; indeed, it was only a matter of time before its break with
the AFL would become formal. In 1917, the Carriage, Wagon and
Automobile Workers Union was suspended from the AFL and in
1918 expelled, thus finally ending a twenty-seven-year association.[12]

President William Logan of the Carriage, Wagon and Automobile
Workers understood the situation perfectly as he reported to his
union's members that the cause of

> all the trouble between our organization and the AF of L has been
> because of the fact that we stood uncompromisingly for industrial
> unionism. It was hardly possible for us, as an organization, to claim
> jurisdiction over all the workers in our industry, without stepping
> upon the toes and coming in conflict with other trade union organi-
> zations also claiming jurisdiction over workers employed in different
> branches of our industry.[13]

During this period of AFL infighting, the membership being
fought over was by no means large. The struggle was more over
principle than it was over actual members. By 1915, membership
increased to 3,000. Furthermore, union leaders complained that most
of their members were apathetic, did not attend meetings, and had
little continuing interest in the life of the union. "The average seems
to think that all a union is for is to conduct strikes, and that unless
conditions get so bad that nothing but a strike will change them,
there is no need for him to organize."[14]

The Carriage, Wagon and Automobile Workers Union's greatest
strength came in the period of labor upsurge immediately after World
War I, although it in no way represented the threat to the auto
industry that unions did in some other industries at the same time.

On January 1, 1919, the United States government cancelled all wartime restrictions on automobile production. As the auto industry shifted back into production for civilian use, it had an acute need for labor to meet the demand for cars that developed in the immediate postwar period. Some of this demand was met by servicemen who had been auto workers before the war and returned to the auto factories after the war. The Selective Service reported that 35,000 automobile factory workers and automobile and gasoline engine mechanics had been drafted during the war. During a five-week period in the spring of 1919, 1,361 servicemen registered with the United States Employment Service in Detroit and 1,092 were immediately placed in Detroit auto factories. Many returned to the auto factories without such formalities. All through 1919 and into the spring of 1920 employment in the auto industry rose continuously, and auto companies expressed a keen interest in both black southern workers and workers from the rural areas of Michigan, Ohio, Indiana and from the soft coal areas of Pennsylvania. The auto industry estimated that 33,000 auto workers came to Detroit in the six months between April 1919 and October 1919. These, with their families, added an estimated 75,000 people to the city's population, severely aggravating the housing shortage, but finding ready jobs in the booming auto plants.[15]

The demand for auto workers after World War I created a short-lived workers' market in which workers shopped around in an attempt to maintain their high wartime wages. Auto labor turnover increased and efficiency went down. "We had a bigger turnover after the war than during the war," said Ford's Samuel Marquis. "We had an attitude of certain indifference to the job and an attitude that resented any attempt, not only on the part of the man who would give any instructions, however kindly and well meant it might be, it was 'If you don't like it, why there is another job I can get,' and walked out." Lowered efficiency in the face of a labor shortage was estimated by some auto manufacturers to range from 20% to 35% of wartime efficiency levels.[16]

If turnover and lower efficiency were troublesome to the auto manufacturers, their problems were minor compared to those of employers in other industries. As auto manufacturers looked around the country in 1919, they saw enough labor unrest to provoke serious concern. The Seattle general strike and major strikes in the coal and steel industries were powerful object lessons to auto employers about the dangers of unionization. On the one hand, they cut off needed materials for auto production; on the other hand, they portended a labor situation that might become a reality for them if auto workers became organized. Early in February 1919, the National Automobile Chamber of Commerce discussed with its members a "general undercurrent of unrest" among labor. Throughout 1919, manufacturers employed spies to report on what the men were saying in the plants and at meetings of unions, socialist groups, the IWW, and the popular Detroit Labor Forum. Auto manufacturers also had their own operatives to report on the progress of the steel strike, a matter of great interest to them since steel was crucial to automobile production. Adding to a national wave of antilabor and antiradical activity, the Detroit police commissioner announced the creation of a special force of 1,000 Detroit policemen armed with rifles and machine guns, who were ready to deal with any agitation or activity seeking to establish a "reign of Bolshevism in America."[17]

In the context of labor shortage and booming demand for automobiles, the Carriage, Wagon and Automobile Workers Union had a brief but impressive growth in membership activity. From a membership of 3,000 in 1915, the union grew rapidly after the war to a membership of between 40,000 and 45,000 in 1920. The immediate postwar period saw strikes involving auto workers in more than twenty-five plants around the country. Compared to the enormous upheaval in the steel industry or the citywide strike activity of the Seattle general strike, auto worker strikes were often small and short-lived. On the other hand, in the context of a period of labor upheaval, they seemed both more positive to the union and more threatening to industry executives than they really were. The Carriage, Wagon and Automobile Workers Union carried out strikes in Detroit, Flint, Milwaukee, Grand Rapids, and New York City.[18]

In the spring of 1919, the Wadsworth Manufacturing Company in Detroit reneged on a previous agreement to allow workers to choose freely from among themselves those who would represent them on shop committees to talk with management. The Wadsworth management wanted to place some restrictions on the process of free choice. The Wadsworth workers, feeling betrayed and also resenting a company shift from day work to piecework, refused to accept this change in the rules, and the company locked them out. The Detroit local of the Carriage, Wagon and Automobile Workers Union, Local 127, soon turned this lockout into a strike with a clearcut demand for collective bargaining through worker representatives of their own choosing. Wadsworth manufactured sedan bodies for Ford and Ford employees were used as strike breakers in an attempt to keep production rolling. The strike dragged on into the summer, colored by sporadic violence between strikers and strike-breakers, until a spectacular and mysterious fire swept the Wadsworth plant in August. The strike was resolved to no one's satisfaction by the plant's destruction, amidst charges from both sides that the other had set the fire.[19]

Also in the spring of 1919, the Carriage, Wagon and Automobile Workers Union joined a strike of machinists organized by the International Association of Machinists (IAM) at the Willys-Overland plant in Toledo where 13,000 workers were employed. In March 1919, the Willys-Overland management announced an increase in weekly hours from forty-four to forty-eight, accompanied by a decrease in wages. When the Willys workers refused to work under the new conditions the company locked them out and insisted that the higher hours and lower wages were a precondition for continued employment. Led by the machinists, the Willys-Overland workers turned the lockout into a strike, establishing three shifts for round the clock picketing. The strikers presented the company with their demands for an eight-hour day, one-half day on Saturday, and no reduction in pay. On May 9, the Willys-Overland management tried to move strikebreakers across the picket lines. The strikebreakers, most of whom were either black workers or local high school students, were met with stones and fists. On May 10, 500 World War I veterans were deputized as extra police and succeeded in restoring order and moving the strike breakers into the plant. For two weeks, strike breakers operated the Willys-Overland plant while the strikers grew increasingly frustrated with their ineffective picketing. On June 3, a battle erupted between strikers and strikebreakers in which the strikers threw bricks and were met with a hail of bullets from the deputy police. Three bystanders were killed and many others, strikers and bystanders, injured. Following the violence, Federal Judge John Killits, invoking the Clayton Anti-Trust Act, enjoined the strikers against further interference with the strikebreakers and limited picketing to United States citizens. Several United States deputy marshals were dispatched to enforce the injunction, strikebreakers successfully entered the plant; within a few days, production returned to normal, and the strike was broken.[20]

Both the Wadsworth and the Willys-Overland strikes began as company attempts to regain control over areas of company policy—shop committees, hours, wages—that had been relaxed during the war to meet the need to recruit labor and satisfy the government's interest in wartime labor relations. Both resulted in lockouts when workers refused to relinquish wartime gains and both became strikes as workers' organizations—both the Carriage, Wagon and Automobile Workers Union and the Machinists Union—moved to articulate demands and organize resistance. Neither resulted in workers' victories; they were instead indications of workers' willingness to fight to maintain gains previously granted and to join and work with unions for that goal.

The most successful of the postwar strikes took place in the unlikely city of New York where auto workers in more than 100 body shops went on strike for a forty-four-hour week and an increase in pay. The strike lasted seventeen weeks in the best-organized shops, from the fall of 1919 into the winter months of 1920, and resulted in a winning contract and an auto workers' local with 2,500 members. The New York workers were employed in shops that built luxury bodies and required a higher proportion of skilled workers than did most Detroit and other midwestern shops. The skilled workers were not only more likely to feel their traditional rights and fight for them, but also to respond to the union message, and in New York succeeded in giving at least one example of the possibility and the value of carpenters, painters, and upholsterers joining in one body and one action and taking it on to victory.[21]

Auto employers responded to the postwar conditions and to their increasingly militant workers by attempting to create a new and dependably structured work environment that would be more under their control. The auto manufacturers' attempt to introduce discipline, lower wages, longer hours, and more intensive production standards after World War I was greatly aided by the advent of the short-term 1920-1921 depression. Where at least a few workers had been willing to defy their employers by striking in the labor-short, strike-heavy atmosphere of 1919, by mid-1920, when many workers were unemployed and many others worked greatly reduced hours, thoughts of striking were temporarily put aside.

The 1920-1921 depression was a major crisis for auto workers. Only its brief duration kept it from producing the despair and total misery of the early 1930s' Great Depression. Beginning in April 1920, auto industry employment dropped steadily until late 1921. From March 1920 to January 1921, the industry's employment index declined from 118 to 37. In 1919, the auto industry produced 1,934,000 motor vehicles with a work force of 343,115; in 1921, it produced 1,683,916 motor vehicles with a work force of 212,777. By June 1920, Detroit auto factories were averaging only 50% of their predepression production; by December, Nash, Willys-Overland, Packard, Dodge, Studebaker, Reo, Maxwell-Chalmers, Buick, and

Ford all had plants which were closed entirely. Other factories were reduced to skeleton crews of a few managers and superintendents.[22]

By the summer of 1920, Detroit's housing shortage was temporarily eased, with reports of hundreds of available dwellings. By October, the city counted 54,000 unemployed; by the end of 1920, the Michigan Manufacturers Association noted that between 100,000 and 200,000 people had left Detroit returning to Midwest farms and coal mines. Most of those leaving the city were probably single men who came to Detroit during and immediately after the war and who still had strong ties to families living elsewhere. Workers with families to support found it more difficult to pick up and move. For them, times were difficult indeed. Many were forced to curtail or postpone plans to buy homes as they were not able to keep up the payments. As one worker explained to Henry Ford, "Very many of your employees attempted to buy houses at high prices with big payments and interest, figured on roomers and tenants to help. And now between layoffs and loss of roomers many cannot make their payments, have no funds for fuel and winter clothing."[23]

While the situation in 1920 and 1921 was gloomy, it had its bright spots for auto employers. "Plenty of labor available now," exulted Hudson's Roy Chapin in August 1920, and efficiency "has improved considerably in the past three months." For workers, the brief depression brought lower wages, speed-up, and the end of the personal paternalism of the prewar period, symbolized by the 1921 closing of the Ford Sociological Department. A United States Department of Labor study disclosed wage rate reductions from 10% to 30%. For the unemployed auto workers, of course, reductions in pay were of little immediate interest. For them, wages became a real concern when business improved late in 1921 and they were rehired at lower rates than those previously received. In addition, they found greatly intensified production norms. "When the men came back in 1921," reported W. C. Klann of the Ford Motor Company, ". . . they had to work twice as hard to keep their job. [*sic*] They all came back and they just doubled production."[24]

Throughout the postwar period, a preponderance of the Carriage, Wagon and Automobile Workers Union's strength around the country was in body shops. Body making still employed many crafts formerly used in building carriages. Carpenters, painters, and upholsterers all had craft traditions of union membership that helped attract them to the auto union. After World War I, auto manufacturers lowered wages of many skilled worked employed in body shops, bringing their wages more in line with other auto production workers. The most impressive of the union's early postwar strikes, Wadsworth and the New York shops, had taken place in body shops, and the 1921 strike that ended the postwar era and marked the beginning of a rapid decline in unionization was also a strike of body workers.

The Fisher Body strike began in February 1921, after a series of pay cuts beginning in November 1920. The union's organizing success of 1919 had yielded gains at Fisher Body, especially among painters and trimmers. Here the workers had become used to a conference committee that consulted regularly with the Fisher management to settle grievances. The pay cuts were followed by attempts to exact more work per hour and to require overtime. When the workers attempted to use their elected committee to reach an agreement, the company refused to talk. With the auto industry into its postwar depression and high unemployment, the likelihood of a successful strike was slim. The union leaders opposed a strike, but the members were firm in thinking that pay cuts had gone too far and, against the advice of their leaders, they voted to strike. Fisher Body was able to break the strike by reducing production (no great sacrifice since orders were few) and by using strikebreakers for the little work that continued. In April, most strikers returned, the strike was lost and with it the remnants of Carriage, Wagon and Automobile Workers Union's strength in the auto industry.

After the strike, the union rapidly lost membership and greatly declined in importance. Much of its loss of impetus was due to the depression conditions facing workers. The combined hostility of employers and the AFL also helped to destroy any potential the union had for becoming a strong voice for all auto workers. By late spring of 1921, the union was reduced to welfare activities for the unemployed (furnishing free meals and running a food commissary), for it was unable to operate as an offensive organization in the factories. When auto business improved, the union was virtually finished.[25]

Throughout its history, the Carriage, Wagon and Automobile Workers Union was beset by contradictions. In spite of its motto, "One industry, one jurisdiction, one union," and in spite of its insistence that membership be open to all auto workers regardless of sex, nationality, or race, the fact that its strength remained primarily among skilled workers doomed it to ineffectiveness as an industrial union. Strikes often involved only one or two shops within a factory because only those workers had been organized. After World War I, the union leaders consistently opposed strikes and advocated arbitration and conciliation. This policy made them difficult to distinguish from the AFL which also favored labor-management cooperation. The union also opposed, in principle, signing contracts between employers and the union on the grounds that such contracts tied workers' hands. The IWW maintained a similar principle. But most workers wanted written contracts. The union also had an extremely idealistic attitude toward union shops, an attitude typical of skilled workers; union shops were discouraged as "detrimental to the morale of the organization." A union shop, it was claimed, made "the workers depend more or less upon the employer to compel those who are hired to join the organization" and thus had "a tendency to influence the workers to lean upon the agreement as a crutch and thereby spoil their self-reliance."[26]

In 1926, William Logan resigned as union president, and offered some parting advice. He noted that the industry had changed.

> Where once we had men to deal with who were skilled or semiskilled and who felt a certain degree of independence, we now have a large body of workers to deal with who are not skilled or who cannot use their skill if they have it and who are specialists performing an operation over and over to a greater degree than ever before. They lack the feeling of independence that comes to a skilled mechanic.

Logan, himself a trimmer who had started out as a furniture upholsterer, understood that his union had never succeeded in acquiring these unskilled workers as members and warned that the union could never be successful with craftsmen only. "Mass production," he continued, "must be met with mass organization. This of course will not be the work of a day or a month, but we must commence to alter our program to fit changing conditions in the industry." And Logan felt it necessary to strike a final blow against apathy. "Last but not least, we must wake up our own rank and file to the need of attendance at meetings. No one can do anything with a member who stays home on meeting nights."[27]

Whereas the Carriage, Wagon and Automobile Workers Union understood the necessity for industrial unionism but failed to accomplish it, the AFL failed both in conception and accomplishment in the auto industry. The activities of the AFL in the auto industry during the 1920s present one of the most dismal episodes in the Federation's entire history. After the expulsion of the Carriage, Wagon and Automobile Workers in 1918, the AFL largely ignored the auto industry. Those auto workers who belonged to AFL unions did so more as a way of keeping their options open if they returned to their craft outside the auto industry than they did as a means of union protection within the auto industry. If the AFL was largely uninterested in the automobile workers, the workers were equally indifferent to the AFL as an organization they might consider joining. The AFL in the 1920s had developed a policy of cooperation with practices of scientific management as part of its policy of furthering workers' interests through cooperation with employers. The AFL's strategy was to convince employers of the greater efficiency of organized workers. The policy was particularly unlikely to attract workers in an industry where the minute job divisions of scientific management allowed for the much hated practice of speed-up. Of course, the idea was not really to attract workers but to persuade the companies to recognize the AFL unions as collective bargaining agents, thereby avoiding the process of attaining union recognition through organizing the workers to demand it for themselves. In pursuit of this strategy of labor-management unity, the Detroit Federation of Labor, an umbrella of AFL unions in Detroit, even went so far as to ask the city's employers to make regular financial contributions to the Federation. A somewhat bemused General Manager of the Maxwell Motor Car Company asked advice of Hudson's Roy Chapin about the visit of "a representative of the Detroit Federation of Labor" who asked for "a financial contribution" and "represented that all of the leading motor manufacturers of Detroit made annual contributions to the Federation and that the money was used, in part at least, to combat radicalism in union ranks."[28]

The Detroit Federation of Labor itself was somewhat more sympathetic to organizing auto workers than the national AFL. This is not surprising given its postion in an open shop city whose major industry was auto. At various times, it petitioned the AFL to begin organizing in the auto industry but without much success. In particular, the Detroit Federation of Labor was not openly hostile to the Auto Workers Union in the way that its parent organization was. One union organizer remembered that Frank Martel, president of the Detroit Federation of Labor, "often gave us verbal encouragement. I think he sincerely hoped we would organize the automobile workers." In 1925, Martel gave active support to an Auto Workers Union sponsored campaign to achieve free speech areas— spaces where union organizers could set up soap boxes—in front of Detroit auto factories. Martel was arrested as a speaker in this drive. During the 1933 Briggs strike, Martel used his considerable political connections to vouch for jailed strikers to help get them released pending bail. While Martel could be utterly clear on the need for an auto workers' union, telling one complaining Ford worker there was "only one answer" to Ford workers' complaints and "that is for them to organize themselves into a union and deal collectively with the Ford Motor Company," he could also expend considerable futile time and effort petitioning auto manufacturers to relieve unemployment in Detroit by refusing jobs to outsiders.[29]

In 1926, the AFL held its national convention in Detroit and announced the inauguration of a campaign to organize the auto workers into AFL federal unions. AFL president William Green and Metal Trades Department president James O'Connell were by this time convinced that auto workers could not be organized into craft unions, at least not initially. Green and O'Connell sought to organize auto workers into federal unions. The campaign, however, turned out to be more announcement than event. The craft unions were afraid that their jurisdictional claims might be overruled, and, in addition, had no real desire to incorporate into their unions unskilled and semiskilled workers—many of them the despised "new immigrants." Unskilled workers, they suggested, did not have staying power when it came to unions and would not be committed members. That they might also be foreigners, blacks, or tinged with radicalism was no doubt also not in their favor. AFL leaders occasionally suggested that unskilled workers had made a poor decision in choosing to work in automobile factories, a decision that the more discriminating trade unionists would be careful to avoid. In response to a question from S. M. Levin, a university professor and an expert on auto industry employment policies, William Green replied that the AFL was not really concerned with labor relations in the automobile industry.

> The American Federation of Labor has taken no action in regard to Mr. Ford's labor policy. Union men do not desire to work for Mr. Ford as his espionage system is very objectionable. So far as his attacks on trade unions are concerned, they have no effect on the wage earners. They are simply used by labor-baiting employers to bolster up their own opposition to organized labor."[30]

As late as 1932, the AFL continued to express a contemptuous attitude toward the noncraft workers in the automobile industry. When Wyndham Mortimer requested help from the Cleveland Federation of Labor in continuing to organize the workers at White

Motors he was informed by the Federation that "no one can organize that bunch of hunkies out there."[31]

Without the support of their member unions, the AFL campaign to organize the auto industry had little chance of succeeding. Whatever campaign took place was concentrated more on attempts to make employers more conciliatory toward the idea of unions than on actually organizing the workers. The Detroit Federation of Labor aided the AFL in its plan of acquiring union recognition through labor management cooperation with a plea to employers that cited the need for workers to be organized if Detroit were to remain a prosperous city.

> The intelligent employer will not oppose this step. The first automobile factory to be properly organized is going to have a tremendous advantage over its competitors. Unionization will have the effect of reducing waste and the wastage in the automobile industry is away above average. Those who oppose the unionization of the automobile industry are really interfering with the future prosperity of Detroit.[32]

Apparently the auto manufacturers were unconvinced. Faced with a campaign that was having little success in enlisting workers or employers, O'Connell was forced to report failure by 1928. "While we have not given up hope that sooner or later we may be able to reach some of the employers who will be willing to sit down and confer with us, up to the present we are not in a position to even report progress." In fact, rather than sitting down and conferring with the AFL, auto employers responded by organizing a Citizens' Committee of Detroit to collect funds to fight union organizing. Alerting Detroit employers to the danger of an AFL attempt to unionize auto factories, they appealed for funds on the grounds that "If they are successful, it means untold hardships for our workmen and the expenditure of millions of dollars by our Employers."[33]

After the failure of the 1921 Fisher Body strike, the Carriage, Wagon and Automobile Workers Union declined rapidly in membership and entered gradually the Communist phase of its history when it was known as the Auto Workers Union. Both before and after World War I, and until William Logan's 1926 resignation as president, the leaders of the Carriage, Wagon and Automobile Workers Union were Socialists and made no secret of the fact. Ideological discussions of the class struggle and the coming socialist commonwealth were familiar fare to the union's members. During 1922,

Logan accepted Edgar Owens's offer from the Workers party (the aboveground organization of the then-underground Communist Party) that Owens would bring twenty-five to thirty Communists into the Auto Workers Union as hard-working union members if Logan would permit Owens to work for the union. This created a situation in the early 1920s in which the main leadership of the union was still Socialist but many of its organizers were Communists. The Communists rapidly acquired a position of strength in the union, especially in Detroit where by 1926 the Communist Party had established shop nuclei in the Ford, Dodge, and Fisher Body plants. By 1927, Communists claimed additional nuclei in Chrysler, Murray Body, Briggs, Buick, Packard, and Durant Hayes-Hunt.[34]

Relations between Communists and Socialists in the Auto Workers Union were not without conflict. They disagreed over the proper attitude to be taken toward the national presidential election in 1924, the Socialists supporting La Follette and the Communists opposing him. In addition, Logan's opposition to spontaneous strikes was criticized by Communists who thought that spontaneous strikes should be used as a means of educating the workers and organizing them into the union. The Communist position was always that the union should give every possible aid to strikers whenever strikes occurred.

In 1926, the Communists were strong enough to begin moving into union leadership positions. Communist Phil Raymond, who had been working in Detroit auto plants since 1924 and who was to become the most important 1920s Communist auto organizer, ran for secretary of the Auto Workers Union, successfully defeating Socialist Lester Johnson. The following year the remaining Socialist officers resigned leaving only Arthur Rohan, in the newly created office of executive secretary, as the only Socialist officer in a Communist-dominated union. Phil Raymond became the leader of the Detroit Local 127, and by the end of the decade even Rohan had left the leadership, displaced by Communist Alfred Goetz who became the head of the national Auto Workers Union.[35]

The Auto Workers Union never succeeded in enlisting large numbers of auto workers into its ranks; judged on the basis of membership figures, it would be deemed a failure. It did, however, succeed in establishing enough shop nuclei to create a vital daily presence that paved the way for a new spurt of labor activity beginning in 1933. Although union membership figures are impossible to obtain, from 1929 to 1933 the union probably never had more than 1,500 members and only between 200 and 800 members from

1930 to 1932. Table VII-2 estimates the membership of the Auto Workers Union from 1926 through 1934.

The Auto Workers Union attempted to combine daily efforts to organize a union with educational attacks against capitalism. When strikes arose spontaneously, the strikers sometimes called upon the union for help, but the short-lived strikes of the 1920s resulted in no significant increase in union membership. Most of the more than twenty-five strikes in which the Auto Workers Union was involved between 1926 and 1930 started spontaneously without union instigation. When walkouts occurred, the union offered its services, articulating demands, distributing handbills, scheduling speakers, and providing legal aid. The union tried to turn walkouts into effective strikes and to organize the striking workers into the Auto Workers Union. In these two aims they were seldom successful, but they did become known. For example, oil sanders at Fisher Body's Flint plant walked out in 1928 protesting a pay cut. Guided by the Auto Workers Union, the oil sanders compiled a list of demands including a pay increase, a better grinding compound, hot water for washing, and no reprisals against strikers. After several days, the strike spread to other departments, the company offered a raise to nonstrikers and

TABLE VII–2
Auto Workers Union Membership, 1926–1934

Year	Number of Members
1926	3,000
1929	1,500
1930	100
1931	175
1932	800
1933	1,500
1934	885

Figures compiled from: Edward Levinson, *Labor on the March* (New York; University Books, 1938), p. 42; Leo Wolman, *Ebb and Flow in Trade Unionism* (New York: National Bureau of Economic Research, 1936), p. 144; *Auto Workers News,* April 1932; Henry Kraus Collection, box 1, WSU; Roger Keeran, *The Communist Party and the Auto Workers Unions* (Bloomington, IN: Indiana University Press, 1980), p. 94.

fired the striking oil sanders, thereby breaking the strike. In the case of a walkout of the trimmers after wage cuts at Graham-Paige and Murray Body, the strikers initially turned to the Detroit Federation of Labor for aid. Rebuffed, they then turned to the Auto Workers Union, which instructed the strikers in the procedures of electing a strike committee and running strike meetings. There the strikers voted to accept a compromise proposal and returned to work.[36]

The most important of the pre-1933 strikes involving the Auto Workers Union was the 1930 strike of metal finishers at Fisher Body's Flint plant, which spread to include all plant workers, an estimated 3,000 workers. The metal finishers walked out due to the usual reason for a walkout, a reduction in piecework rates. News of the walkout spread rapidly to Detroit and later that day a corps of Auto Workers Union leaders arrived in Flint to offer leadership. Attending a mass meeting called by Phil Raymond, the strikers agreed to engage in mass picketing and in militant attempts to bring out other Fisher Body workers. The next day strikers roamed throughout the plant and persuaded the other workers to join the strike. The following morning, thousands of pickets appeared before the Fisher No. 1 plant blocking traffic and carrying signs which proclaimed, "In 1776 we fought for liberty; today we fight for bread." Flint police and Michigan state troopers intervened to break up the picket lines, charging into the crowds with horses and arresting the leaders, including Raymond. The following Monday, mass picketing was again disrupted by police arrests and dispersal of picketers and the strike was effectively ended.[37]

The Auto Workers Union held lunchtime meetings outside plants at which it tried to work on specific plant issues to reach large numbers of workers. Probably a majority of workers in the auto industry came into contact with Auto Workers Union speakers, activities, or newspapers at some time or another. One of the union's most successful practices was the production and distribution of shop newspapers. Beginning with the publication of the *Ford Worker* in 1926, the Auto Workers Union followed with papers at Dodge, Fisher Body, Briggs, and Chrysler. Concentrating on exposing specific grievances at each plant, the shop papers were lively, written in the workers' vernacular, and extremely popular. The union also engaged in more careful and clandestine activity with small numbers of workers who were felt to be particularly receptive to the union's message and worth cultivating as union members and as potential Communist Party members. One practice was to distribute pamphlets to a very few trusted workers in factories and have them use their judgment as to which workers would be good to approach. Meetings could then be held in private homes in an attempt to avoid black-listings and firings.[38]

Evaluating a small, radical union's influence in a large, unorganized industry during a time when few workers showed much interest in any type of union, much less a radical one, is difficult. Since it represented the only continuing union presence, the Auto Workers Union probably had influence beyond its numbers in helping prepare workers to look favorably upon unions when faced with the 1930's Great Depression. One worker described the importance of the union's and other left groups' education work:

> They used to hold classes in public speaking. They were developing people in the sense of giving them confidence to get up on their feet and speak; they were getting some training in public speaking, they were getting some ideas, some background of the labor movement. All of this meant that when the upsurge came, you had people in factories and around Detroit who were able to get up and present an intelligent case for unionism and the ideas in the union movement as they saw them.[39]

In addition, the Auto Workers Union, by its consistent advocacy of working-class unity and industrial unionism helped suggest the cure for the natural cleavages in the auto industry's work force. In the 1920s, many workers may not have been ready to imagine organizations which would include young and old, men and women, blacks and whites, foreigners and natives, northerners and southerners, but at least they had been exposed to the idea that they must overcome their differences if they were to be successful against the companies. Frank Marquart was perhaps typical of many. He thought that in the 1920s he "had the same kind of prejudices that most workers had." Attending the meetings of the Auto Workers Union and other left groups, he began to think seriously about abandoning his prejudices. "For the first time I became confronted with the idea that people who work for a living should not think in terms of discrimination."[40]

Early in 1929, the Auto Workers Union called a conference to which they invited representatives of the Detroit Federation of Labor and specific trade unions with members in the auto industry to discuss the inauguration of a major new drive to organize workers in the auto industry into an industrial union. The Detroit Federation of Labor and the other unions did not respond favorably to the invitation, but the Auto Workers Union used the conference as an occasion to articulate specific principles of organization in the auto industry, among them the extreme importance of not neglecting the foreign born, black, female, and younger members of the work force. Certainly 1929 was not a propitious year for a major organizing drive, nor did the Auto Workers Union have the resources for such a drive even under the best of circumstances. By the year's end, the union had, in fact, lost rather than gained members due to increasing industry unemployment. The union was also plagued by a continuing problem in organizing—the seeming indifference of those workers who most needed representation: the unskilled, the blacks, the women, and the young. "Mass production" had still not been countered with "mass organization."[41]

Chapter Eight

The Great Depression Arrives

The great sit-down strikes that shook the auto industry in 1936 and 1937 and finally brought industrial unionism to one of the nation's largest and most powerful industries had their origins in the depression that swept over the country and its auto workers starting in 1929. The Great Depression of the 1930s crept up on an auto industry that received some early warnings but refused to understand or heed them. Signs of an impending depression in the automobile industry were already present in 1926 and 1927. Production was down slightly in 1926 and considerably in 1927 after Henry Ford eliminated model T production. After Ford introduced the model A in late 1928, however, motor vehicle production reached a record high of more than 5,300,000 in 1929. When layoffs occurred in the fall of 1929, many auto workers thought they could survive a few months of unemployment. "After fourteen years and three months of best endeavor for the Ford Motor Company, I, with thousands of others have been sent home," wrote one Ford worker. "By economy I have a comfortable home nearly paid for. The rental of a few rooms supply most of our needed necessities. I don't think we shall need any help from the Community fund but unless the factories open up before long there will be dire suffering in Detroit."[1]

"Dire suffering" came quickly enough. By 1931, motor vehicle production had dropped to 2,389,738 and in 1932 to 1,331,860, the lowest level of production in the industry's history since 1916. In 1929, the average annual wage of workers in the automobile industry, as figured by the Bureau of Labor Statistics, was $1,638, a figure that had remained fairly steady since 1923, providing an above-

130

average standard of living that might include single-family dwellings, nutritional diets, washing machines, electric irons, radios, and perhaps even an automobile. In 1931, the average annual wage fell to $1,228; in 1933, to $1,035. Everett Francis, working in the trim shop at Fisher Body's Flint plant, kept a careful account book in which he entered his annual wages. Their range from 1927 to 1933 illustrates depression wages in individual terms. Francis was used to steady, above-average wages: $1,783 in 1927; $1,919 in 1928; $1,791 in 1929; $1,708 even in 1930. In 1931, his wages dropped to $1,560 and then fell precipitously in 1932 and 1933 to $752 and $878 respectively. The left-wing Labor Research Association estimated an average auto worker's annual wage in 1931 at a mere $757 and two Department of Labor statisticians figured that auto workers averaged less than $900 pay in 1934. Where hourly wages at the Ford River Rouge plant had averaged 92¢ in 1929, in 1933 the norm was 59¢ per hour. From 1930 to 1932, the average decline in wages in the industry varied from 4.7% for the lowest-paid female workers to 20.4% for some skilled craftsmen. Whether one took the official Bureau of Labor Statistics's figures or the even lower estimates of other researchers, the wage picture was gloomy indeed.[2]

And yet, those workers who had jobs at all were considered the lucky ones. In 1929, employment in the auto industry was almost 450,000. In 1932, it dropped precipitously to 285,000, and by 1933, had fallen still further to 243,000, only 54% of the number employed in the auto industry in 1929. An industrial employment index of the Detroit metropolitan area found the index of Detroit employment (using 1923 through 1925 as 100) for 1929, at 123; for 1930, 92; for 1931, 69; for 1932, 57; and for the first month of 1933, a low of 52.[3]

The Ford Motor Company's Detroit plants employed more than 128,000 people in 1929; by the summer of 1931, only 37,000 workers were employed by Ford in the Detroit area and about one-half of these worked only three days per week. In March 1929 the Willys-Overland Company in Toledo employed 28,000; by the spring of 1932 it employed 3,000. General Motors's Pontiac plant dropped in employment from 29,000 in the spring of 1929 to 14,000 that fall. In Flint, General Motors released no figures, but production was cut to one-seventh of normal in November 1929. Unemployment figures, however, only begin to tell the story since many of the employed worked only part of the week or year. A Bureau of Labor Statistics's study of the automobile industry in 1934 concluded that only one-third of the motor vehicle employees worked throughout the year;

one-fourth had less than six months work; and another one-fourth worked between six and ten months, an employment pattern similar to that for 1932 and 1933. The Detroit Mayor's Unemployment Committee found that the number of days worked per week dropped by 50% in Detroit's manufacturing establishments from 1929 to 1932.[4]

Everyone suffered from great uncertainty. Lines of workers often formed outside plant gates during the night. Huddled around fires, men waited through cold nights, their feet wrapped in newspapers inside oversize shoes, hoping that their vigilance would pay off in a day's work. Others, prepared for a day's work, arrived in the morning with their lunches but spent the morning waiting outside or in small factory area cafes, never called for work. The trip to the factory became a charade of going to work as usual, but there was no work and no pay envelope at the week's end. In some factories, those who had jobs guarded them against lay-offs by letting it be known that they were buying cars. Others got jobs on the word of auto dealers that they were buying cars and should be given employment. Rumors flew about jobs for sale. Sometimes, $50 or $75 slipped to the employment manager resulted in employment, at least until someone else came with $50.[5]

Auto workers responded to the early 1930s lay-offs in a variety of desperate and ingenious ways. Some took to the road, riding the rails and chasing after job rumors and finding purpose in movement even if the jobs failed to materialize or amount to much. Others returned to the greater security of relatives who still lived on farms or were still employed. Still others grabbed at any employment available. They dug ditches, shined shoes, drove taxis, drove milk trucks, or entered the profession that seemed to belong especially to the depression, undertaking. Insurance companies were always willing to take on salesmen, but one laid-off worker who tried it found "more people were selling their insurance than were buying it."[6]

Inside the auto factories a great emphasis was placed on efficiency and cost cutting as the antidote to falling profits. Whereas the auto industry had prided itself on its modern techniques and increasingly high productivity during the 1920s, it saw efficiency in the early depression as the key to survival. "There has been so much saved by the efficient processes in the automotive industry," boasted John Willys of the Willys-Overland's Toledo plant in late 1930, "that I believe our profits this year will be just as large as last year." The pace of work intensified even over the high speed of the 1920s, with lay-offs serving to weed out those who could not maintain the pace.

One worker realized that the harder he worked the more he endangered his job because it would take fewer men to do it. A worker was, he commended, "constantly in fear of a resulting layoff from, maybe, his own effort." When workers were rehired after lay-offs, seniority played no part in determining who would be rehired. As one worker described it, "The workers were being fired if they slowed down and were unable to make production. They were dismissed in lieu of getting younger blood into the plants, someone who could produce more and accumulate more wealth for the companies." Another commented succinctly, "You either had to put out or get out . . . you thought you were lucky to hold your job." Foremen met workers' complaints about worsening working conditions with the perennial request to look out the window at the line of job seekers and the standard refrain of, "if you cannot do the job, there is somebody in that line who can." Many plants combined speed-up with a shift from piecework to day rates, keeping wages low as production increased at a rate that one study estimated from two- to three-times its predepression rate. Some workers were even forced to work overtime for no pay in order to keep their jobs.[7]

The precarious security of the 1920s became a thing of the past, recalled with fondness and compared to a bitter present. Houses almost purchased were lost. The Detroit Mayor's Unemployment Committee studied 1,164 families in 1932 and found 145 who were buying homes on mortgages. Of these 145, seventy-seven either had their mortgages foreclosed or were in arrears on their payments. In one Detroit factory alone, 40% of the homeowners were no longer owners by 1932. Approximately one-third of all families owning homes were delinquent in their tax payments. Unemployment had a domino effect. Not only might homeowners lose jobs, but their roomers upon whose rent they depended for mortgage payments lost their jobs too. Roomers often left the city; homeowners' bills came due and could not be paid.[8]

The problem was not that auto workers were worse off than other workers; in some respects they fared better. Even in 1932, the auto industry paid the second highest wages of any industry in the contry and by 1935 it was back to its mid-1920s position of first. It was simply that workers in general took a terrible beating and for auto workers, this especially meant loss of security and the modicum of comfort they had obtained in the 1920s through grueling work at relatively high wages. The Ford Medical Department found workers' resistance to infection eroded by undernourishment. Many auto workers had to turn to welfare agencies for help, and most of the corporate liberal benefits of bonuses, savings plans, and insurance afforded by the auto companies in the 1920s disappeared after 1929.[9]

Individual agreements between employee and company could no longer be relied upon. Clara and Henry Ford received pitiful letters from disabled employees who had been promised employment for life and now found those promises meaningless. Ford had previously built a reputation for humane hiring of his injured employees. The depression found the disabled some of the first to be laid off. Other injured employees failed to receive agreed-upon compensation and had no recourse beyond pleading letters. Often, workers were too proud to beg for special consideration. One Polish worker's wife wrote in 1931 on behalf of her husband who had been laid off for nine months, "Won't you try and do something for my husband . . . if you can't reinstate him, won't you at least let me work in his place. We are in such a desperate position that God alone can see. Won't you try and do something for our children's sake." The letter concluded with the deference typical of missives to the Fords, "I thank you very kindly for your precious time." A hospitalized Ford worker wondered if, "the Factory could place my wife at something until I could be able to go back on my job." And the wife of an unemployed Ford worker whose husband "stood in line hours at a time and is never permitted to enter the employment office" expressed bitterness at "being forgotten when so many are hired who have never been there before. We only ask fair treatment not expecting favors. We have three children and have tried so many times to get back there that we are about desperate."[10]

The auto companies were not entirely unmindful of the suffering caused by the depression or of its potential to stimulate radicalism. But their attempts to alleviate the distress of their employees, former and present, were marked by a pitiful futility. Mostly there was talk, and even the talk addressed only the least important problems. Industry leaders discussed share-the-work plans, whereby the existing work would be divided among the available workers, hiring more individuals at less than full-time. Seasonal employment paced to the introduction of new models early in the year had long plagued the auto workers. The depression provided the opportunity for a new discussion of the problem. The Detroit Common Council advised the auto companies to abandon the practice of annual model changes entirely. They also suggested lowering auto prices in winter and raising them in summer to persuade the public to even out its buying practices throughout the year. The Packard Motor Car Company tried to even production throughout the year to avoid the usual employment peaks, but other companies failed to follow its example. Finally, the Automobile Manufacturers Association took the lead in persuading auto makers to introduce new models in the fall instead of at the beginning of the year in order to increase demand during the usually slow fourth quarter. Another Automobile Manufacturers Association proposal called for the government to take and pay for 80% of the nation's automobile factories' output as a means of alleviating unemployment and creating demand. The suggestion of W. H. Burnham, retiring in 1930 as president of the Michigan Manufacturers Association, that the auto manufacturers might create a reserve fund into which a fixed percentage of gross sales would be placed to be used for the relief of employees facing seasonal layoffs, was ignored.[11]

Auto cities based their depression programs on a combination of relief and persuasive measures to get the unemployed to leave the cities and go back where they came from. The Detroit Chamber of Commerce proposed a state "immigration service" to patrol Michigan state lines and turn back migrants seeking work in Detroit. In October 1929, Detroit's Department of Public Welfare carried 156,000 persons on its rolls; in April 1930, the Department was swamped with 728,000 for which to care. The Mayor's Unemployment Committee created a special subcommittee, the Homeless Men's Bureau, to find shelter and food for the many unemployed and unattached men who roamed Detroit's streets. Hundreds of homeless people slept nightly in Detroit's Grand Circus Park and listened daily to the soap box speakers who flocked to the park and its ready audience. Some Detroit families lived in caves dug in the ground and overlaid with a protective covering of brush. In the winter of 1930, the city's municipal lodging homes sheltered 5,000 each night and fed up to 10,000 each day. Other unemployed and homeless workers slept on army cots set up in vacant factory buildings donated by General Motors and Studebaker. The Detroit Mayor's Unemployment Committee attempted to help some of the floating men by operating a free employment service, but its listings fell dismally short of the need. By the winter of 1931, the Detroit Department of Public Welfare added 300 families daily to its relief rolls; at least one-half of these families had never before appealed to any welfare organization. As self-supporting families finally exhausted their resources, they had nowhere else to turn.[12]

City governments also attempted to persuade the auto companies to incur more of the burden of welfare programs claiming, in the case of Detroit, that "the industries which brought this surplus population to Detroit during boom times should not expect the taxpayers to shoulder the entire load of a situation which the small taxpayer, at least, did not bring about." Some auto companies did make an effort toward contributing to the relief of the unemployed, particularly in the very early years of the depression. Most of their efforts, however, were entirely inadequate even to begin meeting the need. In Flint, the Industrial Mutual Association offered more recreational activities for those whose "leisure" time had greatly increased. General Motor's housing subsidiaries reduced the interest rates on their houses. More to the point, General Motors supplied laid-off workers with coupons exchangeable for groceries at local stores. The value of the coupons was expected to be paid back if the worker was rehired.[13]

The heaviest pressure from government and public opinion to do something about the plight of its workers fell on the Ford Motor Company. The city of Detroit argued that many of the Ford workers lived in Detroit although they worked in Dearborn and Highland Park. Ford workers, thus, were on the Detroit relief rolls, but Detroit did not receive taxes from the company. In 1931, the city estimated that more than 15% of the heads of families on its relief rolls were former Ford workers. Ford claimed that he was willing to help meet the relief problem, but that the city counted many who had never worked for the Ford Motor Company as former Ford workers. He also used the opportunity to launch a political attack on Detroit's liberal mayor, Frank Murphy, claiming that the Welfare Department was mismanaged and the welfare rolls full of freeloaders, some of them Ford workers drawing relief while employed full-time. More than one investigation of the alleged welfare fraud found Ford's charges unfounded, but the investigations had little effect on Ford's willingness to aid his unemployed workers.[14]

Ford preferred to ignore the existence of a major depression. He did offer his workers garden plots to supplement their incomes with homegrown vegetables and publicly hoped this would allow people to "recover some of the old security which the land gave its cultivators." This charity proved unpopular with many. Some plots were far from home and entailed considerable inconvenience—not to mention the extra work after the end of an already fatiguing day. Under the direction of Harry Bennett, Ford's harsh and abusive lieutenant, the garden program became a punitive tool whereby workers could be dismissed if they failed to tend their plots and keep them weed free. Even those who enjoyed gardening found it somewhat discouraging when "about the time that your garden was grown to the extent about ready for harvest, you found that the supervisor of your department and his family and friends would come down and help you harvest your little plot of ground and take the cream of the crop home for their own particular use."[15]

Within the city of Dearborn, Ford worked out an arrangement with the mayor's office whereby unemployed Ford workers would be shifted from the city's public relief rolls and put on Ford relief. The benefits of Ford relief consisted of food orders that could be exchanged for 60¢ worth of food a day at the Ford commissary. If a worker were later re-employed at Ford, his relief debts were deducted from his paycheck. In addition, in 1932 the Ford Company agreed to provide food for all of Dearborn's dependents in exchange for a commitment by the Dearborn Council to remove from the general election ballot a referendum issue calling for a special welfare tax.[16]

Ford did continue the activities of his Sociological Department (although greatly abbreviated from the period before 1920), having his investigators go to the homes of those who requested jobs or other assistance to ascertain the worthiness of their entreaties. Investigators' records for nine months during 1930 suggest that the most frequent form of welfare was to provide a lunch on the days of the visitation and to arrange for an assignment of Ford wages to the company in exchange for needed treatment at Henry Ford Hospital. Some workers were given employment through these investigations. Of the 1,040 families visited between March and November 1930, 367 found employment. While this helped the 367, it did little to dent the growing unemployment figures or shorten the lengthening lines outside the Ford Employment office.[17]

Ford's most publicized relief measure was the renovation of Dearborn's adjacent black community, Inkster. By November 1931 when the Ford program began, Inkster's electricity and police protection had been discontinued. Ford established a commissary in Inkster, paid the families' back bills, renovated houses, and provided decent clothing. He also arranged for jobs at the Ford Motor Company for the adult males with a minimum starting wage of $4 per day, deducting $3 to pay for the improvements in Inkster. Even after Ford abandoned the Inkster project in 1933, some Inkster workers still received only $1 per day working at Ford, with the other $3 going to satisfy past obligations.[18]

While the depression ultimately created the conditions for unionizing the auto industry, the early years of the depression showed few signs of militance. From the fall of 1929 until the early months of 1933, auto workers coped with the increasingly severe conditions of their work in personal and private ways. The only important organizations to come out of these early depression years grew around unemployed auto workers. Organized protest from unemployed workers took place in auto cities starting in early 1930. The Communist Party sponsored unemployment demonstrations in industrial cities around the country on March 6, 1930. Some 50,000 to 100,000 demonstrators gathered in Detroit to demand unemployment insurance; full wages for part-time workers; a moratorium on lay-offs, wage cuts, and speed-up; a seven-hour work day; and emergency relief from the city government. Cleveland, Milwaukee, Grand Rapids, Hamtramck, Kalamazoo, Toledo, Flint, and Pontiac all had sizeable demonstrations of the unemployed, and auto worker were numerous among them. Closely following the March demonstrations, the Communist Party formed Unemployed Councils in the auto cities of Detroit, Hamtramck, Lincoln Park, Pontiac, Grand Rapids, Toledo, and Cleveland. The majority of the Unemployed Councils' time was spent in antieviction efforts and in organizing demonstrations calling for jobs and relief. They also ran soup kitchens with food solicited from local merchants and ran a few halls where homeless men could sleep. In addition, the Unemployed Councils held protest meetings against police brutality, often a feature of unemployed demonstrations, and investigated claims of police brutality against young, unemployed black men who were picked up and held by police for being on the streets at night. Many an auto worker's first experience with organized working-class activity came through participating in an event sponsored by an Unemployed Council.[19]

The most spectacular of these events, news of which spread rapidly to auto workers around the country, was the Ford Hunger March of March 7, 1932. Ford was a natural target for a protest demonstration. Henry Ford had long cultivated a public image as personal, individual head of the Ford Motor Company. More than any other auto manufacturer, Ford was seen as bearing personal responsibility for his workers' plight both in good times and in bad times. While less militant workers wrote letters to Ford believing that if only he knew of their conditions he would help, and more militant workers took to marches and demonstrations; they all shared the belief that Henry Ford could turn things around if he only would.

When the Detroit Unemployed Council announced a march to begin in Detroit and conclude at the Ford River Rouge plant in Dearborn, it intended to do more than dramatize the plight of the unemployed. Many of the marchers' specific demands went beyond jobs and relief, petitioning for changes directly affecting those workers still employed at Ford. In addition to demanding either jobs or 50% of pay for those who remained unemployed, the marchers called for an end to speed-up, two fifteen-minute rest periods, no discrimination against black workers in job assignments, free medical care for Ford workers at the Ford Hospital, an end to the Ford Service Department, a seven-hour day with no loss of pay, and workers' right to organize. Some of these demands spoke directly to the situation of employed workers and clearly pointed to the need for a labor union to promote auto workers' welfare. Thus, the Unemployed Council provided a link in the unionization chain.

As the marchers assembled on Detroit's west side, they carried banners demanding *GIVE US WORK* and *WE WANT BREAD NOT CRUMBS*. As their numbers increased to almost 3,000, they proceeded without incident through Detroit to the Dearborn city line. Instead of being allowed to present their petition, the marchers were met at the Dearborn city line by fifty Dearborn policemen who ordered them not to cross into the city. Defying the police order, the marchers continued into windblown tear gas and on to the Ford employment gate where a battle ensued between marchers, Dearborn police, and Ford servicemen. The marchers, angered by the tear gas and police refusal to allow them to move ahead, picked up rocks and chunks of frozen earth and hurled them at the police, who, with the Ford servicemen, opened fire, killing four marchers and wounding at least fifty others. The Ford Hunger March and its aftermath, a giant funeral parade of 20,000 mourners for its four martyrs, was the high mark of the unemployed organizing in auto. A funeral banner proclaiming *FORD GAVE THEM BULLETS FOR BREAD* was telling evidence of the change in Henry Ford's public image in Detroit and represented for many auto workers the shattering of a final illusion. In 1933, attention finally turned to the plants themselves.

Starting in January 1933, employees of the Briggs Manufacturing Company in Detroit startled the industry by taking a simple walkout over slashed wages and sustaining and building it into a genuine and impressive strike. Briggs was the largest independent body manufacturer in the auto industry, making bodies for Chrysler, Hudson, Graham-Paige, and Ford. Since 1928, the Ford Motor Company had been Briggs's largest customer. All through the late 1920s, Briggs maintained a reputation for exceptionally poor working conditions and low wages. A disastrous explosion and fire in 1927 at the Briggs

Harper Avenue plant resulted in at least twenty-one deaths, charges of company culpability, and a bitter poem in the labor press entitled "Bodies by Briggs." A poor accident record combined with low wages gave Briggs the "worst reputation in Detroit" by 1930. One worker remembered the streetcar conductor in the 1930s announcing, "Briggs slaughterhouse, all off, Mack Avenue." In addition, Briggs workers complained that the depression brought a new and killing speed-up in which employed workers were induced to work faster and faster to ward off unemployment. "After the first layoff of ten percent, the rest worked so much faster that it was necessary to lay off another twenty percent . . . the greater the number of unemployed, the greater the effort on the part of those working. As the depression deepened, the men tended to work close to the limit of their capacities."[21]

Body work was one of the areas of auto production that still required skilled workers long after most assembly and machine work had succumbed to mass-production techniques. Metal finishers, trimmers, molders, painters, and stripers all carried with them skills that had commanded a high price and considerable respect well into the 1920s. By the late 1920s, however, body work had become more routine, especially as bodies became covered with pressed metal panels. Parts of the process of body building became adapted to line construction and others were subdivided. Wages were downgraded accordingly. The decline both in skill and wages intensified in the early depression as many car manufacturers put out more and more of their body work to independent suppliers like Briggs whose reputations for speed-up and working conditions had always been poor. Thus, body workers were faced with a decline in their working conditions while many still remembered the more desirable conditions of the 1920s. They were inclined to be a militant group.[22]

In 1930, and again in 1932, responding to the pressures of the depression, Briggs instituted a series of wage cuts, some as high as 50%. Following the November 1932 wage cuts, the company again instituted wage cuts of 15% for tool and die makers starting on January 6, 1933, at the Mack Avenue plant. Aware of the Mack Avenue plant wage cuts, workers at the Waterloo plant, where the Auto Workers Union had a nucleus, met and decided that a walkout should be staged if wages were cut at the Waterloo plant. On January 9, Auto Workers Union members in the Waterloo plant distributed the following flyer:

No more wage cuts. Wages of the tool and die makers in the Mack Avenue plant have been cut. *We are next.* We are not going to accept it. Refuse to sign your own starvation warrants. If they come to *you,* let us know and we will all go to the office. If the company wants to discuss wages, let them do so with committees elected by the men.

Committee Against Wage Cuts

On January 11, when tool and die makers at the Waterloo plant received notice of a 20% cut in wages, they immediately walked out and began picketing and leafleting at all four of the Briggs plants. This strike action resulted in a surprising success. On January 12, Briggs rescinded the wage cuts at the Mack Avenue plant and the following day company management met with strikers at the Waterloo plant and agreed to revoke the wage cuts there and promised no retaliation against strikers. The Waterloo workers agreed to these conditions and immediately went back to work, flushed with the success of their three-day strike. A week later, on January 20, workers at the Motor Products Company also conducted a successful three-day strike.[23]

Inspired by the success of these brief strikes, metal finishers at the Briggs Highland Park plant walked off the job on January 22. When they reported their actions to a meeting at Finnish Hall led by Auto Workers Union head, Phil Raymond, he advised them to return to work the following day and bring out the entire plant. On January 23, the entire Highland Park plant walked out and by the following day all four of the Briggs plants were out on strike. By the end of January, workers at Murray Body were also on strike and Hudson had shut down in order to avert a strike. Although the immediate occasion for the strike was the cut in wages, as workers got together in strike committees to write up their demands, a flood of grievances flowed out that expressed the feelings of many auto workers in 1933. The strike continued into March, although it was effectively broken sooner than that by using strikebreakers with police escorts. At the height of the strike wave, probably about 12,000 Detroit auto workers were on strike and approximately 100,000 other workers were directly affected as Ford was forced to close some of its operations for lack of bodies.[24]

The strikers' demands centered on a guaranteed hourly wage which would mean an end to "dead time," time when workers were required to be on the job but because of lack of supplies, shut down of lines, or peculiar production schedules, were not actually working and therefore not paid. In addition, they demanded a nine-hour day and a five-day week, time and one-half for overtime, the end of compulsory health and accident insurance, gloves and tools to be furnished by the company, and the recognition of shop committees elected by the workers in each department which would function to settle grievances and would have the power to rule on the necessity for overtime. The company refused to negotiate with the strikers, claiming it would only authorize individual negotiations, and totally rejected the notion of shop committees. It did, however, establish a guaranteed minimum wage of 25¢ an hour with pay for dead time.[25]

The strike arose initially over the company's succession of wage cuts, cuts which had gone so far that many workers felt they had little to lose and much to gain by taking a stand. Briggs workers averaged 35¢ an hour after the January cut in wages and the company deducted from these wages fees for health and accident insurance and the cost of identification badges and some tools. The workers claimed the insurance was worthless and beyond their ability to afford even if it had been of value. When low hourly wages were combined with dead time, they could produce but a paltry weekly paycheck. A widely distributed leaflet of the Briggs strike told of the worker who earned $2.49 for two weeks' work. Insurance payments took $2, leaving him with 49¢. A photo of the check for 49¢ dominated the leaflet which concluded with the calculation that at 12¢ a day for carfare, this worker had lost money working for Briggs.[26]

In an attempt to develop some rudimentary forms of organization, strikers from the various Briggs factories formed a strike committee of 100 members, and a smaller executive committee of twenty-five. With the devotion to democratic procedures typical of early union activity, the strikers agreed that all decisions must be approved by all the strikers. The smaller committees did not have the power to act on their own. Shortly after they had achieved this initial organization, the strikers invited the Auto Workers Union's Phil Raymond to help them organize their strike. Raymond was a known Communist who ran for mayor of Detroit on the Communist Party ticket in 1930. This gave the company an opportunity to claim that the strikers were all Communists, following Communist leadership, and therefore not to be taken seriously.[27]

The question of Communist influence in the Briggs strike was much debated in Detroit in 1933. It seems clear that the vast majority of those who walked off their jobs did so spontaneously in response to wage cuts and walkouts at other plants. They had attended no previous meetings agitating for a strike nor were they Auto Workers Union members. They did work in an industry in which the Auto Workers Union existed, they probably knew of its existence, and a few may have attended some of the union's activities. In the fall of 1932, the Communist Party called a conference in Chicago at which a decision was made to make another assault on the auto industry with particular emphasis on the Ford Motor Company and the Briggs Manufacturing Company. This decision to again attempt to organize in the auto factories represented a shift in Communist Party strategy away from emphasizing the unemployed and toward a new concentration upon vital industries. Such a shift was not easy to accomplish. The depression decimated the ranks of the Auto Workers Union as its members lost their jobs. By April 1932, there were no shop papers left in the auto industry and Communist activity was at a very low level. Nevertheless, by October 1932, the Communists had developed working units at both Ford and Briggs.[28]

During the November 1932 Briggs wage cuts, the Auto Workers Union called a meeting of workers at the Briggs Waterloo plant to protest wage cuts, a meeting attended by two workers. A subsequent meeting drew four workers. Despite this slow beginning, the Auto Workers Union was successful in fighting the Waterloo plant's speed-up introduced in the fall of 1932 of having workers tend two lathes instead of one. A cartoon ridiculing workers who agreed to the extra lathe appeared stuck on the additional lathes and the ensuing commotion resulted in the company dropping the practice. After the first wage cuts in 1933 at the Briggs Mack Avenue plant, members of the Auto Workers Union at the Briggs Waterloo plant called a special meeting attended by twenty-eight workers specially invited because of their trustworthiness and commitment to union organizing. These Briggs Waterloo workers agreed that they would organize a strike when and if the Waterloo plant announced a wage cut. Later committees were established in each floor of the plant committed to a plantwide strike if wages were cut in any department. The Waterloo plant appears to be the only case of organized planning for a strike *before* the wage cuts. In other cases, the Auto Workers Union became active *after* the strike began, although its members in Briggs plants certainly encouraged any strike sentiment that they found. Earl Browder, in a speeech made to workers during the Briggs strike claimed total credit for the Communist Party.

I read that the company officials charge that we Communists are responsible for the strike. . . . That is true, and we glory in the charge. This is one of the most glorious pages in the history of Communism in America. We have been working tirelessly and unceasingly for years to build up an organization among the workers in the automobile industry for the time when we could come out openly and throw this monkey-wrench into the wheels of the industry.[29]

But Browder claimed too much and in fact, this claim was one of the events that eventually turned a majority of the strikers against Communist Party leadership. The strike committee always insisted on its right to Raymond's assistance as a representative of the only active union in their industry. They were undoubtedly expressing most of the strikers' view when they asserted, "This strike is not for political purposes. This strike is against abominable conditions of labor which goaded practically the whole plant to rise in protest. It is a strike for decent American wages and for decent American conditions of labor."[30]

What the Communists provided was experienced leadership, which the mass of strikers accepted in an organizational sense although they independently made their own decisions on specific issues. The Briggs strikers rejected the demands formulated by the Auto Workers Union when they were more militant—and more political—than their own. For instance, the Auto Workers Union's suggested demands were for a six-hour day for most workers and a five-hour day, with full pay, for those engaged in particularly hazardous occupations like oil sanding and spray painting. The Auto Workers Union also called for the company to pay health and accident insurance, to grant equal pay for equal work to blacks and women, and to establish a relief fund for unemployed workers. In response to Raymond's suggestion that large numbers of unemployed workers be used to block plant gates to strike breakers, the strikers divided. Since the Communists had already organized Unemployed Councils in Detroit, they already had organizations that could have been used for strike support and to dramatize solidarity between strikers and the unemployed. While some Briggs workers thought this was a good idea, especially early in the strike, others were fearful of merging causes with the unemployed. Some picketing occurred during the strike by unemployed workers carrying signs that said, "We, the unemployed, will not scab on strikers." Since the unemployed councils were widely known for being Communist led, this

opened another opportunity for red-baiting by the Briggs management, and many strikers were persuaded that outsiders on the picket
lines were a mistake and that picketing should be restricted to Briggs
workers. Most strikers insisted that they would stay out until they
had a firm offer from Briggs in writing, refusing to accept verbal
concessions, and holding out for the right to shop committees. On
the question of when to end the strike, the Communists themselves
were divided with some Party leaders arguing in favor of accepting
Briggs's early verbal offer of a guaranteed hourly minimum, declaring
a victory, and returning to work, while the Communists in the Auto
Workers Union who actually worked in the plants sided with the
mass of strikers who wanted to continue the strike.[31]

After the strike was red-baited for Phil Raymond's presence in
it, the strikers continued to use his talents but not because he was
a Communist. They saw him as a skilled organizer with experience
that they lacked and hence valued. John W. Anderson, a non-
Communist leader at Highland Park, who later joined the IWW and
the Socialist Party, thought that without the aid of the Auto Workers
Union and the International Labor Defense "the strike would have
been broken in a few days with no important gains made." And a
Wobbly striker commented that it was "the ignorance of the mass
of strikers" that led to acceptance of the attack on Raymond. "I am
satisfied," he concluded, "that this was the first move toward the
loss of the strike since it caused a break in our ranks that has never
healed." The strikers, however, finally did give in to charges of
Communist direction and told Raymond that his services were no
longer needed, announcing that, "The Committee has decided that
Raymond and his associates and organization shall have nothing
more whatever to do with this strike. It will be run strictly by Briggs
employees for Briggs employees."[32]

The question of Communist influence, then, is a complicated
one. For Detroiters of 1933, at least those who made up the mayor's
investigating committee, the question revolved around the issue of
whether the strikers had legitimate grievances. Since the committee
decided that Briggs's work conditions warranted a strike, they concluded that Communist influence was not important. The conditions
produced the strike. The fact remains, however, that the Communists
were active in at least the Briggs Waterloo plant before the strike
and the Waterloo plant workers did conduct the first successful strike.
In addition, the Auto Workers Union's leadership in the wake of
the brief strikes of early January at Waterloo and at Motor Products
encouraged other Briggs workers to learn the lessons of the successful

strikes and use them as models. That many auto workers did what the Communists wanted them to do, choosing to join a strike wave that was rapidly gaining momentum after three years of declining conditions of work does not, of course, make them Communists, but neither does the small number of the Communists mean their influence was unimportant.

As the strike was prolonged, that influence diminished. Maintaining unity in a rapidly deteriorating strike situation was difficult—and with more and more plants operating at closer and closer to full capacity—the strikers who were left fell to wrangling among themselves. The most important Communist influence lay not in the specific origins of the Briggs strike, although they were there, but in their long history of keeping the Auto Workers Union alive and with it giving repeated legitimation to the idea that auto workers had rights and that unions existed to secure and protect those rights.[33]

The Briggs strike resulted neither in a permanent union nor in victory for the strikers over their specific demands. The company's granting of a 25¢ per hour minimum wage and abolishing dead time came at the end of the strike's first week, and no further gains had been won by the time the strikers went back to work. Nevertheless, the Briggs strike seemed qualitatively and quantitatively different from other auto walkouts. Leon Pody, a leader of the Highland Park strikers, thought that "in one sense the strike was a lost cause," but also believed that "it was the very start of successful organization of the automobile and allied industries." In size and duration alone, it was the most significant strike the auto industry had then experienced. The strike's ability to mobilize community support in the form of donations of food and milk for strikers was also impressive. Furthermore, the strike indicated that worker militancy in the auto industry was high even before the stimulus to organizing provided by the passage of the National Industrial Recovery Act (NIRA) and its Section 7a in June 1933. Coming after more than three years of depression and the violence of the 1932 Ford Hunger March, it had a more serious cast than the brief walkouts of the 1920s. "Taking up a picket sign and walking the picket line was a difficult emotional experience for workers in 1933," remembered John W. Anderson. "Few of us had ever seen much less walked one. The fear of physical injury or even death in those days were deterrents to workers joining a picket line or engaging in other strike activity."[34]

In summary, the early years of the Great Depression brought misery and unemployment to many automobile workers and created a setting in which continuing to think of the auto industry as a high wage magnet for workers who often considered themselves to be transients in the industry was difficult. The end of the 1920s was the end of an era for auto workers, just as it was for many other Americans. During the 1920s, auto workers had struck a temporary and fragile bargain. In return for relatively high wages and widespread job availability, they accepted grueling and monotonous work. That this bargain was never very stable is attested to by the numerous brief walkouts and attempts to exert control over speed-up in the 1920s. But it held enough to make the industry look remarkably peaceful, especially from the outside.

When auto unemployment began to ease and some workers were called back to work in 1933, they came with a feeling of permanance about their positions and a sense that they had to make the auto industry a home in which they could live. They developed a new seriousness and militancy as they saw the depression destroy what hard work had won, a modicum of comfort and decent living for themselves and their families. They wanted secure wages, secure jobs, a system of seniority, and some control over speed-up, and they began to make a stand with the Briggs strike.

The depression era changed most of the characteristics of auto life that had kept it ununionized for so long. The paternalistic employers, with the exception of Henry Ford, whose image was greatly changed, were all dead. The company paternalism embodied in savings plans and bonuses was also dead. Hourly wages still compared favorably with other industries, but they had fallen dramatically, and too many workers had gone too many hours without any wages. Ethnic diversity was still a feature of auto factory life, but workers in the 1920s were more likely to be second rather than first generation immigrants. They spoke English and they often came from families who had spent a generation or more working in factories. In addition, demonstrating the need for unity in specific union-building struggles was easier than it had been in the calm of the 1920s. Even the few means of resistance that unorganized auto workers employed in the 1920s lost their charm in the Great Depression. Restriction of output, changing jobs, and unorganized walkouts brought the threat of firings and no one wanted to lose an irreplaceable job. It became more important to do it right and in such a way that a lasting protective organization resulted.

In short, all that remained of previous conditions was industry hostility to unionism. That, of course, intensified in the early 1930s, but by itself it was not enough to defeat a growing insurgency and rebellion. In this context, the Briggs strike can be seen as both the last of the 1920s-style walkouts and the first of a more unified and organized union drive. The strike was largely spontaneous in origins and defensive in nature. But in the workers' ability to shut down entire plants, to stay on strike for many weeks, and to articulate wide-ranging demands, the Briggs strike foreshadowed the eventual triumph of the United Automobile Workers (UAW).[35]

Chapter Nine

Conclusion

If the Briggs strike was the first shot in the battle that won unionization, the first three decades of auto worker history must be searched for the preparation they contained for that shot. In the early days of auto manufacture, auto shops employed primarily all-around mechanics and craftsmen to assemble automobiles whose design was undergoing frequent change. These workers were almost all American-born workers whose previous work experience was in the similar shops of the carriage, wagon, marine engine, and machine shops of the Midwest and New England. The first auto shops were small and discipline was relaxed, with often frequent, close, and fairly egalitarian contact between the owner-inventor and his employees. As mass-production techniques came to dominate the auto industry they brought a minute division of labor, interlocking moving assembly lines, a new layer of supervisory personnel, and an emphasis on speed and efficiency. The auto plants of the mass-production era were large, relied upon rigid discipline, and expected their workers to follow a set routine, ask no questions, and leave thinking to the management.

The workers of the earlier era stayed on and made their adjustments to mass production. The enormous expansion of productive capacity which accompanied mass production meant that they were joined by a much larger, new group of workers many of whom were foreign born or part of the surplus agricultural population of the southern and midwestern United States. Their previous work experience was agricultural and very different from the stopwatch precision of the auto factories. Thus two different groups of workers had to adjust to the new conditions of mass production, those who carried with them a tradition of craft and skill, including machine skills, and those who carried a tradition of preindustrial agricultural labor. The first group was the backbone of unionization in the auto industry up until the 1930s. For unionization to succeed, it had to include the second group since their numbers were far in excess of the skilled workers.

The one time at which one might expect that auto workers would have organized themselves to take greater control of their work lives was at the point of increasing domination of mass-production techniques. This did not happen for reasons that are basic to a description of the auto industry from 1914 to 1929. On the one hand, the bitter pill of the new factory life was sweetened in various ways. Even after auto factories became large, impersonal places in which to work, many auto magnates maintained a personal and paternal image with their workers. Henry Ford, Tom and Walter White, John and Horace Dodge, and Ransom Olds all were seen as men who cared about their employees' welfare. Even in those companies where paternalism was not vested in a personal face, General Motors for example, concern for the workers was seen to rest in company plans for recreation, home ownership, and savings plans and bonuses.[1]

In addition, auto wages were good compared to those available in other industries and agriculture. In the depressed agricultural market of the post-World War I era, auto cities took on the look of Mecca. There a young man could make some money quickly and move on, or he could buy a home and settle down with a family. For foreign workers, also, auto wages meant an improvement in standard of living that compared favorably with any other employment available.[2]

If high wages and paternalism were the positive base of the open shop, a diversified work force and antiunionism were its negative base. Auto workers partook of at least three separate cultures: immigrant, black, and native-born white. These separate communities pulled against each other. Blacks were suspicious of white workers' intentions when they spoke of unions. All the leaders of the black community warned that unions were not for black men and were used to exclude them from industries. In addition, black workers saw the auto industry as a place to escape low-paying jobs and southern-style discrimination. Native-born white workers were suspicious of the ability of blacks and immigrants to defend themselves and saw them as more willing than native-born Americans to be pushed around. Immigrants often looked upon native workers as dangerously heedless about job security and freer than themselves to move about from job to job and city to city. Most immigrant workers also saw auto work as a step up from common laborer status, and, for second generation ethnic workers, auto work provided the same opportunity it did for other American workers to provide a decent standard of living. When the Auto Workers Union tried to convince workers of the need for unity across racial and ethnic lines, they found some who would listen but not many who would join the union and try to make that unity a reality.[3]

The auto industry's antiunionism was a model for United States industrial leaders. Detroit was the leading American Plan, open-shop city; and many leaders of other industries envied the effectiveness of the auto industry's hostility to unionism. Company spies, blacklists, private disciplinary forces, and the simple refusal to talk to collective bodies of workers was a stamp of the industry.

Auto workers' failure to achieve unionization should not be seen as total acquiescence to company domination. Auto workers had a sense of limits, of the point beyond which they would not be pushed, which expressed itself most clearly, and occasionally effectively, in actions to thwart speed-up or wage reductions through restriction of output and through spontaneous walkouts. The means at workers' disposal outside of organizational struggle were limited, but they did use them to gain whatever concessions they could and to assert their activity as human beings and negate the passivity that was expected of them as auto workers.

The experience of the 1920s is crucial to understanding the meaning of auto workers' lives for their futures and for industrial America's future. The place to look for the greatest expressions of struggles for workers' control over the productive process is in the previous decade, from 1910 to 1920, when the pace of technological change was at its most intense and the productive process was transformed into one that contained all the elements of modern mass production: division of work into discrete tasks, line production, sophisticated machinery, and a reliance upon a machine-tending work force for most jobs. During this decade, some genuinely skilled workers and craftsmen lost out and found themselves victims of a deskilling process that left them without use for their crafts and skills. But in the main, such craftsmen and skilled workers were swamped by the industry's expansion and its absorption of massive numbers of new workers without crafts or skills for whom auto factory work was an advancement in their economic positions. In this context, older workers might rebel by occasional walkouts and work stoppages and newer ones by pretending not to understand what they were supposed to do. All might participate in making frequent job turnover the industry's major labor headache, but none could make any progress toward returning skill and craft to the industry.

By the 1920s, auto workers and their employers had struck an implicit bargain. In return for relatively high wages, plentiful jobs, a gradually improving standard of living; workers accepted monotony, routinized work, and rigid discipline. In essence, workers accepted that meaning in work was not part of modern industry; meaning was to be found in life outside the factory, along with pride, comfort, and pleasure. One student observer of auto factory life in the mid-1920s commented that the average auto worker "wants a normal mental life off of the job and on the job he prefers easy work. Few have any desire to learn to make a car. Their interest is not in building cars, it is in things outside of their work." While alienating work might produce what Paul Taylor termed "dissatisfaction without knowing why," it did not produce robots. Robots might have been more satisfactory workers given the demands of auto factory life; actual auto workers continued to insist on their human dignity and integrity; it was just that that dignity was not to be found in pride in workmanship. Myron Watkins in 1920 offered a succinct description of this split between pride in individual manhood off the job and lack of pride in work on the job. He described the auto workers he observed going to work in Detroit.

> A stiff straw or a Panama hat, a collar and necktie, a light-colored shirt occasionally of silk, a dark suit of street clothes and polished shoes—these are the rule and not the exception for the young fellows who flock to the machines and benches in the automobile shops. They are proud—but not of their work![4]

The implicit bargain of the 1920s was never simply accepted and adhered to by either side. Both workers and their employers tested out and pushed against its limits. It is in this context that struggles for workers' control took place in the 1920s. While employers pushed for increased speed and greater production, workers pushed for less. They used sporadic walkouts in response to sudden changes in production quotas and restricted output to defend their interests generally. This is a very different notion of workers' control from one that stresses struggles to assert the place of skill and craft in industrial production. Restriction of output was, rather, in defense of health, vigor, and integrity. In part, restricting output as a means of exerting some control over pace was a way of policing the bargain that allowed life outside the factory to compensate for alienating work itself. For if workers left the factories too tired to claim the pleasures of family and city, what had they gained?

In noting that craftsmen set their own proper "stint" of work and that industrial workers in the 1920s continued this practice by restricting output, David Montgomery warns that one should not conclude that "scientific management has changed nothing." For, Montgomery continues, "The customary craftsman's stint had been an overt and deliberate act of collective regulation by workers who directed their own productive operations. The group regulation which replaced it was a covert act of disruption of management's direction of production. The stint had become sabotage." Just so, and the difference is perhaps even more important than the continuity. Auto workers in the 1920s could take pride in "beating the system," but that was not the same thing as reclaiming a system in which pride was based on control over skill and workmanship, a control that management could not claim. Very few in the 1920s expected that. What they did expect or hope might someday be possible, was a system in which they could exact from their employers some respect for their pride and their dignity, as well as for their material well-being.[5]

The depression, then, represented a rupture in the terms of the 1920s agreement so severe that the agreement crumbled. Once auto workers were no longer able to rely on auto employment to provide some security, a reasonable standard of family living, a chance to be proud of one's status as an American auto worker, the only recourse was to renegotiate entirely the bargain and to do so by means of militant union-building.

In that process of union-building some led and some followed. Whether or not a gap exists between leaders and their mass following in sentiment, understanding, or aims, a gap in time, effort, and commitment to the union-building struggle is always found. In Wyndham Mortimer's somewhat frustrated leader's words, "the vast majority were willing to let someone else build the union."[6]

One way to examine the kinds of workers for whom auto work was the most problematic is to look at those who became leaders in creating a union in the 1920s. This is not a perfect formula by any means, for leadership may be a measure of special skills, education, and background as well as a measure of militance and a willingness to challenge the frustrations of working life, but it does provide some sense of the kinds of workers who both felt compelled to organize and were successful in doing so. In 1959, Wayne State University and the University of Michigan's Institute of Labor and Industrial Relations began a joint project to interview individuals whose remembrances would shed light on the auto industry's history of unionization. Out of this oral history project and an additional one on blacks and the labor movement, 103 of those interviewed worked in the auto industry at some time before 1934. I have taken this sample of 103 auto workers active in bringing about unionization of the auto industry to look for some common pattern among them. Information culled from these interviews is summarized in Table IX-1.[7]

Perhaps the depression affected the greatest change for those workers whose position had always been the best and the most

TABLE IX-1
Collective Biographical Description of Early Union Activists

	Percentage of Total N *	Percentage of Native Born	N
Native Born	82%	100 %	82
Midwest	42	51.2	42
South and border states	16	19.5	16
Northeast	5	6.1	5
West	1	1.2	1
		TOTAL N = 100	
Foreign Born	18		18
British Isles	9	50.0	9
Canada	2	11.1	2
Other	7	38.9	7
		TOTAL N = 100	

	Percentage of Total N	N
Years Entered Auto Industry		
1910–1914	1.0	1
1915–1919	11.7	12
1920–1924	27.2	28
1925–1929	46.7	49
1930–1934	12.6	13
	TOTAL N = 103	

	Percentage of Total *N*	*N*
Previous Employment		
Auto only	3.2	2
Carriage and Wagon	1.6	1
Farming	4.8	3
Mining	3.2	2
Railroads	3.2	2
Other industrial	23.8	15
Other Nonindustrial	17.5	11
Multiple categories	42.9	27
	TOTAL *N* =	63
Auto Work		
Body Work	40	28
Assembly and/or machine	21.4	15
Foundry	5.7	4
Tool and die	8.6	6
Other	16.3	17
	TOTAL *N* =	70
Father's Employment		
Auto	20	8
Mining	20	8
Farming	15	6
Railroads	7.5	3
Other blue collar	27.5	11
Other non-blue collar	17.5	7
	TOTAL *N* =	43

* Total *N* is total of those interviewed who provided information about the category. Potential Total *N* is always 103 (the 103 respondents who worked in the auto industry before the 1934 cutoff date).
Source: Oral History Interviews: Unionization of the Auto Industry and Blacks and the Labor Movement, Archives of Labor History and Urban Affairs, Wayne State University. I included all individuals who worked as auto workers at any time before 1934.

mobile, the native-born American workers from the Midwest. They certainly appeared in large numbers among those men who devoted themselves to organizing the UAW. They developed a new attitude of serious militancy as they saw the Great Depression destroy the moderate advances of the 1920s. A composite portrait of someone likely to become a leader in union building would look something like this. He was most likely to be a native-born, white Midwesterner.

He became an auto worker in the 1920s after trying a variety of jobs that might include farming, selling, and nonauto factory jobs; his previous work career was stamped especially by considerable variety and instability. He was frequently a body worker. None of this implies that southern- and foreign-born workers did not become loyal and militant unionists; they did, but they were not to be found in large numbers among the ranks of the leaders. When the time came to sit-down, however, they were there. Unions undoubtedly meant different things to different people. One of the things they meant to those who devoted substantial time, energy, and conviction to their formation in the auto industry was a chance to put meaning into their work lives through their union work that did not exist in the work of making automobiles. One activist described the union as a new frontier, a place for pioneering and adventure. The auto industry in the 1920s was no longer a new frontier, maybe the union could be.[8]

The means that auto workers employed before unionization to resist total company domination always had an aura of "Don't Tread on Me." In its simplest form, this was the worker who quit without notice and found a new job when the strictures of his current job became too much. At its most organized and militant, it was a group of workers laying down their tools and walking out at an announcement of a rate cut, indicating that there was a point beyond which they would not be pushed. Even when they knew their case was hopeless, walking out was better than giving in. What changed in the 1920s was not this spirit of prideful assertion, but rather the conscious need to be effective and to win, and the understanding that winning necessitated organization and the hard, committed, daily persuasion that entailed. The liveliness of the sit-down strikes had its history in the long years of work in which little personal pride could be taken. The pride that had been denied auto workers in their work was restored through their ability to take a united and effective stand to demand that the companies respond to their needs.

Notes

Preface

1. Especially noteworthy are Alfred D. Chandler, Jr., *Giant Enterprise: Ford, General Motors, and the Automobile Industry* (New York: Harcourt, Brace and World, 1964); John B. Rae, *American Automobile Manufacturers* (Philadelphia: Chilton Company, 1959); Keith Sward, *The Legend of Henry Ford* (New York: Holt, Rinehart and Winston, 1948); Allan Nevins, *Ford: The Times, The Man, The Company* (New York: Charles Scribner's Sons, 1954); Allan Nevins and Frank Ernest Hill, *Ford: Expansion and Challenge 1915–1933* (New York: Charles Scribner's Sons, 1957); Allan Nevins and Frank Ernest Hill, *Ford: Decline and Rebirth 1933–1962* (New York: Charles Scribner's Sons, 1963); Arthur Pound, *The Turning Wheel* (Garden City, NY: Doubleday, Doran, 1934); Alfred D. Chandler, Jr., "General Motors," in *Strategy and Structure* (Cambridge, MA: MIT Press, 1962); John B. Rae, *The American Automobile* (Chicago: University of Chicago Press, 1965); Jonathan Hughes, "Henry Ford and the Automobile Age," in *The Vital Few* (Boston: Houghton Mifflin, 1965); Alfred D. Chandler, Jr., and Stephen Salsbury, *Pierre S. Du Pont and the Making of the Modern Corporation* (New York: Harper and Row, 1971).

2. Roger Keeran, *The Communist Party and the Auto Workers Unions* (Bloomington, IN: Indiana University Press, 1980); August Meier and Elliott Rudwick, *Black Detroit and the Rise of the UAW* (New York: Oxford University Press, 1979); Stephen Meyer, III, *The Five Dollar Day: Labor Management and Social Control in the Ford Motor Company, 1908–1921* (Albany, NY: State University of New York Press, 1981); David Brody, *Workers in Industrial America: Essays on the Twentieth Century Struggle* (New York: Oxford University Press, 1980); David Montgomery, *Workers' Control in America* (Cambridge: Cambridge University Press, 1979). For general discussions of the centrality of work in labor history see: David Brody, "The Old Labor History and the New: In Search of an American

Working Class," *Labor History,* 20 (Winter 1979), pp. 111–126; David Montgomery, "To Study the People; The American Working Class," *Labor History,* 21 (Fall 1980), pp. 485–512; Robert Ozanne, "Trends in American Labor History," *Labor History,* 21 (Fall 1980), pp. 513–521.

Chapter One

1. On the auto industry as a worldwide phenomenon, see Mira Wilkins and Frank Ernest Hill, *American Business Abroad: Ford on Six Continents* (Detroit, MI: Wayne State University Press, 1964). On nineteenth-century visitors to Manchester see John F. Kasson, *Civilizing the Machine: Technology and Republican Values in America 1776–1900* (Harmondsworth, England: Penguin Books, 1977), pp. 55–60.

2. Alfred D. Chandler, Jr., *Giant Enterprise: Ford, General Motors, and the Automobile Industry* (New York: Harcourt, Brace and World, 1964), p. 5. The combined motor vehicle and motor vehicle bodies and parts industries ranked first in value of products in 1925. They did not rank first in number of wage earners until 1935.

3. Paul Baran and Paul M. Sweezy, *Monopoly Capital* (New York: Monthly Review Press, 1966), pp. 219–220; Douglas F. Dowd, *The Twisted Dream: Capitalist Development in the United States Since 1776* (Cambridge, MA: Winthrop Publishers, 1974), pp. 89–93; Paul M. Sweezy, "Cars and Cities," *Monthly Review,* 24 (April 1973), pp. 5–12.

4. Dowd, *Twisted Dream,* p. 94; Chandler, *Giant Enterprise,* pp. 13, 95–96; William Serrin, *The Company and the Union* (New York: Alfred A. Knopf, 1973), p. 101.

5. Auto workers have also received less attention from historians. For one study of an auto industry policy and its technological base that reveals a great deal about auto workers themselves see Stephen Meyer III, *The Five Dollar Day: Labor Management and Social Control in the Ford Motor Company 1908–1921* (Albany, NY: State University of New York Press, 1981).

6. On loss of innocence, see especially Henry F. May, *The End of American Innocence: A Study of the First Years of Our Own Time* (New York: Alfred A. Knopf, 1959).

7. John B. Rae, *The American Automobile* (Chicago: University of Chicago Press, 1965), p. 21. The exceptions to this picture of unvarying expansion were the post-World War I recession years of 1920–1921 and the pre-Great Depression year of 1927.

8. Chandler, *Giant Enterprise,* pp. 11–13, 95–96; Rae, *American Automobile,* p. 18; Robert P. Thomas, "Business Failures in the Automobile

Industry, 1895–1910," in J. Von Fenstermaker, ed., *Papers Presented at the Annual Business History Conference* (Kent, OH: Kent State University Bureau of Economic and Business Research, 1965), p. 11.

9. Rae, *American Automobile*, p. 17; Howard R. DeLancy, "The Cole Motor Car Company," *Business History Review*, 30 (September 1956), p. 263; Jack W. Skeels, "Early Carriage and Auto Unions: The Impact of Industrialization and Rival Unionism," *Industrial and Labor Relations Review*, 17 (1963–1964), p. 573. Of those auto makers with a previous history in the wagon and carriage business, Studebaker, Nash, Durant, and the Fisher brothers were the most prominent.

10. Sweezy, "Cars and Cities," p. 5; Rae, *American Automobile*, pp. 51, 89–91.

11. Sweezy, "Cars and Cities," pp. 4–7.

12. John B. Rae, *The Road and the Car in American Life* (Cambridge, MA: MIT Press, 1971), pp. 35–39, 60–73. The Lincoln Highway Association, founded in 1913 promoted the plan of a coast-to-coast highway. Carl Fisher, its originator, was the founder of the Electric Auto-Lite Company of Indianapolis. Henry B. Joy and Ralph Chapin were both prominent supporters of the Association.

13. Chandler, *Giant Enterprise*, pp. 11–13, 23; John B. Rae, *American Automobile Manufacturers* (Philadelphia: Chilton Co., 1959), p. 116.

14. Chandler, *Giant Enterprise*, pp. 13, 95–96; Serrin, *The Company*, p. 101; Dowd, *Twisted Dream*, p. 94. The year 1919 was an exceptional one during which more than four million cars were sold, probably due to Ford's introduction of the Model A in that year.

15. Chrysler Corporation, "The Automobile Industry," in John G. Glover and William Cornell, ed., *The Development of American Industries* (New York: Prentice-Hall, 1933), pp. 650–651; Rae, *Manufacturers*, pp. 58–59; Rae, *American Automobile*, pp. 23–29; Lawrence H. Seltzer, *A Financial History of the American Automobile Industry* (Cambridge, MA: Houghton Mifflin, 1928), p. 30; Clarence W. Burton, *The City of Detroit, Michigan 1701–1922* (Detroit, MI: S. J. Clarke Publishing Co., 1922), vol. I, pp. 566–569; Jane Jacobs, *The Economy of Cities* (New York: Vintage Books, 1969), pp. 123–124; Keith Sward, *The Legend of Henry Ford* (New York: Holt, Rinehart and Winston, 1948), pp. 6–9; Allan Nevins, *Ford: The Times, The Man, The Company* (New York: Charles Scribner's Sons, 1954), pp. 376, 515.

16. Chandler, *Giant Enterprise*, pp. 3–175; Alfred D. Chandler, Jr., *Strategy and Structure* (Cambridge, MA: MIT Press, 1962) pp. 145–191; Serrin, *The Company*, pp. 80–99; Sweezy, "Cars and Cities," pp. 5–6; Alfred D. Chandler, Jr., and Stephen Salsbury, *Pierre S. Du Pont and the Making*

of the Modern Corporation (New York: Harper and Row, 1971), pp. 511–559; Rae, *American Automobile,* p. 105; Rae, *Manufacturers,* p. 191.

Chapter Two

1. Oral history interview with Andrew Montgomery, pp. 1–3, WSU.

2. Oral history interview with Everett Francis, pp. 1–7. WSU.

3. Oral history interview with Bud Simons, pp. 1–2, WSU.

4. Oral history interview with Fred Haggard, pp. 1–2, WSU.

5. Oral history interview with Stanley Nowak, pp. 1–2, WSU.

6. Oral history interview with Nick Di Gaetano, pp. 1–2, WSU.

7. Oral history interview with Shelton Tappes, pp. 1–2, WSU.

8. Oral history interview with Joseph Billups, pp. 1–2, WSU.

9. Oral history interview with Hodges Mason, pp. 1–2, WSU.

10. Employers Association of Detroit, Minutes, February 18, 1913, in accession 940, George Heliker Notes, FMCA. The Employers' Association of Detroit (EAD) was founded in 1902 and quickly came to include most of the major manufacturing companies in the city. With the addition of Henry Ford to membership in 1910, the EAD had the united support of Detroit's auto executives.

11. *Ibid.;* Allan Nevins, *Ford: The Times, The Man, The Company* (New York: Charles Scribner's Sons, 1954), p. 517.

12. Robert W. Dunn, *Labor and Automobiles* (New York: International Publishers, 1929), pp. 62–63; Joel John Lowery, "Labor Relations in the Automobile Industry During the Nineteen Twenties: (M.A. thesis, Michigan State University, 1958), p. 3; John J. Kruchko, *The Birth of a Union Local: The History of UAW Local 674, Norwood, Ohio, 1933–1940* (Ithaca, NY: New York State School of Industrial and Labor Relations, 1972), p. 14; Letter to Mrs. Henry Ford, June 29, 1921, accession 1, box 118, FMCA.

13. Raymond Cole, "The Immigrant in Detroit," pp. 1, 15, prepared for the Detroit Board of Commerce, May 1915, typescript in Michigan Historical Collections, UM. For the notion of a "peasant proletariat" see Caroline Golab, *Immigrant Destinations* (Philadelphia: Temple University Press, 1977), p. 45.

14. *Detroit Free Press,* July 14, 1912.

15. *Detroit Labor News,* December 4, 1914.

16. *Detroit Labor News,* December 4, 1914 and May 29, 1914.

17. Lowery, "Labor Relations," pp. 3–4; Blanche Bernstein, "Hiring Policies in the Automobile Industry," Works Progress Administration National Research Project on Reemployment Opportunities and Recent Changes in Industrial Techniques, in William Ellison Chalmers Collection, box 1, WSU.

18. Albert Meyer, "A Study of the Foreign-Born Population of Detroit 1870–1950" (Department of Sociology and Anthropology, Wayne State University, 1951), p. 24, in DPL. Since Detroit had more auto workers than any other city and a heavy dominace of the auto industry in the life of the city, using general Detroit population statistics to suggest trends important to all auto workers is not unreasonable. It is a crude compensation for the nonexistence before 1920 of Census figures specifically on auto workers and before 1930 on Census figures specifically on Detroit auto workers. The best analysis of the significance for Detroit of population growth and change in ethnic and rural composition is Olivier Zunz, *The Changing Face of Inequality: Urbanization, Industrial Development, and Immigrants in Detroit, 1880–1920* (Chicago: University of Chicago Press, 1983).

19. Cole, "Immigrant in Detroit," p. 2.

20. National Americanization Committee, *Americanizing a City* (New York: National Americanization Committee, 1915), p. 6; Americanization Committee of the Detroit Board of Commerce, *Annual Report,* March 21, 1920, in DPL; Stephen Meyer, III, "Adapting the Immigrant to the Line: Americanization in the Ford Factory, 1914–1921," *Journal of Social History,* 14 (Fall 1980), pp. 67–82; Stephen Meyer, III, *The Five Dollar Day: Labor Management and Social Control in the Ford Motor Company 1908–1921* (Albany, NY: State University of New York Press, 1981), pp. 149–167; Zunz, *Changing Face,* pp. 309–318.

21. National Americanization Committee, *Americanizing A City,* pp. 6–7.

22. *Ibid.,* pp. 10–12; Gregory Mason, "America First: How the People of Detroit Are Making Americans of Foreigners, 1916," in Melvin G. Holli, ed., *Detroit* (New York: Franklin Watts, 1976), pp. 135–142; Robert W. Dunn, *The Americanization of Labor* (New York: International Publishers, 1927), pp. 67, 155; Henry B. Joy "To The Editor," *The Detroit Journal,* February 19, 1916, Henry B. Joy Papers, vol 1, UM; *Factory Facts From Ford* (Ford Motor Company, 1917), p. 54, in FMCA; Meyer, III, "Adapting the Immigrant," pp. 57–79.

23. Letter to Henry Ford, June 21, 1921, accession 1, box 118, FMCA.

24. Letter to Roy Chapin, November 9, 1920, Roy D. Chapin Papers, vol. 32, UM.

25. *Factory Facts From Ford,* 1917, p. 54. This practice was widespread in American industry. Herbert Gutman has provided an example from the English lesson for Polish workers at International Harvester just before World War I. It begins, "I hear the whistle. I must hurry." Herbert G. Gutman, "Work, Culture, and Society in Industrializing America, 1815–1919," *The American Historical Review,* 78 (June 1973), p. 533.

26. Report on Ford's English School, March 1916, accession 1, box 121, FMCA.

27. Accession 571, box 27, FMCA; Cole, "Immigrant in America," p. 14.

28. *Factory Facts From Ford,* 1915, p. 54; Polish Activities League, *A Quarter Century of Social Service* (Detroit, MI: The Conventual Press, 1948), p. 16.

29. Accession 280, box 1, FMCA.

30. To date, the most comprehensive published book on black auto workers is August Meier and Elliott Rudwick, *Black Detroit and the Rise of the UAW* (New York: Oxford University Press, 1979). Meier and Rudwick concentrate on the role of black workers in unionization and early union history. The best work on the preunion period remains Lloyd M. Bailer, "Negro Labor in the Automobile Industry" (Ph.D. diss., University of Michigan, 1943).

31. Lowery, "Labor Relations," p. 4; John Hope Franklin, *From Slavery to Freedom: A History of Negro Americans* (New York: Alfred A. Knopf, 1974), p. 349.

32. Meier and Rudwick, *Black Detroit,* p. 19; Sterling D. Spero and Abram L. Harris, *The Black Worker* [1931.] (Reprint. New York: Atheneum Edition, 1968), p. 140; *The Negro in Detroit,* prepared for the Mayor's Inter-Racial Committee by Detroit Bureau of Governmental Research, 1926, vol. 12, 2, 29, in DPL; Bailer, "Negro Labor," p. 31; Louise Venable Kennedy, *The Negro Peasant Turns Cityward,* Columbia University Studies in History, Economics and Public Law, no. 329 (New York: Columbia University, 1930), p. 127; U. S. Department of Labor, Division of Negro Economics, *The Negro at Work During the World War and During Reconstruction* (Washington: U. S. Government Printing Office, 1921), p. 138. The Detroit Urban League had a Dress Well Club which handed out cards to newcomers advising them: "Don't crowd inside of a street car filled with people in your dirty, greasy overalls. Stay on the platform as do the majority of white men in such apparel or wear a coat over your clothes when you are going back and forth to the foundry." See David Allan Levine, *Internal Combustion: The Races in Detroit 1915–1926* (Westport, CT: Greenwood Press, 1976), pp. 86–90.

33. Negro in Detroit, vol. 2, pp. 14–18; vol. 8, p. 23; Bailer, "Negro Labor," p. 32; U. S. Department of Labor, Division of Negro Economics, *Negro Migration in 1916–1917* (U. S. Government Printing Office, 1919), pp. 27–28, 100–107.

34. Shelton Tappes Interview, p. 2; Interview with Robert C. Mansfield, in Robert W. Dunn Collection, box 1, WSU; Bailer, "Negro Labor," pp. 52–86; Matthew Ward (Charles Denby), *Indignant Heart* (New York: New Books, 1952), p. 30.

35. Bailer, "Negro Labor," pp. 64–69, 151; "The Reminiscences of Willis F. Ward," p. 9, Oral History Section, FMCA: Herbert G. Northrup, *The Negro in the Automobile Industry* (Philadelphia: University of Pennsylvania Press, 1968), p. 13; Shelton Tappes Interview, p. 3.

36. Oral History Interview of Canon Malcolm Dade, pp. 2–4, WSU; Meier and Rudwick, *Black Detroit*, pp. 9–11.

37. Allan Nevins and Frank Ernest Hill, *Ford: Expansion and Challenge 1915–1933* (New York: Charles Scribner's Sons, 1957), pp. 354, 539–540; Northrup, *Negro in the Automobile Industry*, p. 13.

38. J. Herkel, Employment Department to F. Dolson, September 16, 1920, accession 284, box 10, FMCA.

39. *Negro in Detroit*, vol. 3, p. 14; Bailer, "Negro Labor," p. 100; U. S. Department of Labor, *Negro at Work*, p. 43.

40. Bailer, "Negro Labor," p. 126.

41. William Ellison Chalmers, "Labor in the Automobile Industry: A Study of Personnel Policies, Workers Attitudes and Attempts at Unionism" (Ph.D. diss., University of Wisconsin, 1932), p. 184; "The Reminiscences of Frank Hadas," pp. 99, 97, Oral History Section, FMCA.

42. Levine, *Internal Combustion*, p. 137; *Negro in Detroit*, vol. 3, p. 29.

43. Bailer, "Negro Labor," pp. 77–81, 117–118; Lloyd M. Bailer, "The Negro Automobile Worker," *Journal of Political Economy*, 51 (October 1943), p. 421; Glen E. Carlson, "The Negro in the Industries of Detroit" (Ph.D. diss., University of Michigan, 1929), pp. 140–143; Dunn, *Labor and Automobiles*, pp. 69–70.

44. E. P. Thompson, *The Making of the English Working Class* (New York: Pantheon, 1963), p. 9. For the attitudes of established unions towards immigrant labor see Robert Asher, "Union Nativism and the Immigrant Response," *Labor History*, 23 (Summer 1982), pp. 325–348; Olivier Zunz finds Detroit transformed by 1920 "from an ethnically divided city to a metropolis reorganized by ethnicity and class," where "industrialization had cut deep into ethnic autonomy" and "Detroit's space was becoming reorganized according to social class." See Zunz, *Changing Face*, pp. 399–400.

Chapter Three

1. Sidney Olson, *Young Henry Ford* (Detroit, MI: Wayne State University Press, 1963), pp. 182–183; Cy Caldwell, *Henry Ford* (New York: Julian Messner, 1947), p. 86; Henry Ford (in collaboration with Samuel Crowther), *My Life and Work* (Garden City, NY: Doubleday, Page and Co., 1923), p. 80; "The Reminiscences of Frank Bennett," vol. 2, p. 4, Oral History Section, FMCA; "The Reminiscences of John Wondersee," p. 9, Oral History Section, FMCA. William Ellison Chalmers cites one worker who had been with Packard for so long that, "He could remember when the wooden frame for a body was brought to two men working at a stand, a location on the floor, and then all of the various materials necessary were deposited around the body. The two men worked for three and one-half days on the same job, and turned out a complete automobile body at the end of that time." See William Ellison Chalmers, "Labor in the Automobile Industry: A Study of Personnel Policies, Workers' Attitudes and Attempts at Unionism" (Ph.D. diss., University of Wisconsin, 1932), p. 89.

2. Walter P. Chrysler, *Life of an American Workman* (New York: Dodd, Mead, 1937), pp. 133–134.

3. Roy Chapin speech, "Modern Production," n.d. (c. 1917), Roy D. Chapin Papers, vol. 17, UM; "The Reminiscences of Max F. Wollering," pp. 6–7, Oral History Section, FMCA.

4. One should not imagine instantaneous change in all processes at once. Actually some operations continued to be hand work into the 1920s, succumbing to machines only as those machines were invented. See Interview with L. W. Haskell, Assistant Manager of Operations, Dodge Plant of Chrysler Corporation, November 6, 1936, in Edward W. Wieck Collection, box 10, WSU.

5. Duane Yarnell, *Auto Pioneering: A Remarkable Story of Ransom E. Olds* (Lansing, MI: Franklin De Kleine Company, 1949), pp. 83–84; Howard R. De Lancy, "The Cole Motor Car Company," *Business History Review,* 30 (Sept. 1956), p. 265; Chrysler, *American Workman,* p. 135; "The Reminiscences of Max. F. Wollering," p. 24, Oral History Section, FMCA.

6. Max Wollering quoted in Allan Nevins, *Ford: The Times, The Man, The Company* (New York: Charles Scribner's Sons, 1954), p. 326; Keith Sward, *The Legend of Henry Ford* (New York: Holt, Rinehart and Winston, 1948), p. 33. On sequence of machines by 1910, see also L. W. Haskell Interview in Edward A. Wieck Collection, box 10, WSU; Horace L. Arnold and Fay L. Faurote, *Ford Methods and the Ford Shops* (New York: The Engineering Magazine Co., 1919), p. 38. Ford's prominence in developing assembly line, mass-production techniques has obscured the extent to which other companies had experimented with an orderly sequence of operations

and also with a hand-powered assembly line. For evidence from other companies see: Chrysler, *American Workman,* p. 135; Roy Chapin speech, "Modern Production,"; and De Lancey, "The Cole Motor Car Company," p. 265. For an assessment of Ford's contribution see Jonathan Hughes, *The Vital Few: American Economic Progress and its Protagonists* (Boston: Houghton Mifflin, 1965), pp. 323–324; and Daniel Nelson, *Managers and Workers: Origins of the New Factory System in the United States 1880–1920* (Madison, WI: University of Wisconsin Press, 1975), pp. 23–25.

7. Roy Chapin speech, "Modern Production."

8. Nevins, *Ford: The Times,* pp. 447–551; Alfred D. Chandler, Jr., *Giant Enterprise: Ford, General Motors, and the American Automobile Industry* (New York: Harcourt, Brace and World, 1964), p. 26; Arnold and Faurote, *Ford Methods.* The latter has many excellent photographs of the Highland Park plant and of men at work. Additional photographs of auto workers at work are to be found in William Joseph Showalter, "The Automobile Industry: An American Art that has Revolutionized Methods in Manufacturing and Transformed Transportation," *The National Geographic Magazine,* 44 (October 1923), pp. 337–414. For the argument that the development of the Ford assembly line arose from the need for management to gain control over the labor process at a time of a skilled labor shortage see David Gartman, "Origins of the Assembly Line and Capitalist Control of Work at Ford," in Andrew Zimbalist, ed., *Case Studies on the Labor Process* (New York: Monthly Review Press, 1979), pp. 193–205. See also Craig R. Littler, "Taylorism, Fordism, and Job Design," in David Knights, Hugh Willmott, and David Collinson, ed., *Job Redesign: Critical Perspectives on the Labour Process* (London: Gower, 1985), pp. 10–29. The following is a typical journalistic account from 1914 of the new auto factory.

> Of course there was order in that place; of course there was system—relentless system—terrible 'efficiency'—but to my mind, unaccustomed to such things, the whole room with its interminable aisles, its whirling shafts and wheels, its forest of roof-supporting posts and flapping, flying leather belting, its endless rows of writhing machinery, its shrieking, hammering, and clatter, its smell of oil, its autumn haze of smoke, its savage-looking foreign population—to my mind it expressed but one thing, and that thing was delirium. Fancy a jungle of wheels and belts and weird iron forms—of men, machinery and movement—add to it every kind of sound you can imagine; the sound of a million squirrels chirking, a million monkeys quarreling, a million lions roaring, a million pigs dying, a million elephants smashing through a forest of sheet iron, a million boys whistling on their fingers, a million others coughing with the whooping cough, a million sinners groaning as they are dragged to hell—imagine all of this happening at the very edge of Niagara Falls,

with the everlasting roar of the cataract as a perpetual background, and you may acquire a vague conception of that place.

Julian Street, "Detroit the Dynamic," *Collier's,* July 4, 1914, p. 10.

9. Sward, *Legend of Henry Ford,* pp. 38–39; Stephen Meyer, III, *The Five Dollar Day: Labor Management and Social Control in the Ford Motor Company, 1908—1921* (Albany, NY: State University of New York Press, 1981), pp. 9–36; Nevins, *Ford: The Times,* p. 463; Mortimer W. LaFever, "Workers, Machinery and Production in the Automobile Industry," *Monthly Labor Review,* 19 (October 1924), pp. 8–9; Oral History Interview of Clayton Johnson, p. 10; WSU; *Detroit Times,* August 26, 1928; "I was a Painter," in Joe Brown Collection, box 9, WSU; Oral History Interview with Phil Raymond, p. 11, WSU.

10. Oral History Interview of Joe Hattley, p. 3, WSU; LaFever, "Workers, Machinery, and Production," pp. 15–18; Chrysler, *American Workman,* p. 134; Oral History Interview of Lester Johnson, p. 10, WSU; Oral History Interview of Everett Francis, p. 1, WSU.

11. Oral History Interview of Arthur Rohan, pp. 1–2, WSU; Oral History Interview of Everett Francis, p. 305, WSU.

12. Wyndham Mortimer, *Organize! My Life as a Union Man* (Boston: Beacon Press, 1971), p. 40; Arnold and Faurote, *Ford Methods,* pp. 38, 41–42; Sward, *Legend of Henry Ford,* p. 47; Ford, *My Life and Work,* p. 90; Meyer, III, *The Five Dollar Day,* pp. 9–36. For examples from the French automobile industry, see Alain Toraine, "The End of the Road for the Skilled Worker: Automaking at Renault," in Edward Shorter, ed., *Work and Community in the West* (New York: Harper and Row, 1973), pp. 80–87.

13. Arnold and Faurote, *Ford Methods,* pp. 41–42.

14. R. R. Lutz, *The Metal Trades* (Philadelphia: The Survey Committee of the Cleveland Foundation, 1916), p. 80.

15. Nevins, *Ford: The Times,* p. 380; Charles Reitell, "Machinery and its Effect Upon the Workers in the Automobile Industry," *The Annals of the American Academy of Political and Social Science,* 116 (November 1924), p. 39; Arnold and Faurote, *Ford Methods,* p. 41; Louise Venable Kennedy, *The Negro Peasant Turns Cityward,* Columbia University Studies in History, Economics and Public Law, no. 329 (New York: Columbia University, 1930), p. 251; A. T. Court, "Men, Methods and Machines in Manufacturing Motor Vehicles," (Automobile Manufacturers Association, 1939), p. 13, mimeo, DPL.

16. List of trades and occupations, January 31, 1917, accession 62, box 59, FMCA. Of a total 41,200 men listed, 13,177 were machine hands and 4,149 were assemblers. Other job categories of more than 100 men were

inspectors, 1,092; millwrights, 1,065; molders, 1,605; stock men, 1,669; and toolmakers, 1,018. Reitell, "Machinery and Its Effect," p. 39. The job categories are defined as follows: machine tenders (operators of boring mills, drill presses, milling and polishing machines, punch presses, screw machines, sewing machines, planers, shapers, and sheet metal machines); assemblers (no definition); skilled workers (machinists, blacksmiths, die sinkers, painters, and varnishers); inspectors and testers (no definition); helpers (varnish rubbers, trim bench hands, machinist helpers, and blacksmith helpers); laborers (carrying, handling and cleanup). Ford, *My Life and Work,* p. 110.

17. John W. Anderson, "How I Became Part of the Labor Movement," in Alice and Staughton Lynd, eds., *Rank and File* (Boston: Beacon Press, 1973), pp. 43, 46.

18. Chandler, *Giant Enterprise,* pp. 17–18; Oral History Interview of Tom Klasey, p. 3, WSU; Meyer, III, *The Five Dollar Day,* p. 37. For parallel trends in the steel industry, see David Brody, *Steelworkers in America: The Nonunion Era* (Cambridge, MA: Harvard University Press, 1960).

19. Oral History Interview of Mort Furay, pp. 1, 7, WSU.

20. *Ibid.,* p. 8.

21. The number of wage earners in the motor vehicle industry increased as follows: 1909, 75,721; 1919, 343,115; 1929, 447,448. (See Table I-1.)

22. Lutz, *Metal Trades,* p. 88.

23. On deskilling and degradation see Harry Braverman, *Labor and Monopoly Capital: The Degradation of Work in the Twentieth Century* (New York: Monthly Review Press, 1974). For an excellent review of theories about the labor process that includes discussion of Braverman, see Paul Thompson, *The Nature of Work: An Introduction to Debates on the Labour Process* (London: Macmillan, 1983); and Paul Thompson, "Crawling from the Wreckage." Paper prepared for the 4th ASTON/UMIST Conference on Organization and Control of the Labour Process, April 1986. For the importance of skilled workers in auto unionization see Steve Babson, "Pointing the Way. The Role of British and Irish Skilled Tradesmen in the Rise of the UAW," *Detroit in Perspective,* 7 (Spring 1983), pp. 75–96.

24. "The Reminiscences of Frank Hadas," p. 177, Oral History Section, FMCA; "The Reminiscences of E. G. Liebold," p. 237, Oral History Section, FMCA: Ford, *My Life and Work,* pp. 105–106. For a plan to change jobs every three months, see *The Ford Industries* (Ford Motor Company, 1924), p. 114. As early as 1918, Samuel Marquis suggested that frequent job changes would be a good idea. See S. S. Marquis to E. G. Liebold, May 16, 1918, accession 1, box 121, FMCA.

25. Ford, *My Life and Work,* p. 106; S. Wyatt, "Boredom in Industry," *Personnel Journal,* 8 (1919), p. 161; Chalmers, "Labor in the Automobile Industry," pp. 90–92.

26. Oliver M. Zendt in Robert W. Dunn Collection, box 1, WSU.

27. Charles R. Walker and Robert H. Guest, *The Man on the Assembly Line* (Cambridge, MA: Harvard University Press, 1952), pp. 13, 65–66.

28. Eli Chinoy, *Automobile Workers and the American Dream* (Garden City, NY: Doubleday, 1955), p. 86.

29. Allan Nevins and Frank Ernest Hill, *Ford: Expansion and Challenge 1915–1933* (New York: Charles Scribner's Sons, 1957), p. 295; *Pipp's Weekly,* August 25, 1923; Samuel Marquis to E. G. Liebold, May 16, 1918, accession 1, box 121, FMCA.

30. Samuel Marquis to E. G. Liebold, May 16, 1918, accession 1, box 121, FMCA.

31. Babson, "Pointing the Way," pp. 75–86.

32. Reitell, "Machinery and Its Effect," p. 41; Sward, *The Legend of Henry Ford,* p. 78; "The Reminiscences of W. C. Klann," p. 85, Oral History Section, FMCA; "The Reminiscences of Frank Hadas," p. 95, Oral History Section, FMCA; Meyer, III, *The Five Dollar Day,* pp. 95–121.

33. On Taylor and scientific management, see Ed Andrew, *Closing the Iron Cage: The Scientific Management of Work and Leisure* (Montreal: Black Rose Books, 1981); Daniel Nelson, *Frederick W. Taylor and the Rise of Scientific Management* (Madison, WI: University of Wisconsin Press, 1980); on scientific management and American industry in general, see Richard Edwards, *Contested Terrain: The Transformation of the Workplace in the Twentieth Century* (New York: Basic Books, 1979); Don Clawson, *Bureaucracy and the Labor Process: The Transformation of U. S. Industry, 1860–1920* (New York: Monthly Review Press, 1980); David M. Gordon, Richard Edwards, and Michael Reich, *Segmented Work, Divided Workers: The Historical Transformation of Labor in the United States* (Cambridge: Cambridge University Press, 1982); Nelson, *Managers and Workers.*

34. Frederick Winslow Taylor, *The Principles of Scientific Management* (New York: Harper and Brothers, 1919); Touraine, "The End of the Road," pp. 90–96; Reitell, "Machinery and Its Effect," p. 41; Sward, *The Legend of Henry Ford,* p. 78; Nevins, *Ford: The Times,* p. 468; Loren Baritz, *The Servants of Power: A History of the Use of Social Science in American Industry* (Middletown, CT: Wesleyan University Press, 1960), pp. 28–29; E. J. Hobsbawn, "Custom, Wages and Work-Load," in *Labouring Men* (New York: Basic Books, 1964, pp. 417–422; Charles E. Sorensen, *My Forty Years With Ford* (New York: W. W. Norton, 1956), pp. 39–41; Katherine Stone, "The Origins of Job Structures in the Steel Industry," *Radical America,* 7

(November–December 1973), p. 45; David Montgomery, *Workers' Control in America* (Cambridge: Cambridge University Press, 1979), pp. 32–47.

35. Quoted in Edmund Wilson, *The American Jitters* [1932.] (Reprint. Freeport, NY: Books for Libraries Press, 1969), p. 53.

Chapter Four

1. U. S. Congress, Federal Trade Commission, *Report on Motor Vehicle Industry,* 76th Cong., 1st sess., House Document No. 468, pp. 8–10; Paul F. Brissenden, *Earnings of Factory Workers 1899–1927,* Census Monograph X (Washington: Bureau of the Census, 1929), pp. 45, 381; Whitney Coombs, *The Wages of Unskilled Labor in Manufacturing Industries in the United States, 1890–1924,* Studies in History, Economics, and Public Law, no. 283 (New York: Columbia University Press, 1926), pp. 42–48; R. R. Lutz, *The Metal Trades* (Philadelphia: The Survey Committee of the Cleveland Foundation, 1916), pp. 89–91.

2. Ford maintained that piecework led to hurried and careless work. Although Ford wages were not based on piecework, Ford did employ time-study men and would inform workers of the output expected from them. Foremen were also well aware that they were expected to meet production quotas. See "The Reminiscences of Max Wollering," pp. 25–26, Oral History Section, FMCA; and "The Reminiscences of W. C. Klann," p. 151, Oral History Section, FMCA; Roy Chapin speech, "Modern Production," Roy D. Chapin Papers, Vol. 17, UM; Harry Braverman, *Labor and Monopoly Capital: The Degradation of Work in the The Twentieth Century* (New York: Monthly Review Press, 1974), p. 97; Jean Trepp McKelvey, *AFL Attitudes Toward Production 1900–1932,* Cornell Studies in Industrial and Labor Relations, Vol. 2 (Ithaca, NY: New York State School of Industrial and Labor Relations, 1952), p. 13; E. J. Hobsbawn, "Custom, Wages and Work Load," in *Labouring Men* (New York: Basic Books, 1964), pp. 406, 411–412, 425; Herbert Gutman, "Work, Culture, and Society in Industrializing America," *The American Historical Review,* 78 (June 1973), p. 565. For typical statements of the theory and practice of scientific management, see Frederick Winslow Taylor, *The Principles of Scientific Management* (New York: Harper and Brothers, 1919); Dwight T. Farnham, *Scientific Industrial Efficiency* [1917.] (Reprint. Easton, PA: Hive Publishing Company, 1974); Harrington Emerson, *The Twelve Principles of Efficiency* (New York: The Engineering Magazine Co., 1912); U. S. Congress, Commission on Industrial Relations, *Efficiency Systems and Labor,* 64th Cong., 1st Sess., Senate Document No. 415, 1916; Daniel Nelson, *Frederick W. Taylor and the Rise of Scientific Management* (Madison, WI: University of Wisconsin Press, 1980); Ed Andrew, *Closing the Iron Cage: The Scientific Management of Work and Leisure* (Montreal: Black Rose Books, 1981).

3. Interview with Joseph Geschelin, Technical Editor, Chilton Company Automotive Journals, November 4, 1939, in Edward A. Wieck Collection, box 10, WSU; Oral History Interview of Raymond Berndt, p. 2, WSU; Interview with L. W. Haskell, Edward A. Wieck Collection, box 10, WSU; Oral History Interview of Roy H. Speth, p. 2, WSU.

4. Claude E. Hoffman, *Sit-Down in Anderson: UAW Local 663, Anderson, Indiana* (Detroit, MI: Wayne State University Press, 1968), p. 17; William Ellison Chalmers, "Labor in the Automobile Industry: A Study of Personnel Policies, Workers Attitudes and Attempts at Unionism" (Ph.D. diss., University of Wisconsin, 1932), p. 121; *Packard Advanced Training School Lecture Course 1919* (Detroit, MI: Packard Motor Car Co., 1919), p. 63; Detroit Mayor's Non-Partisan Committee, *Report of the Mayor's Non-Partisan Committee on Industrial Disputes (The Fact-Finding Committee) in the Matter of the Strike of the Workers at the Briggs Manufacturing Company, Detroit, Michigan*, February 21, 1933, p. 47. Taylor expressed his disapproval of rate cutting as follows: "After a workman has had the price per piece of the work he is doing lowered two- or three-times as a result of his having worked harder and increased his output, he is likely to entirely lose sight of his employer's side of the case and to become imbued with a grim determination to have no more cuts if soldiering can prevent." Quoted in Braverman, *Monopoly Capital*, p. 99.

5. Interview with L. W. Haskell, Edward A. Wieck Collection, box 10, WSU; Oral History Interview of Tracy M. Doll, pp. 2–3, WSU.

6. *Packard Advanced Training School*, p. 63.

7. Oral History Interview of Tracy M. Doll, p. 3, WSU.

8. Joel John Lowery, "Labor Relations in the Automobile Industry During the Nineteen Twenties," (M.A. thesis, Michigan State University, 1958), pp. 11–12; Mortimer W. La Fever, "Workers, Machinery, and Production in the Automobile Industry," *Monthly Labor Review*, 19 (October 1924), p. 23; Morris L. Marcus notes in Robert W. Dunn Collection, box 1, WSU; Interview with A. F. Sherman, Detroit Editor, *Iron Age*, November 8, 1919, in Edward A. Wieck Collection, box 10, WSU; H. Dubreuil, *Robots or Men?* (New York: Harper, 1930), pp. 72–73.

9. Oral History Interview of Tracy M. Doll, p. 4, WSU; John W. Anderson, "How I Became Part of the Labor Movement," in Alice and Staughton Lynd, ed., *Rank and File* (Boston: Beacon Press, 1973), p. 46; Headrick Paper, in Robert W. Dunn Collection, box 1, WSU; Report of a company spy March 19, 1931, in Harry Ross Collection, box 6, WSU; Frank Martel to Congressman Ernst Lundeen, May 23, 1933, in Metro-Detroit AFL-CIO Collection, box 2, WSU. For more on workers' restriction of output see Chapter VI herein.

10. U. S. Department of Labor, Bureau of Labor Statistics Bulletin No. 438, "Wages and Hours of Labor in the Motor Vehicle Industry: 1925," May 1927, pp. 9–11; Lutz, *Metal Trades*, p. 94; National Industrial Conference Board, *Wages in the United States, 1914–1926*, Research Report No. 120 (New York: National Industrial Conference Board, 1927,) p. 90. "The Reminiscences of W. C. Klann," p. 88, Oral History Section, FMCA: Minutes, Board of Directors, Ford Motor Company, November 25, 1912, accession 85, box 1, FMCA; Oral History Interview of George Addes, p. 1, WSU; Oral History Interview of Orrin Peppler, pp. 1–2, WSU; Robert W. Dunn, *Labor and Automobiles* (New York: International Publishers, 1929), pp. 93–95; Marcus notes in Robert W. Dunn Collection, box 1, WSU; Chen-Nan Li, "A Summer in the Ford Works," *Personnel Journal*, 7 (June 1928), pp. 26–27.

11. W. M. Cunningham, *"J8" A Chronicle of the Neglected Truth About Henry Ford D. E. and the Ford Motor Company* (Detroit, MI: North American Publishing Co., n.d.), p. 36; Li, *Personnel Journal*, 7, pp. 26–27; Edmund Wilson, *The American Jitters* [1932.] (Reprint. Freeport, NY: Books for Libraries Press, 1968), pp. 52–53; Horace Lucien Arnold and Fay Leone Faurote, *Ford Methods and the Ford Shops* (New York: The Engineering Mgazine Co., 1919), p. 60. Some workers continued to eat at their machines well into the 1920s. See Oral History Interview of Ed Lee, p. 9, WSU; and Leheny manuscript in Robert W. Dunn Collection, box 2, WSU.

12. Chalmers, "Labor in the Automobile Industry," p. 19; Oral History Interview with Lew Michener, p. 5, WSU: Daniel Nelson, *Managers and Workers: Origins of the New Factory System in the United States 1880–1920* (Madison, WI: University of Wisconsin Press, 1975), pp. 149–150.

13. *Packard Advanced Training School*, p. 311; Leslie McDonnell, "Life with Uncle Henry," pp. 2–3, Oral History Section, FMCA; Myron W. Watkins, "The Labor Situation in Detroit," *The Journal of Political Economy*, 28 (1920), p. 841; Clayton Fountain, *Union Guy* (New York: Viking Press, 1949), pp. 18–19; Robert Cruden letter, July 1, 1928, cited in Robert W. Dunn Collection, box 1, WSU; Oral History Interview of Shelton Tappes, pp. 1–2, WSU; Andrew Steiger, Thomas Mimms, and Richard Sears notes in Robert W. Dunn Collection, box 1, WSU. For accounts of workers hired for their baseball skills, see Oral History Interview of Norman Bully, p. 2, WSU; Oral History Interview of Jack Jourdan, p 2, WSU; and Tony Lane, "A Merseysider in Detroit," *History Workshop*, issue 11 (Spring 1981), p. 145.

14. Oral History Interview of R. C. Ingram, pp. 3–4; Richard Sears and Morris Marcus notes in Robert W. Dunn Collection, box 1, WSU.

15. Oral History Interview of Charles K. Beckman, p. 5, WSU; Blanche Bernstein, "Hiring Policies in the Automobile Industry," prepared for the Works Progress Administration, 1937, copy in Edward Levinson Collection

(and William Ellison Chalmers Collection), box 2, WSU; Oral History Interview of Louis H. Adkins, p. 2, WSU; Oral History Interview of Charles K. Beckman, pp. 4–5, WSU; Oral History Interview of Bert Foster, p. 20, WSU; Fountain, *Union Guy,* p. 58.

16. Oral History Interview of Ed Lee, p. 11, WSU; Oral History Interview of Charles K. Beckman, p. 5, WSU; Anderson, "How I Became Part of the Labor Movement," pp. 52–53; James Richard McDonnell, "The Rise of the CIO in Buffalo, New York 1936–1942" (Ph.D. diss., University of Wisconsin, 1970), p. 45; Oral History Interview of Tracy Doll, pp. 20–21, WSU; Oral History Interview of George Merrelli, pp. 1–2, WSU; Oral History Interview of Joe Hattley, p. 5, WSU; Oral History Interview of Harvey Kitzman, p. 12, WSU; Oral History Interview of Bert Foster, p. 2, WSU. For Ford letters, see for example letter dated September 1, 1920, to Henry Ford, accession 1, box 120 (the box contains many similar letters), FMCA; see also "A Ford Employee to Mrs. Henry Ford," March 20, 1922, accession 1, box 118, FMCA.

17. Frank Marquart, *An Auto Worker's Journal: The UAW from Crusade to One-Party Union* (University Park, PA: University of Pennsylvania Press, 1975), p. 31; Oral History Interview of Arthur Case, p. 1, WSU; Allan Nevins, *Ford: The Times, The Man, The Company* (New York: Charles Scribner's Sons, 1954), p. 333; Andrew Steiger notes in Robert W. Dunn Collection, box 1, WSU; Oral History Interview of Charles K. Beckman, p. 5, WSU; Oral History Interview of Paul Miley, p. 1, WSU; McDonnell, "The Rise of the CIO in Buffalo," p. 37.

18. Telegram from E. G. Liebold to Henry F. Pringle, *New York Sunday World,* October 15, 1926, accession 285, box 496, FMCA.

> This company has always maintained a strict policy of releasing its employees where we have found the slightest evidence of their using intoxicating liquors not waiting until such use has been carried to a point of intoxication. Furthermore many men are open to discharge for various reasons all of which may be attributed to even mild use of liquor.

Packard Advanced Training School, pp. 52–53; George Edward Lyndon of the *Brooklyn Eagle,* reprinted in *Pipp's Weekly,* August 25, 1923; Allan Nevins and Frank Ernest Hill, *Ford: Expansion and Challenge 1915–1933* (New York: Charles Scribner's Sons, 1957), p. 514; Oral History Interview of Andrew Montgomery, pp. 3–4, WSU; Lowery, "Labor Relations," p. 26.

19. Oral History Interview of Norman B. Matthews, p. 2, WSU; *Packard Advanced Training School,* pp. 31–35; "The Reminiscences of W. C. Klann," p. 151, Oral History Section, FMCA.

20. Thomas Mimms notes in Robert W. Dunn Collection, box 1, WSU; "The Reminiscences of W. C. Klann," p. 84, Oral History Section, FMCA.

21. "The Reminiscences of W. C. Klann," p. 107, Oral History Section, FMCA; McDonnell, "Life with Uncle Henry," p. 26, Oral History Section, FMCA; LaFever, "Workers, Machinery, and Production," p. 6; Lowery, "Labor Relations," pp. 36–38; Nevins and Hill, *Ford: Expansion,* pp. 329, 515–520; Thomas H. Wright, "Why Ford's Men Strike," *Christian Century,* 50 (November 29, 1933), p. 1503.

22. Much has been written about the $5 day. The following are useful sources: Nevins, *Ford: The Times,* pp. 512–567; Henry Ford (in collaboration with Samuel Crowther), *My Life and Work* (Garden City, NY: Doubleday, Page and Co., 1923), pp. 126–130; John R. Lee, "The So-Called Profit Sharing System in the Ford Plant," *The Annals of the American Academy of Political and Social Science,* 65 (May 1916), pp. 297–310; Samuel M. Levin, "Ford Profit Sharing, 1914–1920, I. The Growth of the Plan," *Personnel Journal,* 6 (August 1927), pp. 75–86; Samuel M. Levin, "The End of Ford Profit Sharing," *Personnel Journal,* 6 (October 1927), pp. 161–170; David M. Lewis, "Henry Ford: A Study in Public Relations (1896–1932)" (Ph.D. diss., University of Michigan, 1959); Keith Sward, *The Legend of Henry Ford* (New York: Holt, Rinehart and Winston, 1948) pp. 50–63; Jonathan N. Leonard, *The Tragedy of Henry Ford* (New York: G. P. Putnams', 1932), pp. 24–30; John Kenneth Galbraith, "Was Ford a Fraud," in *The Liberal Hour* (Boston: Houghton Mifflin, 1960); Samuel Marquis speech, "Profit Sharing Plan," June 1916, accession 63, box 1, FMCA. The best overall account is Stephen Meyer, III, *The Five Dollar Day: Labor Management and Social Control in the Ford Motor Company, 1908–1921* (Albany, NY: State University of New York Press, 1981), esp. pp. 95–121.

23. Lee, "The So-Called Profit Sharing System," pp. 304–305; "The Reminiscences of George Brown," p. 85, Oral History Section, FMCA; Meyer, III, *The Five Dollar Day,* pp. 123–147.

24. "The Reminiscences of William P. Baxter," p. 11, Oral History Section, FMCA: Samuel S. Marquis, *Henry Ford, An Interpretation* (Boston: Little, Brown, 1923), pp. 98–99; Meyer, III, *The Five Dollar Day,* pp. 108–109.

25. "The Reminiscences of George Brown," p. 83, Oral History Section, FMCA. The six-month probation period was in effect for new employees and for employees returning to work at Ford after having been previously eligible for the $5 wage. It, therefore, discouraged workers from shopping around for a better job. In 1915, in a statement to the Commission on Industrial Relations, Henry Ford reported a drop in absenteeism from 10% to .3% (accession 62, box 6, FMCA). Ford estimated increased efficiency at 15–20%. Boyd Fisher of the Detroit Board of Commerce estimated that worker efficiency increased by 44%. See "Report on Profit Sharing Plan," June 1914, accession 62, box 58, FMCA.

26. "The Reminiscences of W. Ernest Grimshaw," p. 15, Oral History Section, FMCA.

27. Foremen kept cards, which they passed on to salesmen, on prospective buyers among the workers. "We naturally feel that our own employees who are dependent upon this Co. for their livelihood should give first consideration to the Ford car or truck." See General Letter, August 1, 1923, accession 572, box 30, FMCA: "The Reminiscences of W. C. Klann," p. 88, Oral History Section, FMCA: Alan Stuart notes in Robert W. Dunn Collection, box 1, WSU.

28. Meyer, III, *The Five Dollar Day*, pp. 169–194; Levin, "The End of Ford Profit Sharing," pp. 162–164; Charles E. Sorensen, *My Forty Years With Ford* (New York: W. W. Norton, 1956), p. 145.

29. The *Fortune* survey was taken in 1940, after the great wave of CIO organizing successes, after the "Battle of the Overpass," and when Henry Ford's opposition to unionization was very clear. Still, only 12.3% of those questioned saw Henry Ford as harmful to labor whereas 44.6% thought that John L. Lewis was harmful to labor. The 73.6% who found Ford helpful to labor should be compared with 51.8% for Senator Robert F. Wagner, 49.7% for William Green, and 43.4% for Frances Perkins. *Fortune,* 21 (June 1940), pp. 59–60, 160–163; Sorensen, *My Forty Years with Ford,* p. 1.

30. Wyndham Mortimer, *Organize! My Life as a Union Man* (Boston: Beacon Press, 1971), p. 41; Glen A. Niemeyer, *The Automotive Career of Ransom E. Olds,* Michigan State University Business Studies (Lansing, MI: Michigan State University, 1963), pp. 120–128; Oral History Interview of Norman Matthews, p. 2, WSU; See United Community Services Case Records, WSU, for referrals from company welfare offices; the Dodge study is in Oral History Interview of Frank Tuttle, pp. 4–6, WSU.

31. *Packard Advanced Training School,* pp. 318, 56.

32. For a general discussion of corporate liberalism in the United States see: James Weinstein, *The Corporate Ideal in the Liberal State 1900–1918* (Boston: Beacon Press, 1968); and David Brody, *Workers in Industrial America; Essays on the Twentieth Century Struggle* (New York: Oxford University Press, 1980), pp. 48–81; See also notes on interview with Kroger regarding labor relations at Chevrolet Gear and Axle and Drop Forging Plants in Robert W. Dunn Collection, box 1, WSU.

33. Minutes, Board of Directors, Ford Motor Company, December 18, 1909, accession 85, box 1, FMCA.

34. Lowery, "Labor Relations," p. 46; Nevins and Hill, *Ford: Expansion,* p. 330; Levin, "The End of Ford Profit Sharing," pp. 165–168; "The Reminiscences of J. E. Bossardt," p. 13, Oral History Section, FMCA.

35. Sidney Fine, *Sit-Down: The General Motors Strike of 1936–1937* (Ann Arbor, MI: University of Michigan Press, 1969), pp. 23–24; Gordon W. Davidson, "Industrial Detroit After World War I, 1919 to 1921" (M.A.

thesis, Wayne University, 1953), pp. 63–65; Arthur Pound, *The Turning Wheel* (Garden City, NY: Doubleday, Doran, 1934), pp. 395–396, 402–406.

36. Lawrence H. Seltzer, *A Financial History of the American Automobile Industry* (Cambridge, MA: Houghton Mifflin, 1928), pp. 220–221. Pound, *The Turning Wheel,* pp. 395–396; Fine, *Sit-Down,* p. 23; Davidson, "Industrial Detroit," p. 64; Levin, "The End of Ford Profit Sharing," pp. 165–167.

37. Fine, *Sit-Down,* p. 24; Seltzer, *Financial History,* pp. 221–222; Minutes, Board of Directors, Ford Motor Company, August 21, 1913, accession 85, box 1, FMCA: *Proceedings of Convention,* Carriage, Wagon and Automobile Workers' International, September 1915.

38. "Outline of Suggestion for the Housing of the Employees of Henry Ford at Ford Tractor Plants and of the Employees of Ford Motor Company along the River Rouge," n.d., accession 62, box 28, FMCA; Joseph Oldenburg, "Ford Homes Historic District," *The Dearborn Historian,* 20 (Spring 1980), pp. 31–35; Lee, "The So-Called Profit Sharing System," pp. 65, 304.

39. Oldenburg, "Ford Homes," pp. 31–35; Lee, "The So-Called Profit Sharing System," p. 304.

40. *Pipp's Weekly,* May 16, 1925; Fine, *Sit-Down,* p. 23.

41. Sward, *Legend of Henry Ford,* pp. 229–230; Nevins, *Ford: The Times,* p. 519; Niemeyer, *Ransom E. Olds,* p. 127; Chalmers, "Labor in the Automobile Industry," pp. 66–70; *Ford News,* March 15, 1928, p. 52; Letter to Executive Committee of the Ford Motor Company from the Henry Ford Trade School, August 20, 1917, accession 62, box 15, FMCA; "The Reminiscences of E. G. Liebold," p. 204, Oral History Section, FMCA: *The Ford Industries,* 1924, p. 24; "The Reminiscences of Frederick Searle," pp. 6–13, Oral History Section, FMCA; Report of December 17, 1926, accession 285, box 635, FMCA; Henry Ford (in collaboration with Samuel Crowther), *Today and Tomorrow* (Garden City, NY: Doubleday, Page and Co., 1926), p. 183; General Motors Institute of Technology, *Bulletin,* 1928–1929, p. 3, in Henry Kraus Collection, box 16, WSU.

42. Lowery, "Labor Relations," pp. 13–14; Oral History Interview of Ted La Duke, pp. 1–2, WSU; Cunningham, *"J8",* pp. 114–115; Joe Brown to Robert Cruden, March 17, 1936, Vertical File, Joe Brown Collection, WSU; "Compensation Manuscript," Richard Frankensteen Collection, box 2, WSU; Anderson, "How I Became Part of the Labor Movement," p. 52; Oral History Interview of Joseph Piconke, p. 7, WSU; Oral History Interview of Adam Poplawski, p. 2, WSU.

43. Interview with N, November 19, 1934, Vertical File, Brown Collection, WSU; "Poisoning from Chromium Compounds," Dunn Collection, box 1, WSU; Interview with N, July 11, 1935, Vertical File, Brown Collection,

WSU; Edwin P. Norwood, *Ford Men and Methods* (Garden City, NY: Doubleday, Doran, 1931), pp. 61–63.

44. Oral History Interview with Shelton Tappes, p. 5, WSU; Arnold and Faurote, *Ford Methods*, p. 330; Jack (RBC) to R. D. Chapin, August 8, 1916, Chapin Papers, vol. 9, UM; Hoffman, *Sit-Down in Anderson*, p. 19; Oral History Interview of Jack Jourdon, p. 14, WSU.

45. Minutes, Executive Committee, Ford Motor Company, November 1, 1916, accession 85, box 5, FMCA.

46. F. E. Lingemann to Roy Chapin, December 20, 1919, vol. 27, Chapin Papers, UM.

47. Nevins and Hill, *Ford: Expansion*, p. 511; Lowery, "Labor Relations," p. 15.

48. Employees' Liability and Workmens' Compensation Commission of the State of Michigan, *Report*, 1911 (in DPL). *Packard Advanced Training School*, p. 356; Lowery, "Labor Relations," p. 12.

49. Report of Safety Activities 1922, accession 572, box 27, FMCA; Oral History Interview of Roy Speth, pp. 2–3, WSU.

50. National Safety Council, *Transactions*, 1927, vol. 1, p. 443, Robert W. Dunn Collection, box 1, WSU.

51. Report of Rouge Hospital, accession 38, box 51, FMCA; For Ford employment figures see Nevins and Hill, *Ford: Expansion*, Appendix III, p. 687; Oral History Interview of Ken Bannon, pp. 2–3, WSU; Accident Reports, accession 38, box 66, FMCA; Medical Department Annual Accident Reports for 1929, 1930, 1931, accession 572, box 27, FMCA; Erskine Caldwell, *Some American People* (New York: Robert M. McBride, 1935), p. 164. Caldwell's impression of the dangers of auto life is summed up in the following:

> In working-class Detroit you are known by your hands. If you have all your fingers intact, you are either a non-automobile worker, or a new worker, or an exceptionally lucky automobile worker. If you have one finger missing, it serves as an identification device. But when two fingers have been torn free from your hands, you are an outcast. The hiring departments look at the state of your hands before they look at the color of your skin. There is no use in filling out an application blank for an automobile plant job if you are eight-fingered. You are done for. You may as well get out of Detroit and stay out. The finishing touch has been put on you for the rest of your life.

Caldwell, *Some American People*, p. 169.

52. Lowery, "Labor Relations," pp. 12–13; Roger Keeran, *The Communist Party and the Auto Workers Unions* (Bloomington: Indiana University Press, 1980), p. 52.

53. Operative's Report, 1906, accession 940, box 16, FMCA; *The Ford Industries,* p. 119, accession 62, box 59, FMCA; *Packard Advanced Training School,* p. 354; Nevins and Hill, *Ford: Expansion,* p. 511.

54. GMC Industrial Relations Section, "Safety Instructions for Employees," August 1926, in Robert W. Dunn Collection, box 1, WSU; Minutes, Safety Committee, Ford Motor Company, August 19, 1920, accession 284, box 10, FMCA; Packard claimed 95% of all minor accidents resulted from the carelessness or ignorance of workers. See *Packard Advanced Training School,* p. 362.

55. "Testimony of Leon Pody before Subcommittee of Mayor's Unemployment Committee," Vertical File, Joe Brown Collection, WSU. Pody mentions the need for frequent checks of the set screws used to put on disc grinders. If the screws were not secure they could fly off. Also, buffers needed to be tightened down with a wrench. To save time, workers would stick in the end of a file instead. With increasing speed the file would jump out. *Report of the Mayor's Non-Partisan Committee;* "Eye Hazards," in Robert W. Dunn Collection, box 1, WSU; G. A. Kuechenmeister, "My Experience with Goggles," John Zaremba Collection, box 9, WSU; Robert Cruden, "Ask the Man Who Works There," 1928, Robert W. Dunn Collection, box 2, WSU. There may also have been some feeling that goggles and other safety devices were less than manly, that a man takes his chances. Safety measures that depended on a worker taking precautions, rather than having those precautions built into the machines, were likely to take a long time to be widely accepted.

56. The Michigan Workmens' Compensation Law included no coverage for illness, as opposed to accidents, until 1937. Robert Cruden to Joe Brown, January 5, 1936, Vertical File, Joe Brown Collection, WSU; "Compensation Manuscript," Richard Frankensteen Collection, box 2, WSU; Health Fumes Interview, 1934, Vertical File, Joe Brown Collection, WSU; "The Reminiscences of William P. Baxter," p. 15, Oral History Section, FMCA.

57. *Pipp's Weekly,* February 9, 1924; "Compensation Manuscript," Richard Frankensteen Collection, box 2, WSU.

58. Brody, *Workers in Industrial America,* pp. 48–81. Charles Reitell, "Machinery and Its Effect Upon the Worker in the Automotive Industry," *The Annals of the American Academy of Political and Social Science,* 116 (November 1924), p. 43.

Chapter Five

1. Stephen Meyer, III, *The Five Dollar Day: Labor Management and Social Control in the Ford Motor Company, 1908–1921* (Albany, NY: State University of New York Press, 1981), pp. 169–194.

2. Accession 572, box 27, FMCA; Allan Nevins, *Ford: The Times, The Man, The Company* (New York: Charles Scribner's Sons, 1954), p. 553.

3. "The Reminiscences of E. G. Liebold," p. 226, Oral History Section, FMCA; Accession 572, box 27, FMCA.

4. *Helpful Hints and Advice to Employees* (Detroit, MI: Ford Motor Company, 1915), p. 13.

5. Andrew Steiger notes, Robert W. Dunn Collection, box 1, WSU; Tony Lane, "A Merseysider in Detroit," *History Workshop*, issue 11 (Spring 1981), p. 143.

6. "Report to the Health Officer on Housing and Health in Detroit," The Detroit Board of Health, 1916, pp. 8–10, DPL; "The Reminiscenses of George Brown," p. 94, Oral History Section, FMCA; *Pipp's Weekly*, June 5, 1920.

7. Samuel Marquis testimony, accession 293, box 1, FMCA; I. Paul Taylor, *Prosperity in Detroit* (Highland Park, MI: By the Author, 1920), pp. 30, 35–56, 68.

8. *Pipp's Weekly*, June 5, 1920; Report on Mayor's Housing Conference, accession 940, box 5, FMCA; Nevins, *Ford: The Times*, p. 559; Samuel Marquis testimony, accession 293, box 1, FMCA; Carl Crow, *The City of Flint Grows Up* (New York: Harper and Brothers, 1945), p. 70; *Pipp's Weekly* March 1928, April 1928, and August 18, 1923; David Allan Levine, *Internal Combustion: The Races in Detroit 1915–1926* (Westport, CT: Greenwood Press, 1976), pp. 42–43; National Industrial Conference Board, *The Cost of Living Among Wage-Earners Detroit, Michigan September 1921* (New York: National Industrial Conference Board, 1921).

9. Wyndham Mortimer, *Organize! My Life as a Union Man* (Boston: Beacon Press, 1971), p. 43.

10. W. Jett Lauck and Edgar Sydenstricker, *Conditions of Labor in American Industries* (New York: Funk and Wagnalls, 1917), p. 368; U. S. Congress, Federal Trade Commission, *Report on Motor Vehicle Industry*, 76th Cong., 1st Sess., House Document No. 468, p. 8; For John Anderson's savings, see John W. Anderson, "How I Became Part of the Labor Movement," in Alice and Staughton Lynd, eds., *Rank and File* (Boston: Beacon Press, 1973), p. 44. He says "From June 1925 until September 1926 I held eight different jobs and saved over twelve hundred dollars." National Industrial Conference Board, *Cost of Living Among Wage-Earners*.

11. In 1917, 24,553 Ford workers were married; 9,335 were single. Accession 572, box 27, FMCA; Andrew J. Steiger, "Autos and Jobs," *Nation,* 126 (May 2, 1928), p. 506.

12. U. S. Congress, *Report on Motor Vehicle Industry,* p. 8. In Table V–4 I have converted monthly figures to yearly ones by multiplying by twelve in order to facilitate comparison with average annual wage figures. This is not always accurate, however, because many auto workers did not work all year. Hence, the income column in Table V–4 might be larger than it should be.

13. "Standards of Living of Employees of Ford Motor Company in Detroit," *Monthly Labor Review,* 30 (June 1931), pp. 11–54; J. W. Nixon, "How Ford's Lowest-Paid Workers Live," *Social Service Review* 5 (March 1931), pp. 37–46; The *Monthly Labor Review* article comments, "It was very difficult to find families that met or even closely approached these requirements. All told, 1,740 married men receiving about $7 per day were selected by the company as prospects. These men were interviewed in the factory by trained agents of the bureau. The great majority of the prospects had to be rejected for various reasons—the average wage for the year was too high or too low, or the men worked less than 225 days in the year. Many families had boarders and lodgers, or dependents in or outside the family other than the wife and children. Often it was found that families had more or fewer children than the number decided on for the standard, or had children above the age limit. In many families, the wife or children worked and contributed money to the family fund and many families lived considerably above or below the wage income of the husband." (p. 12).

14. U. S. Congress, *Report on Motor Vehicle Industry,* p. 8; "Standards of Living," pp. 20, 39–40, 44, 48, 49; On streetcars, see also *Pipp's Weekly,* February 1926, November 1928, May 1929.

15. "Standards of Living," pp. 49–51.

16. Frank Stricker, "Affluence for Whom?—Another Look at Prosperity and the Working Classes in the 1920s," *Labor History,* 24 (Winter 1983), pp. 5–33. The quote is from pp. 17, 33. Others who "did well" were printers, workers in the building trades, and workers in the railroad operating crafts.

17. Letter to Henry Ford, November 11, 1923, accession 1, box 118, FMCA.

18. United Community Services Case Records, box 9, July 25, 1914 and December 1917, WSU.

19. United Community Services Case Records, boxes 7, 9, 10, 11, 12, 13, 32, WSU. I used those with any indication of an auto worker in the family.

20. The rent would be more than one-third of the family income if the man earned $30 a week. His employment was sporadic enough by 1926 that rent may have represented considerably more than one-third income. Detroit Mayor's Inter-Racial Committee, *The Negro in Detroit,* prepared by Detroit Bureau of Governmental Research, 1926), vol. 12, pp. 17–18.

21. *The Negro in Detroit,* vol. 12, pp. 20–21.

22. Cecile Whalen, "Detroit, Shifting Scenes and Population," n.d., DPL; Walter E. Kreusi, "Hamtramck, A Survey of Social, Educational and Civic Conditions with Some Recommendations," 1915, pp. 5–10, DPL; Sister Mary Remigia Napolska, *The Polish Immigrant in Detroit to 1914* (Chicago: Polish Roman Catholic Union of America, 1946), pp. 63–67; National Industrial Conference Board, *Cost of Living Among Wage-Earners.*

23. Kreusi, "Hamtramck," p. 5; Napolska, *Polish Immigrant,* p. 63; Lois Rankin, "Detroit Nationality Groups," *Michigan History Magazine,* 23 (Spring 1939), pp. 180–182; Arthur Evans Wood, *Hamtramck: A Sociological Study of a Polish-American Community* (New Haven, CT: College and University Press, 1955), pp. 22, 151–155, 207.

24. Wood, *Hamtramck,* p. 46.

25. *Ibid.,* pp. 174–191.

26. Levine, *Internal Combustion,* p. 50; *Pipp's Weekly,* June 5, 1920; Report on Mayor's Housing Conference, accession 940, box 5, FMCA.

27. *Negro in Detroit,* vol. 5, p. 1 (citing 1919 report made for Research Bureau of Associated Charities), p. 10.

28. Lloyd M. Bailer, "Negro Labor in the Automobile Industry" (Ph.D. diss., University of Michigan, 1942), p. 35; The Americanization Committee, *Annual Report,* March 31, 1921, DPL; Taylor, *Prosperity in Detroit,* p. 30.

29. *Negro in Detroit,* vol. 5, pp. 6, 10.

30. *The Negro in Detroit,* vol. 4, pp. 1–6, 8; Glen E. Carlson, "The Negro in the Industries of Detroit," (Ph.D. diss., University of Michigan, 1929), p. 82; Detroit Housing Commission, *First Annual Report,* 1933–1934, DPL; Americanization Committee of the Detroit Board of Commerce, *Annual Report,* March 21, 1920, DPL; Arna Bontemps and Jack Conroy, *They Seek a City* (Garden City, NY: Doubleday, Doran, 1945), p. 219; *Pipp's Weekly,* November 23, 1929, March 1928, April 1928, August 18, 1923; Levine, *Internal Combustion,* pp. 129–130. Levine estimates some black residents paid 40% to 50% of their incomes for housing (pp. 125–126).

31. *Negro in Detroit,* vol. 5, p 22.

32. *Ibid.,* pp. 3–13.

33. Bailer, "Negro Labor," p. 37. On the Ossian Sweet case see Levine, *Internal Combustion.* For another housing incident see Oral History Interview of the Reverend Charles Hill, pp. 1–2, WSU.

34. Albert Mayer, "A Study of the Foreign-Born Population of Detroit 1870–1950," (Wayne University Department of Sociology and Anthropology, 1951), p. 62.

35. *Negro in Detroit,* vol. 7, pp. 6–7, vol. 10, pp. 105, 94; Louise Venable Kennedy, *The Negro Peasant Turns Cityward,* Columbia University Studies in History, Economics and Public Law, no. 329 (New York: Columbia University Press, 1930), p. 204; Ulysses W. Boykin, *A Hand Book on the Detroit Negro* (Detroit, MI: The Minority Study Association, 1943), p. 32; Napolska, *Polish Immigrant,* p. 63; Rankin, "Detroit Nationality Groups," pp. 129–205; Kreusi, "Hamtramck," pp. 5–7. Some black churches also played the roles of employment counselors, housefinders, and general advisors on urban life. Such activities were not entirely motivated by a simple desire to be helpful. In the eyes of some church members, such services were seen as teaching migrants acceptable urban behavior so that the more established black population would not be embarassed by them. Some older residents were sufficiently embarassed anyway to want to separate themselves from the new migrants and some denominational differences along class lines resulted.

36. Report of Sociological Department, October 12, 1914, accession 62, box 59, FMCA; Chen-Nan Li, "A Summer in the Ford Works," *Personnel Journal,* 7 (June 1928), p. 30.

37. "Standards of Living," pp. 48–49; Li, "A Summer in the Ford Works," pp. 31–33; Taylor, *Prosperity in Detroit,* p. 113; *The Negro in Detroit,* vol. 7, p. 19; Clayton Fountain, *Union Guy* (New York: Viking Press, 1949), p. 30; Peter Friedlander, *The Emergence of a UAW Local, 1936–1939: A Study in Class and Culture* (Pittsburgh, PA: University of Pittsburgh Press, 1975), p. 26.

38. John Parker, "A History of the Packard Motor Car Company from 1899 to 1929" (M.A. thesis, Wayne University, 1949), p. 83; William Ellison Chalmers, "Labor in the Automobile Industry: A Study of Personnel Policies, Workers Attitudes and Attempts at Unionism" (Ph.D. diss., University of Wisconsin, 1932), p. 93; Oral History Interview of Paul Russo, p. 2, WSU; Sidney Fine, *Sit-Down: The General Motors Strike of 1936–1937* (Ann Arbor, MI: University of Michigan Press, 1963), pp. 25–26; Clarence H. Young and William A. Quinn, *Foundation for Living* (New York: McGraw Hill, 1963), p. 47; "Minutes of the Conference on Organization of the Auto Workers," January 13, 1929, p. 6, Robert W. Dunn Collection, box 2, WSU.

39. Anderson, "How I Became Part of the Labor Movement," p. 52; Oliver Zendt notes in Robert W. Dunn Collection, box 1, WSU; Matthew

Ward (Charles Denby), *Indignant Heart* (New York: New Books, 1952), p. 31.

40. *Pipp's Weekly,* April 28, 1923.

41. On fatigue, see also Thomas Mimms notes, Robert W. Dunn Collection, box 1, WSU, "It was the longest 8 hours that I ever experienced. I was tired; my fingers, hands and arms ached, and my back was hurting. It seemed that no punishment could be worse than doing work like that." Thomas H. Wright, "Why Ford's Men Strike," *Christian Century,* 50 (November 29, 1933), p. 1504.

Chapter Six

1. Joyce Shaw Peterson, "Auto Workers and Their Work, 1900–1933, *Labor History,* 22 (Spring 1981), pp. 213–236; David Montgomery, *Workers' Control in America* (Cambridge: Cambridge University Press, 1979), pp. 32–47, 113–138; Stephen Meyer, III, *The Five Dollar Day; Labor Management and Social Control in the Ford Motor Company, 1908–1921* (Albany, NY: State University of New York Press, 1981), pp. 67–94. Both Montgomery and Meyer employ categories similar to mine with respect to the period before 1920. I believe that these categories of worker resistance work also for the 1920s, the decade *par excellence* of labor peace.

2. See Chapter III herein.

3. For company attempts to combat high turnover, see Chapter IV herein; Oral History Interview of Lester Johnson, p. 16, WSU; Oral History Interview of Raymond Berndt, pp. 8–9, WSU; Statement of Henry Ford before the Industrial Commission, accession 62, box 6, FMCA. In March 1913, Ford discharged 1,276 workers, 870 quit, and 5,156 fell into the category of five-day men. *Factory Facts From Ford* (1917), p. 45; Yearly Report Highland Park Factory, accession 572, box 28, FMCA; Henry Ford (in collaboration with Samuel Crowther), *My Life and Work* (Garden City, NY: Doubleday, Page and Co., 1923), p. 111; *Packard Advanced Training School Lecture Course 1919* (Detroit, MI: Packard Motor Car Company, 1919), pp. 402–403.

4. O. W. Blackett, "Factory Labor Turnover in Michigan," *Michigan Business Studies,* 2 (November 1928); Myron W. Watkins, "The Labor Situation in Detroit," *Journal of Political Economy,* 28 (1920), p. 851; Andrew J. Steiger, "Autos and Jobs," *Nation,* 126 (2 May 1928), p. 505.

5. A 1949 study of the auto industry found that absenteeism correlated with indices of mass production. Jobs with a high mass production score had higher rates of absenteeism than jobs with a low mass production score. See Charles R. Walker and Robert H. Guest, *The Man on the Assembly*

Line (Cambridge, MA: Harvard University Press, 1952). Minutes, Executive Committee, Ford Motor Company, November 1, 1916, accession 85, box 5, FMCA.

6. *Packard Advanced Training School,* pp. 100–119, 287. Many of the employers' complaints about abuse of tools seem reminiscent of the complaints of southern slaveholders, including the attempt to develop especially sturdy "slaveproof" tools. Packard allocated $50,000 per month to cover loss due to scrap, and this was not sufficient.

7. *Packard Advanced Training School,* pp. 119, 116, 103.

8. Watkins, "Labor Situation in Detroit," p. 842.

9. *Packard Advanced Training School,* pp. 138–139; William Ellison Chalmers, "Labor in the Automobile Industry: A Study of Personnel Policies, Workers Attitudes and Attempts at Unionism" (Ph.D. diss., University of Wisconsin, 1932), pp. 127, 160–165; Oral History Interview of Louis Adkins, p. 2, WSU; See Montgomery, *Workers' Control,* pp. 32–47 on the practice of restriction of output as widespread in American industry and a way of breaking in immigrant workers to the American workers' code. See also Michael Burawoy, *Manufacturing Consent: Changes in the Labor Process under Monopoly Capitalism* (Chicago: University of Chicago, 1979) on worker schemes to "make out."

10. Stanley B. Mathewson, *Restriction of Output Among Unorganized Workers* (New York: Viking Press, 1931), pp. 43–44, 59–61, 118–119. Mathewson studied output restriction in several industries. I have used only his automobile plant cases. See Montgomery, *Workers' Control,* pp. 113–138 for additional discussion of output restriction in American industry in general.

11. Mathewson, *Restriction of Output,,* pp. 86–87, 78, 61; Henry Kraus, *The Many and the Few: A Chronicle of the Dynamic Auto Workers* (Los Angeles: Plantin Press, 1947), pp. 7–9; Frank Marquart, *An Auto Worker's Journal; The UAW from Crusade to One-Party Union* (University Park, PA: Pennsylvania State University Press, 1975), p. 24. For similar practices among electrical workers see Ronald W. Schatz, *The Electrical Workers: A History of Labor at General Electric and Westinghouse 1923–1960* (Urbana, IL: University of Illinois Press, 1983).

12. Walter Ulrich, "On the Belt," League for Industrial Democracy Leaflet No. 6 (1929), p. 8.

13. On the distinction between job control and control over skills see Paul Thompson, *The Nature of Work: An Introduction to Debates on the Labour Process* (London: Macmillan, 1983), pp. 106–108. For an interpretation similar to mine, see Don Clawson, *Bureaucracy and the Labor Process: The Transformation of U. S. Industry, 1860–1920* (New York: Monthly Review Press, 1980). Clawson contends that "American workers did not go

on to develop an analysis that defended their right to control production
. . . workers tended to concede that management had a right to give orders
that workers should obey. The same workers who conceded management's
right to give orders then struggled to evade or sabotage those orders." (p.
156).

14. List of strikes in Detroit, between 1912 and 1922, copied from files
of Employers' Association of Detroit, accession 940, box 6, FMCA. The list
notes 24 strikes in Detroit auto plants out of a total of 243 strikes in Detroit
between 1912 and 1922. "Report of Struggles," Henry Kraus Collection, box
1, WSU. This manuscript lists 25 walkouts between 1926 and 1928. Almost
all were a response to wage cuts and most lasted less than one day. "Sporadic
Strikes," Robert W. Dunn Collection, box 1, WSU. This lists 15 strikes in
Detroit auto plants from 1927 to 1928. "Auto Industry Strikes," Joe Brown
Collection, box 23, WSU. This list of 107 strikes and one lockout between
1904 and 1921 found 33 plantwide walkouts, 52 involving a single department, and 11 involving two departments. These various lists of strikes
compiled by people close to the auto industry indicate that Florence Peter-
son's total of two for 1927 and two for 1928 is an undercount even accounting
for her requirement that the strike last for more than one day. See Florence
Peterson, *Strikes in the United States, 1880–1936,* U. S. Department of
Labor, Bulletin No. 651. State of Michigan, *24th Annual Report of the Bureau
of Labor and Industrial Statistics,* 1907; Allan Nevins, *Ford: The Times,
The Man, The Company* (New York: Charles Scribner's Sons, 1954), p. 513;
Minutes, Employers Association of Detroit, April 18, 1911, copy in accession
940, box 6, FMCA; John W. Anderson, "How I Became Part of the Labor
Movement," in Alice and Staughton Lynd, eds., *Rank and File: Personal
Histories by Working-Class Organizers* (Boston: Beacon Press, 1973), p. 44.

15. Clayton Fountain, *Union Guy* (New York: Viking Press, 1949), pp.
28–29.

16. Oral History Interview of Ted La Duke, p. 2, WSU.

17. Chalmers, "Labor in the Automobile Industry," pp, 128–129, 208–213;
Oral History Interview of John W. Anderson, p. 2, WSU; "Report of
Struggles," Henry Kraus Collection, box 1, WSU; Oral History Interview of
Joe Hattley, p. 1, WSU.

18. Robert W. Dunn, *Labor and Automobiles* (New York: International
Publishers, 1929), p. 180; John Parker, "A History of the Packard Motor
Car Company from 1899 to 1929," (M.A. thesis, Wayne University, 1949),
p. 81.

19. United Automobile, Aircraft and Vehicle Workers of America, President's Report, *Convention Proceedings,* 1926.

20. "Lozier Round Robin Petition" and "Brief Summary of Events in
Connection with the Recent Walk-Out," a report to the Lozier Automobile

Company of Plattsburgh, New York, 1910, in Automotive History Collection, DPL; George Douglas Blackwood. "The United Automobile Workers of America 1935–1951" (Ph.D. diss., University of Chicago, 1951), pp. 16–18; "The Reminiscences of W. C. Klann," pp. 134–137, Oral History Section, FMCA; Dunn, *Labor and Automobiles*, pp. 188–189; Joel John Lowery, "Labor Relations in the Automobile Industry During the Nineteen Twenties" (M.A. thesis, Michigan State University, 1958), p. 58.

21. Carter Goodrich's concept of a "frontier of control" is useful here. Auto workers struggled to maintain as much control as possible around this frontier, but they had little ability to place skill within that frontier. See Carter L. Goodrich, *The Frontier of Control: A Study in British Workshop Politics* (London: G. Bell and Sons, 1920).

22. Nevins, *Ford: The Times*, pp. 377–378, 516; "The Reminiscences of Chester M. Culver," pp. 10–15, Oral History Section, FMCA (Culver was the director of the Employers' Association of Detroit); Employers' Association of Detroit Brochure, n.d. (c. 1926), DPL; Chalmers, "Labor in the Automobile Industry," pp. 188–191; George Heliker notes, accession 958, FMCA; Edward A. Wieck, "Auto Under the NRA," Mary Van Kleeck Collection, WSU.

23. Oral History Interview of James G. Couser, p. 4, WSU.

24. Dunn, *Labor and Automobiles*, p. 149; Wyndham Mortimer, *Organize! My Life as a Union Man* (Boston: Beacon Press, 1971), p. 43; Blackwood, "The United Automobile Workers," pp. 20–21; Anthony Luchek, "Company Unions, F.O.B. Detroit," *Nation*, 142 (January 15, 1936), p. 74.

25. Headrick Notes, Robert W. Dunn Collection, box 1, WSU.

26. Horace Lucien Arnold and Fay Leone Faurote, *Ford Methods and the Ford Shops* (New York: The Engineering Magazine Co., 1919), p. 328; Roy Chapin to Samuel Crowther, January 18, 1923, Roy D. Chapin Papers, vol. 45, UM; Fountain, *Union Guy*, pp. 18, 20; Matthew Ward (Charles Denby), *Indignant Heart* (New York: New Books, 1952), p. 29.

27. For discussion of the transition from preindustrial to industrial modes of production and its meaning for workers see E. P. Thompson, *The Making of the English Working Class* (New York: Pantheon, 1963); E. P. Thompson, "Time, Work Discipline and Industrial Capitalism," *Past and Present*, 38 (1967), pp. 56–97; E. J. Hobsbawn, *Labouring Men: Studies in the History of Labour* (New York: Basic Books, 1964); Herbert Gutman, "Work, Culture and Society in Industrializing America, 1815–1919," *The American Historical Review*, 78 (June 1973), pp. 531–588. On skilled workers as union builders, see Steve Babson, "Pointing the Way. The role of British and Irish Skilled Tradesmen in the Rise of the UAW," *Detroit in Perspective*, 7 (Spring 1983), pp. 75–96.

28. George Heliker notes, accession 958, FMCA.

29. Lloyd M. Bailer, "Negro Labor in the Automobile Industry," (Ph.D. Dissertation, University of Michigan, 1941), pp. 174–180, 190; Chalmers, "Labor in the Automobile Industry," p. 187; Herbert R. Northrup, *The Negro in the Automobile Industry,* Report No. 1, The Racial Policies of American Industry (Philadelphia: Industrial Research Unit, Department of Industry, Wharton School of Finance and Commerce, University of Pennsylvania, 1968), p. 191; August Meier and Elliott Rudwick, *Black Detroit and the Rise of the UAW* (New York: Oxford University Press, 1979); Oral History Interview of Joseph Billups, p. 5, WSU.

Chapter Seven

1. "The Reminiscences of Joseph Galamb," p. 148, Oral History Section, FMCA. "Mr. Ford said he would lick the I.W.W. by paying the men the $5.00 a day." Ford himself denied that the IWW had anything to do with it. See also Stephen Meyer, III, *The Five Dollar Day; Labor Management and Social Control in the Ford Motor Company, 1908-1921* (Albany, NY: State University of New York Press, 1981), pp. 91–94; Henry Faigin, "The Industrial Workers of the World in Detroit and Michigan from the Period of Beginnings through the World War" (M.A. thesis, Wayne University, 1937), pp. 1–101; Philip S. Foner, *History of the Labor Movement in the United States,* vol. 4, *The Industrial Workers of the World, 1905-1917* (New York: International Publishers, 1965), pp. 383–390.

2. Copy of report of operative for Employers' Association of Detroit, 1912, accession 940, box 5, FMCA; Minutes, Employers' Association of Detroit, February 20, 1912, in George Heliker notes, accession 940, box 6, FMCA.

3. Oral History Interview of John Panzer, p. 23, WSU.

4. Faigin, "The Industrial Workers of the World," pp. 1–101; Foner, *The Industrial Workers of the World,* pp. 383–390.

5. Minutes, Employers' Association of Detroit, February 17, 1914, in George Heliker notes, accession 940, box 6, FMCA; "My Story," Matilda Robbins Collection, box 1, WSU; Melvyn Dubofsky, *We Shall Be All: A History of the Industrial Workers of the World* (Chicago: Quadrangle Books, 1969), p. 287; "The IWW Tells Its Own Story," IWW Collection, box 146, WSU.

6. Walter E. Kreusi, "Report Upon Unemployment in the Winter of 1914-1915 in Detroit and the Institutions and Measures of Relief," (1915), pp. 9–10; on the 1919 steel strike, see David Brody, *Labor in Crisis; The Steel Strike of 1919* (Philadelphia: J. B. Lippincott, 1965); on Seattle general strike, see Harvey O'Connor, *Revolution in Seattle* (New York: Monthly Review Press, 1964).

7. Wm. P. Movell to Samuel Gompers, September 18, 1912, reel 36; AFL Executive Council Minutes, September 22, 1913, reel 4 and October 18, 1912, reel 4; W. A. Logan to Frank Morrison, June 25, 1913, reel 36; all in American Federation of Labor Records: The Samuel Gompers Era (microfilm edition, 1979), Microfilming Corporation of America.

8. "Organization Program for General Recruiting Union," April 21, 1932, IWW Collection, series 7, box 1, WSU; W. E. Chalmers to Dear Selig [Perlman], November 9, 1933, Phillips Garman Collection, box 3, WSU.

9. Jack W. Skeels "Early Carriage and Auto Unions: The Impact of Industrialization and Rival Unionism," *Industrial and Labor Relations Review,* 17 (1963–1964), pp. 566–583; Edward Levinson, *Labor on the March* (New York: University Books, 1938), pp. 41–42; James O. Morris, *Conflict Within the AFL* (Ithaca, NY: Cornell University, 1958), pp. 22–24; W. A. Logan, "The Automobile Workers' Union," *Michigan Socialist,* September 22, 1916. I have referred to this union as the Carriage and Wagon Workers Union before 1913, the Carriage, Wagon and Automobile Workers Union from 1913 to 1921, and the Auto Workers Union after 1921. Its actual name in the 1920s was the United Automobile, Aircraft and Vehicle Workers of America, but it was universally known as the Auto Workers Union.

10. Oral History Interview of Phil Raymond, pp. 10–11, WSU. Many of the unions who claimed auto workers were building trades unions with very little interest in or appreciation of conditions inside auto factories.

11. *Carriage and Wagon Workers Journal,* July 1, 1899.

12. For early examples of such jurisdictional disputes, see for example: C. A. Peterson to Samuel Gompers, May 23, 1902, and May 27, 1902, American Federation of Labor Records, reel 36. The nine craft unions who objected to the aspirations of the Auto Workers Union were those of the blacksmiths, sheet metal workers, metal polishers, painters, pattern makers, machinists, carpenters, electrical workers, and upholsterers. Levinson, *Labor on the March,* pp. 41–42; Morris, *Conflict Within the AFL,* pp. 22–24; Skeels, "Early Carriage and Auto Unions," pp. 571–575.

13. President's Report, *Convention Proceedings,* United Automobile, Aircraft and Vehicle Workers of America, September 1918. For appraisals of Logan, see Oral History Interview of Lester Johnson, pp. 4–5, WSU; and Oral History Interview of Larry Davidow, p. 4, WSU.

14. *Proceedings of Convention,* Carriage, Wagon and Automobile Workers' International, September 1915.

15. Irving Bernstein, *The Automobile Industry, Post War Developments, 1918–1921,* U. S. Department of Labor, Bureau of Labor Statistics, Historical Study No. 52, September 1942, pp. 20–45; Gordon W. Davidson, "Industrial Detroit After World War I, 1919 to 1921" (M.A. thesis, Wayne University,

1953), pp. 44–47; "The Reminiscences of Chester M. Culver," p. 40, Oral History Section, FMCA.

16. Samuel Marquis Testimony, accession 293, box 1, FMCA; J. L. Vette to Roy Chapin, October 15, 1919, Roy D. Chapin Papers, vol. 26, UM.

17. Roy Chapin to Harvey Gibson, August 17, 1920, Roy D. Chapin Papers, vol. 31, UM; Samuel Marquis Testimony, accession 293, box 1, FMCA; "The Reminiscences of George Brown," p. 116, Oral History Section, FMCA; Davidson, "Industrial Detroit," pp. 72–83; National Automobile Chamber of Commerce to Roy Chapin, February 1, 1919, Roy D. Chapin Papers, vol. 22, UM; Report of Operative to E. G. Liebold on 1919 steel strike in Canton, Ohio, October 16, 1919, accession 940, box 16, FMCA; *The Proletarian,* April 1919; Oral History Interview of I. Paul Taylor, p. 1;, WSU; Frank Marquart, *An Auto Worker's Journal; The UAW from Crusade to One-Party Union* (University Park, PA: Pennsylvania State University Press, 1975), p. 27.

18. The 45,000 figure is from Morris, *Conflict Within the AFL,* p. 24; the 40,000 figure is from Philip Taft, *Organized Labor in American History* (New York: Harper and Row, 1964), p. 484; "Sporadic Strikes," Robert W. Dunn Collection, box 1, WSU; Meyer, III, *The Five Dollar Day,* p. 193; "Auto Industry Strikes," Joe Brown Collection, box 23, WSU; "Auto Industry History 1916–1921," Edward Levinson Collection, box 1, WSU; Excerpts from *Auto Workers News,* 1919, Edward Levinson Collection, box 1, WSU.

19. Oral History Interview of Lary Davidow, pp. 1–2, WSU; Meyer, III, *The Five Dollar Day,* p. 186; *Auto Workers News* excerpts for May 15, June 19, August 7 (1919), Edward Levinson Collection, box 1, WSU.

20. "Strikes by Machinists Union," Joe Brown Collection, Vertical File, WSU; Bernstein, *Automobile Industry,* p. 33; Joel John Lowery, "Labor Relations in the Automobile Industry During the Nineteen Twenties" (M.A. thesis, Michigan State University, 1958), pp. 52–56; "Sporadic Strikes, notes from *Auto Workers News* of May 22, June 19, June 26, July 17 (1919), Robert W. Dunn Collection, box 1, WSU.

21. Lowery, "Labor Relations," pp. 58–59; George Douglas Blackwood, "The United Automobile Workers of America 1935–1951" (Ph.D. diss., University of Chicago, 1951), pp. 17–18; "Sporadic Strikes," Robert W. Dunn Collection, box 1, WSU; Art Rohan to Mr. Levinson, February 11, 1945, Edward Levinson Collection, box 1, WSU.

22. U. S. Department of Commerce, Bureau of the Census, *Fifteenth Census of the United States, Manufactures: 1929,* II; and *Sixteenth Census of the United States, Manufactures: 1939,* II; Bernstein, *Automobile Industry,* pp. 54–55; Davidson, "Industrial Detroit," pp. 126–134; R. H. Megarle,

"Detroit Losing Working Men," *Michigan Manufacturer and Financial Record,* June 12, 1920.

23. Allan Nevins and Frank Ernest Hill, *Ford: Expansion and Challenge 1915–1933* (New York: Charles Scribner's Sons, 1957), p. 157; John B. Rae, *American Automobile Manufacturers* (Philadelphia: Chilton Company, 1959), p. 136; Keith Sward, *The Legend of Henry Ford* (New York: Holt, Rinehart and Winston, 1948), pp. 77–79; Bernstein, *Automobile Industry,* pp 55, 71; Davidson, "Industrial Detroit," p. 134; Letter to Mr. and Mrs. Henry Ford, November 10, 1920, accession 1, box 120, FMCA.

24. Roy Chapin to Harvey Gibson, August 17, 1920, Roy D. Chapin Papers, vol. 31, UM; U. S. Department of Labor, Bureau of Labor Statistics, *Wages and Hours of Labor in the Automobile Motor Vehicle Industry: 1922,* Bulletin No. 348 (October 1923) pp. 9–10; "The Reminiscences of W. C. Klann," p. 153, Oral History Section, FMCA; Bernstein, *Automobile Industry,* pp. 54–55; Meyer, III, *The Five Dollar Day,* p. 197.

25. Lowery, "Labor Relations," p. 58; William Ellison Chalmers, "Labor in the Automobile Industry: A Study of Personnel Policies, Workers Attitudes and Attempts at Unionism," (Ph.D. diss., University of Wisconsin, 1932, p. 227; Robert W. Dunn, *Labor and Automobiles* (New York: International Publishers, 1929), p. 191; Skeels, "Early Carriage and Auto Unions," p. 282; Oral History Interview of I. Paul Taylor, p. 4, WSU. Taylor thought that the strike originated with provocateurs aiming to break the union. I find no evidence that this was true. Oral History Interview of Lester Johnson, p. 18, WSU; "Sporadic Strikes," notes from *Auto Workers News* of February 10, February 17, February 24, March 3, March 17, March 24, March 31, April 14 (1921), Robert W. Dunn Collection, box 1, WSU; Oral History Interview of Larry Davidow, p. 5, WSU; Wm. A. Logan to Edward Levinson (in reply to "your letter of 3–4–45"), Edward Levinson Collection, box 1, WSU.

26. Logan, "Auto Workers Union," *Michigan Socialist,* September 22, 1916; Maurice Dutton Savage, *Industrial Unionism in America* (New York: The Ronald Press, 1922), pp. 282–283, 195–196. The Union was so open that at times it included furniture upholsterers, milk wagon drivers, and mattress workers. In some ways its philosophy seems more of a throw back to the Knights of Labor than a precursor of the CIO. United Automobile, Aircraft and Vehicle Workers of America, *Convention Proceedings,* September 1920; On Logan's opposition to strikes, see also Oral History Interview of Lester Johnson, p. 12, WSU. Johnson was Logan's long-time co-worker, serving as secretary of the union.

27. United Automobile, Aircraft and Vehicle Workers of America, *Convention Proceedings,* President's Report, September 1926; Oral History Interview of Arthur Rohan, p. 36, WSU, has more on Logan.

28. Chalmers, "Labor in the Automobile Industry," p. 244; Frank Martel to S. O. Denton, March 26, 1930, Wayne County AFL-CIO Collection, series 1, box 2, WSU; Morris, *Conflict Within the AFL,* p. 57; Jean Trepp McKelvey, *AFL Attitudes Toward Production 1900–1932,* Cornell Studies in Industrial and Labor Relations, vol. 2 (Ithaca, NY: New York State School of Industrial and Labor Relations, 1952), p. 78; General Manager, Maxwell Motor Company to R. D. Chapin, July 22, 1919, Roy D. Chapin Papers, vol. 25, UM.

29. Minutes, Detroit Federation of Labor, January 21, 1931, and May 31, 1933, Wayne County AFL-CIO Collection, series 1, box 10, WSU; Oral History Interview of Arthur Rohan, p. 24, WSU; *Detroit Labor News,* May 29, 1925; on Martel, see Oral History Interview of Ed Hall, p. 8, WSU; Frank Martel to Honorable Christopher Stein, Judge of Recorder's Court, March 1, 1933, Metro-Detroit AFL-CIO Collection, box 2, WSU; Frank Martel to Mr. John L. O'Ryan, October 24, 1931, Metro-Detroit AFL-CIO Collection, box 4, WSU; William Ellison Chalmers to Selig Perlman, November 9, 1933, Phillips Garman Collection, box 3, WSU; "Briggs Plant Gets Ford Ultimatum," *New York Times,* January 21, 1933.

30. William Green to S. M. Levin, May 5, 1925, copy in accession 940, box 5, FMCA.

31. For a description of the 1926 campaign see Philip Taft, *The A. F. of L. from the Death of Gompers to the Merger* (New York: Harper and Brothers, 1959), pp. 95–105; John Fitch, "Collective Bargaining and the Automobile Industry," William Ellison Chalmers Collection, box 1, WSU; Morris, *Conflict Within the AFL,* pp. 56–63; Philip A. Raymond to Robert W. Dunn, March 2, 1928, Robert W. Dunn Collection, box 2, WSU; Wyndham Mortimer, *Organize! My Life as a Union Man* (Boston: Beacon Press, 1971), p. 54.

32. *Detroit Labor News,* May 7, 1926.

33. "Auto Industry—Unionization" folder, Joe Brown Collection, Vertical File, WSU; Letter from Citizens' Committee of Detroit, April 25, 1928, Phillips Garman Collection, box 3, WSU.

34. Roger Keeran, *The Communist Party and the Auto Workers Unions* (Bloomington, IN: Indiana University Press, 1980), pp. 35–36; Oral History Interview of I. Paul Taylor, pp. 10–11, WSU; Oral History Interview of Lester Johnson, pp. 4–5, WSU.

35. Keeran, *The Communist Party and the Auto Workers Unions,* pp. 37–39, 45–46; Oral History Interview of Lester Johnson, pp. 13–15, WSU; on Rohan's philosophy of organizing see Oral History Interview of Arthur Rohan, pp. 24–25, WSU.

36. Lowery, "Labor Relations," pp. 82–84; "History of the Auto Workers Union," (1934), Henry Kraus Collection, box 1, WSU; Keeran, *The Com-*

munist Party and the Auto Workers Unions, p. 57; Chalmers, "Labor in the Automobile Industry," pp. 209–211; "Report of the General Executive Secretary Pro-Tem." n.d. (c. 1928), Robert W. Dunn Collection, box 2, WSU; *Auto Workers News,* August 1928.

37. Keeran, *The Communist Party and the Auto Workers Unions,* pp. 79–80; Henry Kraus, *The Many and the Few: A Chronicle of the Dynamic Auto Workers* (Los Angeles: Plantin Press, 1947), p. 7; Sidney Fine, *Sit-Down: The General Motors Strike of 1936–1937* (Ann Arbor, MI: University of Michigan Press, 1969), pp. 65–66; Chalmers, "Labor in the Automobile Industry," pp. 211–212; Oral History Interview of Jack Palmer, pp. 1–5, WSU; Oral History Interview of Phil Raymond, pp. 6–7, WSU; Oral History Interview of Herbert Richardson, p. 3, WSU; Oral History Interview of Alexander Cook, pp. 1–5, WSU.

38. Chalmers, "Labor in the Automobile Industry," p. 269; Keeran, *The Communist Party and the Auto Workers Unions,* pp. 40–43; IWW Collection series 7, box 1, WSU.

39. Oral History Interview of Frank Marquart, p. 6, WSU; Marquart, *An Auto Worker's Journal,* p. 38.

40. Oral History Interview of Frank Marquart, p. 7; Marquart, *An Auto Worker's Journal,* pp. 38–39.

41. Mention is made of receiving credentials to attend the Auto Workers Union conference in Minutes, Detroit Federation of Labor, December 5, 1928, Wayne County AFL-CIO Collection, series 1, box 10, WSU. On January 4, 1929 Frank Martel wrote to William Green commenting on the Auto Workers Union invitation.

> When the first one [invitation] was received by the central body it was placed on file without any comment. This letter has not been before the central body and it will not be taken there. I have hesitated in saying anything directly to the local unions in the way of discouraging their attendance at this meeting because, as you know, sometimes taking too much recognition of a meeting of this kind might have an effect contrary to that which is most to be desired.

Green replied on January 18: "As the undertaking is clearly under communist patronage, I do not see why you should feel any hesitancy about so advising local trade unions." Both letters are in Wayne County AFL-CIO Collection, series 1, box 1, WSU; "Minutes of the Conference on Organization of the Auto Workers," January 13, 1929, Robert W. Dunn Collection, box 2, WSU; Phil Raymond, "Report on Automobile Industry, 1929," Henry Kraus Collection, box 1, WSU; Minutes, Auto Workers Conference, March 8, 1930, Henry Kraus Collection, box 1, WSU.

Chapter Eight

1. Quoted in James Cousens to E. G. Liebold, November 12, 1929, accession 572, box 14, FMCA.

2. Standard of Living of Employees of Ford Motor Company in Detroit," *Monthly Labor Review*, 30 (June 1930), pp. 1209–1252; U. S. Department of Commerce, Bureau of the Census, *Census of Manufactures*, 1929 and 1939; U. S. Congress, House, Federal Trade Commission, *Report on Motor Vehicle Industry*, House Document No. 468, 76th Cong., 1st Sess., 1939, pp. 8, 668; Everett Francis account book, Everett Francis Collection, box 1, WSU; Labor Research Association, "How the Crisis Hit the Auto Workers," Joe Brown Collection, box 8, WSU; Maurice Sugar, "Bullets—Not Food For Ford Workers," *Nation*, 134 (March 23, 1932), p. 333; Samuel M. Levin, "Ford Profit Sharing, 1914–1920, I. The Growth of the Plan," *Personnel Journal*, 6 (August 1927), p. 101; N. A. Tolles and M. W. LaFever, "Wages, Hours, Employment, and Annual Earnings in the Motor Vehicle Industry, 1934," *Monthly Labor Review*, 42 (March 1936), p. 521; Roger Keeran, *The Communist Party and the Auto Workers Union* (Bloomington, IN: University of Indiana Press, 1980), p. 63.

3. *Census of Manufactures*, 1939; Irving Bernstein, *The Lean Years: A History of the American Worker 1920–1933* (Boston: Houghton Mifflin, 1960), p. 317; Industrial Employment Index, William Ellison Chalmers Collection, box 1, WSU. I have computed yearly averages by averaging the twelve middle-of-the-month indexes for each year. Sidney Fine, *Frank Murphy, The Detroit Years* (Ann Arbor, MI: University of Michigan Press, 1975), pp. 246–253 is especially good on the impact of the depression on Detroit.

4. Bernstein, *Lean Years*, pp. 254–256; Keeran, *The Communist Party and the Auto Workers Union*, p. 61; Tolles and LaFever, "Wages, Hours, Employment," p. 521; Sub-Committee of the Detroit Mayor's Unemployment Committee, *The Effects Upon Detroit of the Three Years of the Depression*, 1932, p. 9, DPL.

5. Oral History Interview of Bud Simons, p. 3, WSU; Helen Hall, "When Detroit's Out of Gear," *Survey*, 64 (April 1, 1930), p. 10; *Detroit Worker*, April 15, 1930; Oral History Interview of Joseph Ferris, p. 3, WSU; Oral History Interview of Fred Haggard, p. 3, WSU; "The Reminiscences of Willis F. Ward," pp. 15–16, Oral History Section, FMCA; Oral History Interview of Ed Lee, p. 11, WSU; John W. Anderson, "How I Became Part of the Labr Movement," in Alice and Staughton Lynd, eds., *Rank and File: Personal Histories by Working Class Organizers* (Boston: Beacon Press, 1973), p. 51; Interview with unidentified auto workers in Maurice Sugar Collection, box 54, WSU; Oral History Interview of Patrick O'Malley, p. 4, WSU.

6. Frank Marquart, *An Auto Worker's Journal; The UAW from Crusade to One-Party Union* (University Park, PA: Pennsylvania State University

Press, 1975), pp. 40–44; Oral History Interviews of Frank Marquart, pp. 3–4; William Humphreys, p. 1; Russell Merrill, p. 1; James M. Cleveland, p. 1; Clayton Johnson, p. 1; Martin Jensen, p. 2; Richard Harris, p. 2; George Addes, p. 2; Leon Pody, p. 1; Harvey Kitzman, p. 2; John Eldon, pp. 2–3; Frank Manfred, p. 4; all WSU.

7. *Detroit Worker,* February 15, 1930; Allan Nevins and Frank Ernest Hill, *Ford: Expansion and Challenge 1915–1933* (New York: Charles Scribners' Sons, 1957), p. 587; Oral History Interviews of Michael Manning, p. 1; Everett Francis, pp. 6–7; Joseph Ferris, p. 5; Joseph Ditzel, pp. 1–2; R. C. Ingram, p. 4; Tracy M. Doll, p. 4; Fred Haggard, p. 3; all WSU; Thomas C. Cochran, *The Great Depression and World War II 1929–1945* (Glenview, IL: Scott Foresman, 1968), p. 80; "How the Crisis Hit the Auto Workers," Brown Collection, box 8, WSU; Oral History Interview of George Addes, p. 3, WSU.

8. *The Effect Upon Detroit of the Three Years of the Depression,* p. 4; Fine, *Murphy,* p. 247.

9. Nevins and Hill, *Ford: Expansion,* p. 586.

10. Letter to E. G. Liebold, April 21, 1931, accession 285, box 1309, FMCA; Letter to Mrs. Ford, September 10, 1931, accession 1, box 118, FMCA; Letter to Mrs. Ford, June 13, 1932, accession 1, box 118, FMCA.

11. Accession 6, FMA includes considerable correspondence on share the work plans; *Michigan Federationist,* January 1930; Report of the Mayor's Labor Committee, January 7, 1930, City of Detroit, *Journal of the Common Council,* vol. 2, pp. 3665–3666, DPL; Letter from Automobile Manufacturers Association to Herbert Hoover, July 30, 1932, accession 572, box 14, FMCA.

12. Arna Bontemps and Jack Conroy, *They Seek a City* (Garden City, NY: Doubleday, Doran, 1945), pp. 221–222; *Detroit Free Press,* March 2, 1931; Keeran, *The Communist Party and the Auto Workers Unions,* p. 62, Anderson, "How I Became Part of the Labor Movement," p. 51; Fine, *Murphy,* pp. 271–282; *The Effect Upon Detroit of the Three Years of the Depression,* pp. 3–4; *Detroit Times,* December 15, 1931; Oral History Interview of Mr. and Mrs. Joseph Billups, pp. 38–39, WSU.

13. *Detroit News,* April 26, 1931; Clayton Fountain, *Union Guy* (New York: Viking Press, 1949), p. 42.

14. Fine, *Murphy,* pp. 309–311.

15. "Spare Time Gardens," accession 572, box 14, FMCA; *Detroit News,* August 23, 1931; Oral History Interview of Lew Michener, pp. 3–4, WSU.

16. Keith Sward, *The Legend of Henry Ford* (New York: Holt, Rinehart and Winston, 1948), p. 230; Carl Raushenbush, *Fordism, Ford and the Workers, Ford and the Community* (New York: League for Industrial Democracy, 1937), p. 49.

17. During the nine months from March through November 1930 the Ford Welfare Department paid out a total of $9,921 for groceries, fuel, clothing, and Henry Ford Hospital charity cases. To balance the account, the investigators arranged for $14,615 in assigned wages to be paid to the company in return for hospital care, a balance of almost $4,700 in Ford's favor. The summaries of investigations made by the Sociological Department during the months of March through November 1930 are in accession 572, box 14, FMCA.

18. Sidney Fine, *Sit-Down: The General Motors Strike of 1936–1937* (Ann Arbor, MI: University of Michigan Press, 1969), pp. 26–27; Sward, *Legend of Henry Ford,* pp. 223–230; *The Ford Worker,* August 1932; *Business Week,* July 8, 1931; Raushenbush, *Fordism,* pp. 49–50; Percy Llewellyn Interview (by George Heliker) in accession 940, FMCA; Fine, *Murphy,* pp 309–311.

19. Keeran, *The Communist Party and the Auto Workers Unions,* pp. 71–75; A Detroit leaflet urging attendance at the March 6 rally concluded with these demands: "Against Imperialist war! For the defense of the Soviet Union! Workers of Detroit! Organize and Fight! Refuse to Starve! Join the Detroit Unemployed Council! Join Trade Union Unity League and the Auto Workers Union! Read the Daily Worker! Join the Communist Party! Come With Your Wife and Children!" Leaflet (along with newspaper clippings of unemployed demonstration) is in Harry Ross Collection, box 8, WSU; Oral History Interview of Mr. and Mrs. Joseph Billups, p. 6, WSU; Interview with Shelton Tappes, pp. 6–9, in Maurice Sugar Collection, box 54, WSU.

20. Sward, *Legend of Henry Ford,* pp. 231–236; Keeran, *The Communist Party and the Auto Workers Unions,* pp. 71–74; Bernstein, *Lean Years,* pp. 432–434; Harry Bennett (as told to Paul Marcus), *We Never Called Him Henry* (New York: Fawcett Publications, 1951), pp. 91–94; Jonathan Hughes, *The Vital Few* (Boston: Houghton Mifflin, 1965), pp. 346–348; Fine, *Murphy,* pp. 403–409; Edward A. Wieck, "The Automobile Under the NRA," pp. 17–19, August 1935, in Mary Van Kleeck Collection, box 28, WSU; Robert Cruden, "Bloody Monday at Ford's," pp. 30–36, in Robert W. Dunn Collection, box 1, WSU; "Statement of Workers" (participants descriptions), in Maurice Sugar Collection, box 53, WSU; Maurice Sugar, *The Ford Hunger March* (Berkeley, CA: Meiklejohn Civil Liberties Institute, 1980); Wm. Reynolds, "The Ford Hunger March and Massacre," in Maurice Sugar Collection, box 53, WSU: Robert W. Dunn Collection, box 3, WSU, contains a file of newspaper clippings. The best overall account is Alex Baskin, "The Ford Hunger March—1932," *Labor History,* 13 (Summer 1972), pp. 321–360.

21. *Detroit Worker,* July 1, 1930; Labor Research Association, "Memo on the Briggs Manufacturing Company," Robert W. Dunn Collection, box 3, WSU; "Bodies by Briggs," *Auto Workers News,* June 1927; Oral History Interview of Ken Morris, p. 4, WSU; "The Reminiscences of A. M. Wibel,"

p. 256, Oral History Section, FMCA; Fine, *Murphy,* p. 413 reports a common expression in Detroit: "If poison doesn't work, try Briggs;" Anderson, "How I Became Part of the Labor Movement," p. 47.

22. "Why Auto Body Workers are [more] Militant than Other Auto Production Workers," Joe Brown Collection, box 19, WSU; "Body Workers," Phillips Garman Collection, box 3, WSU; Joseph Brown, "Body by Fisher," Robert W. Dunn Collection, box 2, WSU; Oral History Interview of Everett Francis, p. 4, WSU; see Nelson Lichtenstein, "Auto Worker Militancy and the Structure of Factory Life," *The Journal of American History,* 67 (September 1980), pp. 335–353 for a continuation of these trends into the 1940s.

23. Robert Cruden, "The Great Ford Myth," *The New Republic,* 70 (March 16, 1932), p. 116; Federated Press Releases, January and February, 1933; *Industrial Worker,* January 24, 1933 and February 7, 1933; Joe Brown, "The Story of the Forerunners of the Present Briggs Strike," *Detroit Leader,* February 11, 1933; all above in Joe Brown Scrapbook, vol. 1, WSU; Leaflet is in Joe Brown Collection, box 19, WSU. See also "Briggs Strike," Joe Brown Collection, box 19, WSU. Because the short strikes of early January were not reported in the press, the expression "Briggs Strike" usually refers to the period beginning on January 23, 1933.

24. Approximately 6,000 Briggs workers; 3,000 Hudson workers; 1,600 Motor Products workers; and an undetermined number of Murray Manufacturing Company workers were on strike at some time during the two-and-one-half-week period from January 20 to February 7. Estimating 1,400 strikers for Murray gives a total of 12,000. The figure of 100,000 Ford workers is in *Time,* February 13, 1933. The following sources are useful in providing a general outline of the chronology and major issues of the Briggs strike: Keeran, *The Communist Party and the Auto Workers Unions,* pp. 83–95, is the best overall account. See also Folders on Briggs strike, box 19, and Scrapbook, vol. 1, Brown Collection, WSU; *Report of the Mayor's Non-Partisan Committee on Industrial Disputes (The Fact Finding Committee) in the Matter of the Strike of the Workers at the Briggs Manufacturing Company, Detroit, Michigan,* February 21, 1933, DPL; Phillip Bonosky, *Brother Bill McKie: Building the Union at Ford* (New York: International Publishers, 1953), pp. 99–103; Fine, *Murphy,* pp. 412–421; Samuel Romer, "The Detroit Strike," *The Nation,* 136 (February 15, 1933), pp. 167–168; Oral History Interview of Leon Pody, pp. 3–15, WSU.

25. *Report of the Mayor's Non-Partisan Committee,* p. 28; "Demands of the Briggs Strikers," Joe Brown Collection, box 19, WSU.

26. Leaflet in Joe Brown Collection, box 19, WSU.

27. Report of the Mayor's Non-Partisan Committee," p. 21.

28. *Ibid.,* p. 30; Keeran, *The Communist Party and the Auto Workers Unions,* pp. 81–83; *Michigan Worker,* December 3, 1932.

29. "The Briggs Waterloo Strike," Henry Kraus Collection, box 1, WSU; Phil Raymond, "The Briggs Auto Strike Victory," *Labor Unity,* March 1933, pp. 21–24; Keeran, *The Communist Party and the Auto Workers Unions,* pp. 77–78; *Detroit News,* February 6, 1933; John Schmies, "The Lessons of the Briggs Auto Strike," *Daily Worker,* January 31, 1933.

30. Federated Press Release, February 1, 1933, Scrapbook, vol. 1, Brown Collection, WSU.

31. "Auto Workers Union organizes for strike," Kraus Collection, box 1, WSU; see *Report of the Mayor's Non-Partisan Committee,* p. 33, for a slightly different version of the Auto Workers Union suggested demands. "Summary of Briggs Waterloo Strike," and Briggs strike leaflet in Henry Kraus Collection, box 1, WSU; Anderson, "How I Became Part of the Labor Movement," p. 58; *Michigan Worker,* April 19, 1933; *Detroit News,* February 3, 1933.

32. *Report of the Mayor's Non-Partisan Committee,* p. 2; Anderson, "How I Became Part of the Labor Movement," p. 58; "A Brief History of the Briggs Strike" by a Briggs Striker, p. 2, IWW Collection, box 145, WSU; *Detroit News,* February 7, 1933.

33. Keeran, *The Communist Party and the Auto Workers Unions,* pp. 91–95 on divisions in the strike.

34. Oral History Interview of Leon Pody, pp. 13–15, *Detroit News,* January 30 and February 10, 1933; Anderson, "How I Became Part of the Labor Movement," p. 65.

35. For the effect of the Great Depression on the American labor movement in general, see Robert H. Zieger, *American Workers, American Unions, 1920–1985* (Baltimore, MD: Johns Hopkins University Press, 1986).

Chapter Nine

1. Wyndham Mortimer, certainly no advocate of auto work as the good life, found White Motors "really a good place to work. For the first time in my life I was enjoying my work. I had regular hours. I was home with my family in the evenings. I was able to get a full night's rest." Wyndham Mortimer, *Organize! My Life as a Union Man* (Boston: Beacon Press, 1971), p. 42; For discussions of auto industry paternalism, see Oral History Interview of Frank Tuttle, pp. 4–6, WSU; Oral History Interview of Norman R. Matthews, p. 2, WSU; Glen A. Niemeyer, *The Automotive Career of Ransom E. Olds,* Michigan State University Business Studies (Lansing, MI: Michigan State University, 1963), pp. 125–126; Mortimer, *Organize!,* pp. 41, 47–49.

2. Union organizers themselves attributed to the high wages of the auto industry some of their lack of success. See "The Auto Workers," outline

for an article by Phil Raymond, 1931, Henry Kraus Collection, box 1, WSU; "Organization Program for General Recruiting Union Detroit Branch Industrial Workers of the World, April 21, 1932," IWW Collection, series 7, box 1, WSU; Report of General Executive Secretary—Pro Tem, Robert M. Dunn Collection, box 2, WSU.

3. Edmund Wilson found an American worker distinguishing himself and his attitude toward working at Ford from the foreign workers. "Some of those wops with their feet wet and no soles to their shoes are glad to get under a dry roof—but not for me!" Edmund Wilson, *The American Jitters* [1932] (Reprint. Freeport, NY: Books for Libraries Press, 1968), p. 53; another auto worker who tried to interest his friends in the plight of Sacco and Vanzetti found "I never could interest anybody in the shop. The attitude of most of these people around me that I would talk to about it was, 'Well, they were only a couple of Dagos. Let them hang.'"; Oral History Interview of James Couser, p. 3, WSU; on the possibility of common foreign ethnicity working to favor working-class militancy and unionization, see Victor R. Greene, *The Slavic Community on Strike* (Notre Dame, IN: University of Notre Dame Press, 1968).

4. In David Brody's concise formulation:

> The workingman might have been deprived of pride in, and control over, his job; but he was granted access to the goods of the productive system beyond the dreams of earlier generations. If his share in making a Chevrolet was the endless repetition of a single task, the assembly line worker stepped into one of those machines and drove it home at the end of the day.

David Brody, *Workers in Industrial America* (New York: Oxford University Press, 1980), p. 65. While I estimate that only about one-half of all auto workers owned cars in the 1920s, the point is, nonetheless, well taken. For a theory of how such bargains are connected to concepts of justice see Barrington Moore, Jr., *Injustice; The Social Bases of Obedience and Revolt* (White Plains, NY: M. E. Sharpe, 1978). See also Thomas B. Mimms notes, Robert W. Dunn Collection, box 1, WSU; Oral History Interview of I. Paul Taylor, p. 9, WSU; Myron W. Watkins, "The Labor Situation in Detroit," *The Journal of Political Economy,* 28 (1920), p. 841.

5. David Montgomery, *Workers' Control in America* (Cambridge: Cambridge University Press, 1979), p. 116; For comments on unionization as assertion of dignity see Oral History Interviews of Norman Bully, p. 31; Russell Leach, p. 3; Ken Morris, p. 13; all WSU.

6. For discussion of leaders and followers see Robert Zieger, "Memory Speaks: Observations on Personal History and Working-Class Culture," *The Maryland Historian,* 8 (Fall 1977), pp. 5–8; Mortimer, *Organize!,* p. 50.

7. A certain bias exists in using the oral history interviews as representative of early union activists. Individuals, of course, were free to refuse to be interviewed and some did. Some had already died by the time the interviews were conducted in the 1960s. A type of in-group bias is inherent in following up on suggestions of likely interviewees made by those already interviewed. The project sought individuals who had "played an important role in the development of auto unionism," were "able to articulate their experiences," and were available to be interviewed. For further descriptions of the project, see Jack W. Skeels, "Oral History Project on the Development of Unionism in the Automobile Industry," *Labor History*, 5 (Spring 1964), pp. 209–212; and Warner W. Pflug, *A Guide to the Archives of Labor History and Urban Affairs Wayne State University* (Detroit, MI: Wayne State University Press, 1974), pp. 139–167. The following individuals comprise the 103 who worked in the auto industry before 1934 and are represented in Table IX–1: George Addes, Louis Adkins, John W. Anderson, John Bartee, Charles Beckman, J. A. Beni, Raymond Berndt, Joseph Billups, Merlin Bishop, Norman Bully, Ed Carey, Arthur Case, James M. Cleveland, Dick Coleman, Joseph Coles, Charles Conway, Alexander Cook, James Couser, Nick Di Gaetano, Joseph Ditzel, Tracy Doll, John Eldon, Frank Fagan, Joseph Ferris, Bert Foster, Everett Francis, Richard Frankensteen, Elmer Freitag, Mort Furay, Dan Gallagher, Catherine Gelles, Murvel Grant, Fred Haggard, Ed Hall, Matthew Hammond, Richard Harris, Joe Hattley, Arthur Hughes, William Humphreys, R. C. Ingram, L. Forest Innis, Martin Jensen, Clayton Johnson, Lester Johnson, Jack Jourdon, Robert Kanter, Harvey Kitzman, Tom Klasey, Ted La Duke, William Lattimore, Ed Lee, Al Leggat, Frank Manfred, Michael Manning, Frank Marquart, Hodges Mason, Norman Matthews, Joseph Mattson, John McGill, George Merrelli, Russell Merrill, Lew Michener, Paul E. Miley, Andrew Montgomery, Wyndham Mortimer, Stanley Nowak, James Oddie, Clayton O'Donohue, Patrick O'Malley, John Panzer, Joseph Pagano, Jack Palmer, William Payne, Orrin Peppler, Joseph Piconke, Leon Pody, Adam Poplawski, Phil Raymond, Herbert Richardson, John Ringwald, Arthur Rohan, James Roland, Harry Ross, Paul Russo, Sam Sage, Frank Sahorske, Walter Schilling, Bud Simons, Sam Smith, Harry Southwell, Roy Speth, William Stevenson, Carl Swanson, Shelton Tappes, R. J. Thomas, Hugh Thompson, Frank Tuttle, Art Vega, Ray Vess, Frank Wallemann, Jack Wilse, Elmer Yenney, John Zaremba; all WSU.

8. The number of native-born workers is substantially in excess of their presence in the auto worker population in general in 1930 (68.3%) and very substantially in excess of their presence in the Detroit auto worker population (54.7%). Very few of those interviewed provided information about where their parents were born. The fact that they did not comment on parents' birthplace, combined with their names, suggests almost all had native-born parents. Peter Friedlander's study of a UAW local in Hamtramck found that the native-born American workers remained aloof from joining or organizing the union in its early days. In this plant, the first push for

unionism came from the second generation immigrant workers. The prominence of second generation Poles in this case might be true in many other local situations especially where the plant work force was heavily non-native. See Peter Friedlander, *The Emergence of a UAW Local, 1936–1939: A Study in Class and Culture* (Pittsburgh, PA: University of Pittsburgh Press, 1975), pp. 37–45, 86–98; For the union as pioneering see Oral History Interview of Ken Morris, p. 13, WSU; of those 43 who gave information about their father's work, twenty reported close relatives who were involved in unions. A family union connection gave workers a head start on their own union activism.

Bibliography

Archives and Library Abbreviations

DPL   Detroit Public Library
FMCA Ford Motor Company Archives
UM   Michigan Historical Collections, University of Michigan
WSU   Archives of Labor History and Urban Affairs, Wayne State University

Collections in Archives

Archives of Labor History and Urban Affairs, Wayne State University

Dorothy Hubbard Bishop Collection

Joe Brown Collection

William Ellison Chalmers Collection

Nick DiGaetano Collection

Robert W. Dunn Collection

Everett Francis Collection

Richard Frankensteen Collection

Nat Ganley Collection

Phillips L. Garman Collection

IWW Collection

L. K. Kirk Collection

Henry Kraus Collection

Edward Levinson Collection

Frank Marquart Collection

Metro-Detroit AFL-CIO Collection

Matilda Robbins Collection

Harry Ross Collection

Maurice Sugar Collection

United Community Services Collection

Mary Van Kleeck Collection

Mary Heaton Vorse Collection

Edward A. Wieck Collection

John Zaremba Collection

Oral History Interviews: Unionization of the Auto Industry, Blacks and
the Labor Movement

Ford Motor Company Archives

Fair Lane Papers, Accession 1

Henry Ford Office Papers, Accession 2

Edsel Ford Papers, Accession 6

Production Records, Accession 38

Sociological Department, Accession 55

Henry Ford Office Papers, Accession 62

Rev. S. S. Marquis Papers, Accession 63

General Letters, Accession 78

Corporate Papers, Accession 85

Secretary's Offfice, Accession 162

George R. Brubaker Papers, Accession 185

Industrial Relations Sociological Department, Accession 280

Henry Ford Office Papers, Accession 284

Henry Ford Office Papers, Accession 285

Sociological Department, S. S. Marquis, Accession 293

Office off the Treasurer, Accession 459

Selected Research Papers, Accession 572

Industrial Relations, Accession 616

F. E. Searle Papers, Accession 690

Research Notes, Accession 940

George Heliker Papers, Accession 958

Oral History Section

Labadie Collection, University of Michigan

Michigan Historical Collections, University of Michigan

Roy D. Chapin Papers

Henry B. Joy Papers

American Federation of Labor Records: The Samuel Gompers Era (microfilm edition, 1979), Microfilming Corporation of America

Books

Andrew, Ed. *Closing the Iron Cage: The Scientific Management of Work and Leisure.* Montreal: Black Rose Books, 1981.

Arnold, Horace Lucien, and Faurote, Fay Leone. *Ford Methods and the Ford Shops.* New York: The Engineering Magazine Co., 1919.

Baran, Paul, and Sweezy, Paul M. *Monopoly Capital.* New York: Monthly Review Press, 1966.

Baritz, Loren. *The Servants of Power: A History of the Use of Social Science in American Industry.* Middletown, CT: Wesleyan University Press, 1960.

Beasley, Norman. *Knudsen.* New York: McGraw Hill, 1947.

———, and Stark, George W. *Made in Detroit.* New York: G. P. Putnams' Sons, 1957.

Bennett, Harry (as told to Paul Marcus). *We Never Called Him Henry.* New York: Fawcett Publications, 1951.

Bernstein, Irving. *The Lean Years: A History of the American Worker 1920–1933.* Boston: Houghton Mifflin, 1960.

———. *Turbulent Years: A History of the American Worker 1933–1941.* Boston: Houghton Mifflin, 1970.

Blauner, Robert. *Alienation and Freedom.* Chicago: University of Chicago Press, 1964.

Bonosky, Phillip. *Brother Bill McKie: Building the Union at Ford.* New York: International Publishers, 1953.

Bontemps, Arna, and Conroy, Jack. *They Seek a City.* Garden City, NY: Doubleday, Doran, 1945.

Borth, Christy. *Masters of Mass Production*. New York: Bobbs Merrill, 1945.

Boykin, Ulysses W. *A Hand Book on the Detroit Negro*. Detroit, MI: The Minority Study Associates, 1943.

Brandes, Stuart D. *American Welfare Capitalism, 1880–1940*. Chicago: University of Chicago Press, 1976.

Braverman, Harry. *Labor and Monopoly Capital: The Degradation of Work in the Twentieth Century*. New York: Monthly Review Press, 1974.

Brissenden, Paul Frederick, and Frankel, Emil. *Labor Turnover in Industry*. New York: Macmillan, 1922.

Brody, David. *Labor in Crisis: The Steel Strike of 1919*. Philadelphia: J. B. Lippincott, 1965.

———. *Steeelworkers in America, the Nonunion Era*. Cambridge, MA: Harvard University Press, 1960.

———. *Workers in Industrial America: Essays on the Twentieth Century Struggle*. New York: Oxford University Press, 1980.

Bunge, William. *Fitzgerald: Geography of a Revolution*. Cambridge, MA: Schenkman Publishing Co., 1971.

Burawoy, Michael. *Manufacturing Consent: Changes in the Labor Process Under Monopoly Capitalism*. Chicago: University of Chicago Press, 1979.

Burlingame, Roger. *Backgrounds of Power: The Human Story of Mass Production*. New York: Charles Scribner's Sons, 1949.

———. *Henry Ford*. New York: Alfred A. Knopf, 1954.

Burton, Clarence W., ed. *The City of Detroit, Michigan 1701–1922*. Vols. 1 & 2. Detroit, MI: S. J. Clarke, 1922.

Caldwell, Cy. *Henry Ford*. New York: Julian Messner, 1947.

Caldwell, Erskine. *Some American People*. New York: Robert M. McBride, 1935.

Catlin, George B. *The Story of Detroit*. Reprinted from the *Detroit News*, January 1–August 23, 1923.

Chandler, Alfred D., Jr. *Giant Enterprise: Ford, General Motors, and the Automobile Industry*. New York: Harcourt, Brace and World, 1964.

———. *Strategy and Structure*. Garden City, NY: Doubleday, 1962.

———, and Salsbury, Stephen. *Pierrre S. Du Pont and the Making of the Modern Corporation*. New York: Harper and Row, 1971.

Chinoy, Ely. *Automobile Workers and the American Dream*. Garden City, NY: Doubleday, 1955.

Chrysler, Walter P. (in collaboration with Boyden Sparks). *Life of an American Workman.* New York: Dodd, Mead, 1937.

Clawson, Don. *Bureaucracy and the Labor Process: The Transformation of U. S. Industry, 1860–1920.* New York: Monthly Review Press, 1980.

Cochran, Thomas C. *The Great Depression and World War II 1929–1945.* Glenview, IL: Scott Foresman, 1968.

Coombs, Whitney. *The Wages of Unskilled Labor in Manufacturing Industries in the United States, 1890–1924.* Studies in History, Economics, and Public Law, no. 283. New York: Columbia University Press, 1926.

Cormier, Frank, and Eaton, William. *Reuther.* Englewood Cliffs, NJ: Prentice-Hall, 1970.

Crow, Carl. *The City of Flint Grows Up.* New York: Harper and Brothers, 1945.

Cunningham, W. M. *"J8" A Chronicle of the Neglected Truth About Henry Ford D. E. and the Ford Motor Company.* Detroit, MI: North American Publishing Co., n.d.

Denison, Merrill. *The Power to Go.* Garden City, NY: Doubleday, 1956.

Donovan, Frank. *Wheels for a Nation.* Thomas Y. Crowell, 1965.

Dowd, Douglas F. *The Twisted Dream: Capitalist Development in the United States Since 1776.* Cambridge, MA: Winthrop Publishers, 1974.

Dubofsky, Melvyn. *We Shall Be All: A History of the Industrial Workers of the World.* Chicago: Quadrangle Books, 1969.

Dubreuil, H. *Robots or Men?* New York: Harper and Brothers, 1930.

Dunbar, Willis Frederick. *Michigan: A History of the Wolverine State.* Grand Rapids, MI: William B. Eerdmans, 1965.

Dunn, Robert W. *The Americanization of Labor.* New York: International Publishers, 1927.

———. *Labor and Automobiles.* New York: International Publishers, 1929.

Edwards, Richard. *Contested Terrain: The Transformation of the Workplace in the Twentieth Century.* New York: Basic Books, 1979.

Emerson, Harrington. *The Twelve Principles of Efficiency.* New York: The Engineering Magazine Co., 1912.

Epstein, Ralph C. *The Automobile Industry.* Chicago: A. W. Shaw, 1928.

Erskine, Albert Russell. *History of the Studebaker Corporation.* South Bend, IN: Studebaker Corporation, 1918.

Farnham, Dwight T. *Scientific Industrial Efficiency.* 1917. Reprint. Easton, PA: Hive Publishing Co., 1974.

Feldman, Herman. *Racial Factors in American Industry.* New York: Harper and Brothers, 1931.

Fine, Sidney. *The Automobile Under the Blue Eagle.* Ann Arbor, MI: University of Michigan Press, 1963.

————. *Frank Murphy: The Detroit Years.* Ann Arbor, MI: University of Michigan Press, 1975.

————. *Sit-Down: The General Motors Strike of 1936–1937.* Ann Arbor, MI: University of Michigan Press, 1969.

Florence, P. Sargent. *Economics of Fatigue and Unrest.* New York: Henry Holt, 1924.

Foner, Philip S. *History of the Labor Movement in the United States.* Vol. 4, *The Industrial Workers of the World, 1905–1917.* New York: International Publishers, 1965.

Forbes, B. C., and Foster, O. D. *Automotive Giants of America.* New York: B. C. Forbes Publishing Co., 1926.

Ford, Henry (in collaboration with Samuel Crowther). *Moving Forward.* London: William Heinemann, 1931.

———— (in collaboration with Samuel Crowther). *My Life and Work.* Garden City, NY: Doubleday, Page and Co., 1923.

———— (an authorized interview by Fay Leone Faurote). *My Philosophy of Industry.* New York: Coward-McCann, 1928.

———— (in Collaboration with Samuel Crowther). *Today and Tomorrow.* Garden City, NY: Doubleday, Page and Co., 1926.

Fountain, Clayton. *Union Guy.* New York: Viking Press, 1949.

Franklin, John Hope. *From Slavery to Freedom: A History of Negro Americans.* New York: Alfred A. Knopf, 1974.

Friedlander, Peter. *The Emergence of a UAW Local, 1936–1939: A Study in Class and Culture.* Pittsburgh, PA: University of Pittsburgh Press, 1975.

Friedman, Georges. *The Anatomy of Work.* Glencoe, IL: The Free Press, 1961.

————. *Industrial Society.* Glencoe, IL: The Free Press, 1955.

Gilbert, James. *Designing the Industrial State: The Intellectual Pursuit of Collectivism in America, 1880–1940.* Chicago: Quadrangle, 1972.

Golab, Caroline. *Immigrant Destinations.* Philadelphia: Temple University Press, 1977.

Goodrich, Carter L. *The Frontier of Control: A Study in British Workshop Politics.* London: G. Bell and Sons, 1920.

————, et al. *Migration and Economic Opportunity.* Philadelphia: University of Pennsylvania Press, 1936.

Gordon, David M.; Edwards, Richard; and Reich, Michael. *Segmented Work, Divided Workers: The Historial Transformation of Labor in the United States.* Cambridge: Cambridge University Press, 1982.

Greene, Victor R. *The Slavic Community on Strike.* Notre Dame, IN: University of Notre Dame Press, 1968.

Haber, Samuel. *Efficiency and Uplift: Scientific Management in the Progressive Era 1890–1920.* Chicago: University of Chicago Press, 1964.

Hamilton, J. G. De Rulhac. *Henry Ford, the Man, the Worker, the Citizen.* New York: Henry Holt, 1927.

Harris, Herbert. *American Labor.* New Haven, CT: Yale University Press, 1938.

Henri, Florette. *Black Migration: Movement North 1900–1920.* Garden City, NY: Doubleday, 1975.

Hoffman, Claude E. *Sit-Down in Anderson: UAW Local 663, Anderson, Indiana.* Detroit, MI: Wayne State University Press, 1968.

Holli, Melvin G., ed. *Detroit.* New York: Franklin Watts, 1976.

Howe, Irving, and Widick, B. J. *The UAW and Walter Reuther.* New York: Random House, 1949.

Hughes, Jonathan. *The Vital Few: American Economic Progress and Its Protagonists.* Boston: Houghton Mifflin, 1965.

Jacobs, Jane. *The Economy of Cities.* New York: Vintage Books, 1969.

Keeran, Roger. *The Communist Party and the Auto Workers Unions.* Bloomington, IN: Indiana University Press, 1980.

Kennedy, E. D. *The Automobile Industry.* New York: Reynal and Hitchcock, 1941.

Kennedy, Louise Venable. *The Negro Peasant Turns Cityward.* Columbia University Studies in History, Economics and Public Law, no. 329. New York: Columbia University Press, 1930.

Kraus, Henry. *The Many and the Few: A Chronicle of the Dynamic Auto Workers.* Los Angeles: Plantin Press, 1947.

Kruchko, John G. *The Birth of a Union Local: The History of UAW Local 674, Norwood, Ohio, 1933 to 1940.* Ithaca, NY: New York State School of Industrial and Labor Relations, 1972.

Lauck, W. Jett, and Sydenstricker, Edgar. *Conditions of Labor in American Industries.* New York: Funk and Wagnalls, 1917.

Leggett, John C. *Class, Race, and Labor: Working-Class Consciousness in Detroit.* New York: Oxford University Press, 1968.

Lenski, Gerhard. *The Religious Factor: A Sociological Study of Religion's Impact on Politics, Economics, and Family Life.* Rev. ed. Garden City, NY: Doubleday, 1963.

Leonard, Jonathan Norton. *The Tragedy of Henry Ford.* New York: G. P. Putnams', 1932.

Levine, David Allan. *Internal Combustion: The Races in Detroit 1915–1926.* Westport, CT: Greenwood Press, 1976.

Levinson, Edward. *Labor on the March.* New York: University Books, 1938.

Lewis, Edward E. *The Mobility of the Negro.* Studies in History, Economics and Public Law, no. 342. New York: Columbia University Press, 1931.

Long, J. C. *Roy D. Chapin.* N.p., 1945.

Longstreet, Stephen. *A Century on Wheels: The Story of Studebaker.* New York: Henry Holt, 1952.

Lutz, R. R. *The Metal Trades.* Philadelphia: The Survey Committee of the Cleveland Foundation, 1916.

MacManus, Theodore F., and Beasley, Norman. *Men, Money, and Motors.* New York: Harper and Brothers, 1929.

Marquart, Frank. *An Auto Worker's Journal: The UAW from Crusade to One-Party Union.* University Park, PA: Pennsylvania State University Press, 1975.

Marquis, Samuel S. *Henry Ford, An Interpretation.* Boston: Little, Brown, 1923.

Mathewson, Stanley B. *Restriction of Output Among Unorganized Workers.* New York: Viking Press, 1931.

McKelvey, Jean Trepp. *AFL Attitudes Toward Production 1900–1932.* Cornell Studies in Industrial and Labor Relations, Vol. 2. Ithaca, NY: New York State School of Industrial and Labor Relations, 1952.

McLaughlin, Doris B. *Michigan Labor: A Brief History from 1818 to the Present.* Ann Arbor, MI: Institute of Labor and Industrial Relations, The University of Michigan and Wayne State University, 1970.

Meier, August, and Rudwick, Elliott. *Black Detroit and the Rise of the UAW*. New York: Oxford University Press, 1979.

Merz, Charles. *And Then Came Ford*. Garden City, NY: Doubleday, Doran, 1929.

Meyer, Stephen, III. *The Five Dollar Day: Labor Management and Social Control in the Ford Motor Company, 1908-1921*. Albany, NY: State University of New York Press, 1981.

Montgomery, David. *Workers' Control in America*. Cambridge: Cambridge University Press, 1979.

Moore, Barrington, Jr. *Injustice: The Social Bases of Obedience and Revolt*. White Plains, NY: M. E. Sharpe, 1978.

Morris, James O. *Conflict Within the AFL*. Ithaca, NY: Cornell University Press, 1958.

Mortimer, Wyndham. *Organize! My Life as a Union Man*. Boston: Beacon Press, 1971.

Muste, A. J. *The Automobile Industry and Organized Labor*. Baltimore, MD: Christian Social Justice Fund, n.d., [1936].

Napolska, Sister Mary Remigia. *The Polish Immigrant in Detroit to 1914*. Chicago: Polish Roman Catholic Union of America, 1946.

National Americanization Committee, *Americanizing a City*. New York: National Americanization Committee, 1915.

National Industrial Conference Board. *The Cost of Living Among Wage-Earners Detroit, Michigan September 1921*. New York: National Industrial Conference Board, 1921.

————. *Wages, Hours and Employment in American Manufacturing Industries July 1914-January 1924*. Research Report No. 69. New York: National Industrial Conference Board, 1924.

————. *Wages in the United States, 1914-1926*. Research Report No. 120. New York: National Industrial Conference Board, 1927.

Nelson, Daniel. *Frederick W. Taylor and the Rise of Scientific Management*. Madison, WI: University of Wisconsin Press, 1980.

————. *Managers and Workers: Origins of the New Factory System in the United States 1880-1920*. Madison, WI: University of Wisconsin Press, 1975.

Nevins, Allan. *Ford: The Times, The Man, The Company*. New York: Charles Scribner's Sons, 1954.

————, and Hill, Frank Ernest. *Ford: Expansion and Challenge 1915-1933*. New York: Charles Scribner's Sons, 1957.

————, and Hill, Frank Ernest. *Ford: Decline and Rebirth 1933–1962.* New York: Charles Scribner's Sons, 1963.

Niemeyer, Glenn A. *The Automotive Career of Ransom E. Olds.* Michigan State University Business Studies. Lansing, MI: Michigan State University, 1963.

Noble, David F. *America by Design: Science, Technology, and the Rise of Corporate Capitalism.* New York: Oxford University Press, 1977.

Northrup, Herbert R. *The Negro in the Automobile Industry.* The Racial Policies of American Industry, Report No. 1. Philadelphia: Industrial Research Unit, Department of Industry, Wharton School of Finance and Commerce, University of Pennsylvania, 1968.

Norwood, Edwin P. *Ford Men and Methods.* Garden City, NY: Doubleday, Doran, 1931.

Olson, Sidney. *Young Henry Ford.* Detroit, MI: Wayne State University Press, 1963.

Ozanne, Robert. *A Century of Labor-Management Relations at McCormick and International Harvester.* Madison, WI: University of Wisconsin Press, 1967.

Packard Advanced Training School Lecture Course 1919. Detroit, MI: Packard Motor Car Co., 1919.

Pflug, Warner. *The UAW in Pictures.* Detroit, MI: Wayne State University Press, 1971.

Polish Activities League. *A Quarter Century of Social Services.* Detroit, MI: The Conventual Press, 1948.

Pound, Arthur. *The Automobile and an American City.* Detroit, MI: Wayne State University Press, 1962.

————. *The Turning Wheel.* Garden City, NY: Doubleday, Doran, 1934.

Rae, John B. *The American Automobile.* Chicago: University of Chicago Press, 1965.

————. *American Automobile Manufacturers.* Philadelphia: Chilton Company, 1959.

————, ed. *Henry Ford.* Englewood Cliffs, NJ: Prentice-Hall, 1969.

————. *The Road and the Car in American Life.* Cambridge, MA: MIT Press, 1971.

Raushenbush, Carl. *Fordism, Ford and the Workers, Ford and the Community.* New York: League for Industrial Democracy, 1937.

Savage, Maurice Dutton. *Industrial Unionism in America.* New York: The Ronald Press, 1922.

Schatz, Ronald W. *The Electrical Workers: A History of Labor at General Electric and Westinghouse 1923–1960*. Urbana, IL: University of Illinois Press, 1983.

Seltzer, Lawrence H. *A Financial History of the American Automobile Industry*. Cambridge, MA: Houghton Mifflin, 1928.

Serrin, William. *The Company and the Union*. New York: Alfred A. Knopf, 1973.

Simonds, William Adams. *Henry Ford—His Life, His Work, His Genius*. Indianapolis, IN: Bobbs Merrill, 1943.

————. *Henry Ford Motor Genius*. Garden City, NY: Doubleday, Doran, 1929.

Sinclair, Upton. *The Flivver King*. Detroit, MI: United Automobile Workers of America, 1937.

Sloan, Alfred, Jr. (in collaboration with Boyden Sparks). *Adventures of a White-Collar Man*. New York: Doubleday, Doran, 1941.

————. *My Years with General Motors*. Garden City, NY: Doubleday, 1963.

Smitter, Wessel. *F.O.B. Detroit*. New York: Harper and Brothers, 1938.

Sorensen, Charles E. (with Samuel T. Williamson). *My Forty Years with Ford*. New York: W. W. Norton, 1956.

Spero, Sterling D., and Harris, Abram L. *The Black Worker*. 1931. Reprint. New York: Atheneum, 1968.

Stark, George W. *City of Destiny*. Detroit, MI: Arnold-Powers, 1943.

Stolberg, Benjamin. *The Story of the CIO*. 1938. Reprint. New York: Arno, 1971.

Sugar, Maurice. *The Ford Hunger March*. Berkeley, CA: Meiklejohn Civil Liberties Institute, 1980.

Sward, Keith. *The Legend of Henry Ford*. New York: Holt, Rinehart and Winston, 1948.

Taft, Philip. *The A.F. of L. in the Time of Gompers*. New York: Harper and Brothers, 1957.

————. *The A.F. of L. From the Death of Gompers to the Merger*. New York: Harper and Brothers, 1959.

————. *Organized Labor in American History*. New York: Harper and Row, 1964.

Taylor, Frederick Winslow. *The Principles of Scientific Management*. New York: Harper and Brothers, 1919.

Taylor, I. Paul. *Prosperity in Detroit*. Highland Park, MI: By the Author, 1920.

Thomas, William I., and Znaniecki, Florian. *The Polish Peasant in Europe and America*. New York: Alfred A. Knopf, 1927.

Thompson, E. P. *The Making of the English Working Class*. New York: Pantheon Books, 1963.

Thompson, Paul. *The Nature of Work: An Introduction to Debates on the Labour Process*. London: Macmillan, 1983.

Thornthwaite, Warren C. *Internal Migration in the United States*. Philadelphia: University of Pennsylvania Press, 1934.

Walker, Charles R.; Guest, Robert H.; and Turner, Arthur N. *The Foreman on the Assembly Line*. Cambridge, MA: Harvard University Press, 1956.

————; and Guest, Robert H. *The Man on the Assembly Line*. Cambridge, MA: Harvard University Press, 1952.

Ward, Matthew (Charles Denby). *Indignant Heart*. New York: New Books, 1952.

Weinstein, James. *The Corporate Ideal in the Liberal State: 1900–1918*. Boston: Beacon Press, 1968.

Wesley, Charles H. *Negro Labor in the United States 1850–1925*. New York: Vanguard Press, 1927.

Widick, B. J., ed. *Auto Work and Its Discontents*. Baltimore, MD: Johns Hopkins University Press, 1976.

Wilkins, Mira, and Hill, Frank Ernest. *American Business Abroad: Ford on Six Continents*. Detroit, MI: Wayne State University Press, 1964.

Wilson, Edmund. *The American Jutters*. 1932. Reprint. Freeport, NY: Books for Libraries Press, 1968.

Wolman, Leo. *Ebb and Flow in Trade Unionism*. New York: National Bureau of Economic Research, 1936.

Woods, Arthur Evans. *Hamtramck: A Sociological Study of a Polish-American Community*. New Haven, CT: College and University Press, 1955.

Yarnell, Duane. *Auto Pioneering: A Remarkable Story of Ramson E. Olds*. New York: Franklin De Kleine Company, 1949.

Young, Clarence H., and Quinn, William A. *Foundation for Living*. New York: McGraw Hill, 1963.

Zieger, Robert H. *American Workers, American Unions, 1920–1985*. Baltimore, MD: John Hopkins University Press, 1986.

Zunz, Olivier. *The Changing Face of Inequality: Urbanization, Industrial Development, and Immigrants in Detroit, 1880–1920.* Chicago: University of Chicago Press, 1982.

Articles

"Age Distribution of Ford Employees." *Monthly Labor Review,* 31 (December 1930), pp. 1351–1353.

Anderson, John W. "How I Became Part of the Labor Movement." In Alice and Staughton Lynd, eds. *Rank and File: Personal Histories by Working-Class Organizers.* Boston: Beacon Press, 1973, pp. 35–68.

Asher, Robert. "Union Nativism and the Immigrant Response." *Labor History,* 23 (Summer 1982), pp. 325–348.

Babson, Steve. "Pointing the Way. The Role of British and Irish Skilled Tradesmen in the Rise of the UAW." *Detroit in Perspective,* 7 (Spring 1983), pp. 75–96.

Bailer, Lloyd H. "The Negro Automobile Worker." *Journal of Political Economy,* 51 (October 1943), pp. 415–428.

Baskin, Alex. "Ford Hunger March." *Labor History,* 13 (Summer 1972), pp. 331–360.

Bernstein, Irving. "The Growth of American Unions." *American Economic Review,* 44 (June 1954), pp. 301–318.

Blackett, O. W. "Factory Labor Turnover in Michigan." *Michigan Business Studies,* 2 (November 1928).

Boryczka, Ray. "Militancy and Factionalism in the United Auto Workers Union, 1937–1941." *The Maryland Historian,* 8 (Fall 1977), pp. 13–25.

Brody, David. "The Old Labor History and the New: In Search of an American Working Class." *Labor History,* 20 (Winter 1979), pp. 111–126.

Chase, Stuart. "Danger at the A. O. Smith Corporation." *Fortune,* 11 (November 1930), pp. 62–67, 102.

Chrysler Corporation. "The Automobile Industry." In John G. Glover and William Bouch Cornell, eds. *The Development of American Industries,* ch. 31. New York: Prentice-Hall, 1933.

Collins, William. "Automobile Workers Organize." *American Federationist,* 41 (July 1934), pp. 700–742.

Cruden, Robert, "The Great Ford Myth." *The New Republic,* 70 (March 16, 1932), pp. 116–119.

Culver, Chester M. "A Resume of the Last Year in Industrial Detroit." *Detroit Saturday Night,* 1921.

De Lancy, Howard R. "The Cole Motor Car Company." *Business History Review,* 30 (September 1956), pp. 260–273.

Dunn, Robert W. "Automobile Industry, Labor Conditions." *Encyclopaedia of the Social Sciences,* Vol. 2. New York: Macmillan, 1930, pp. 326–328.

Fine, Sidney. "The Ford Motor Company and the N.R.A." *Business History Review,* 32 (Winter 1958), pp. 353–385.

————. "The Tool and Die Makers Strike of 1933." *Michigan History,* 42 (September 1958), pp. 297–323.

————. "The Origins of the United Automobile Workers, 1933–35." *Journal of Economic History,* 18 (September 1958), pp. 249–282.

"Ford Protests Detroit's Bill for Relief of Late Employees." *Business Week,* July 8, 1931, p. 18.

Fuller, Earl G. "The Automobile Industry in Michigan." *Michigan History Magazine,* 12 (April 1928), pp. 280–296.

Galbraith, John Kenneth. "Was Ford a Fraud?" *The Liberal Hour,* Ch. 9. Boston: Houghton Mifflin, 1960.

Gartman, David. "Origins of the Assembly Line and Capitalist Control of Work at Ford." In Andrew Zimbalist, ed. *Case Studies on the Labor Process.* New York: Monthly Review Press,1979, pp. 193–205.

Godwin, Murray. "The Case Against Henry Ford." *American Mercury,* 23 (July 1932), pp. 257–266.

Gutman, Herbert G. "Work, Culture, and Society in Industrializing America, 1815–1919." *The American Historical Review,* 78 (June 1973), pp. 531–588.

Haber, William. "Fluctuations in Employment in Detroit Factories, 1921–1931." *Journal of the American Statistical Association,* 27 (June 1932), pp. 141–152.

Hall, Helen. "When Detroit's Out of Gear." *Survey,* 64 (April 1, 1930), pp. 9–14, 51–54.

Hobsbawm, E. J. "Custom, Wages and Work-Load." *Labouring Men.* New York: Basic Books, 1964, pp. 405–435.

————. "The Labor Aristocracy in Nineteenth-Century Britain." In Peter N. Stearns and Daniel J. Walkowitz, eds. *Workers in the Industrial Revolution: Recent Studies of Labor in the United States and Europe.* New Brunswick, NJ: Transaction Books, 1974, pp. 138–176.

Kellogg, Paul. "When Mass Production Stalls." *Survey*, 59 (March 1, 1928), pp. 683–686, 722–728.

————. "Henry Ford's Hired Men." *Survey*, 59 (February 1, 1928), pp. 549–557, 593–596.

La Fever, Mortimer W. "Workers, Machinery, and Production in the Automobile Industry." *Monthly Labor Review*, 19 (October 1924), pp. 1–26.

Lane, Tony. "A Merseysider in Detroit." *History Workshop*, issue 11 (Spring 1981), pp. 138–153.

Lee, John R. "The So-Called Profit Sharing System in the Ford Plant." *The Annals of the American Academy of Political and Social Science*, 65 (May 1916), pp. 297–310.

Leggett, John C. "Class Consciousness and Politics in Detroit: A Study in Change." *Michigan History*, 48 (December 1964), pp. 289–314.

Levin, Samuel M. "The End of Ford Profit Sharing." *Personnel Journal*, 6 (October 1927), pp. 161–170.

————. "The Ford Unemployment Policy." *American Labor Legislation Review*, 22 (March 1932), pp. 101–108.

————. "Ford Profit Sharing, 1914–1920, I. The Growth of the Plan." *Personnel Journal*, 6 (August 1927), pp. 75–86.

Levine, Daniel. "Gompers and Racism: Strategy of Limited Objectives." *Mid America*, 43 (April 1961), pp. 106–113.

Li, Chen-Nan. "A Summer in the Ford Works." *Personnel Journal*, 7 (June 1928), pp. 18–32.

Lichtenstein, Nelson. "Auto Worker Militancy and the Structure of Factory Life, 1937–1955." *The Journal of American History*, 67 (September 1980), pp. 335–353.

Littler, Craig R. "Taylorism, Fordism and Job Design." In David Knights, Hugh Willmott, David Collinson, eds. *Job Redesign: Critical Perspectives on the Labour Process*. London: Gower, 1985, pp. 10–29.

Logan, W. A. "The Automobile Workers' Union." *Michigan Socialist*, 22 (September 1916).

Luchek, Anthony. "Company Unions, F.O.B. Detroit." *Nation*, 142 (January 15, 1936), pp. 74–77.

MacDonald, Lois. "Labor and Automobiles." *Labor Problems and the American Scene*. New York: Harper and Brothers, 1938, pp. 158–170.

Mandel, Bernard. "Samuel Gompers and the Negro Workers, 1886–1914." *The Journal of Negro History*, 40 (1955), pp. 34–60.

Megargle, R. H. "Detroit Losing Working Men." *Michigan Manufacturer and Financial Record,* June 12, 1920.

Meyer, Stephen. "Adapting the Immigrant to the Line: Americanization in the Ford Factory, 1914–1921." *Journal of Social History,* 14 (Fall 1980), pp. 67–82.

Montgomery, David. "To Study the People: The American Working Class." *Labor History,* 21 (Fall 1980), pp. 485–512.

Moore, D. A. "The Automobile Industry." In Walter Adams, ed. *The Structure of American Industry,* Ch. 8. New York: Macmillan, 1954.

Niebuhr, Reinhold. "Ford's Five-Day Week Shrinks." *Christian Century,* 44 (June 9, 1927), pp. 713–714.

————. "How Philanthropic is Henry Ford?" *Christian Century,* 43 (December 9, 1926), pp. 1516–1517.

Nixon, J. W. "How Ford's Lowest-Paid Workers Live." *Social Service Review,* 5 (March 1931), pp. 37–46.

Oldenburg, Joseph. "Ford Homes Historic District." *The Dearborn Historian,* 20 (Spring 1980), pp. 31–50.

Ozanne, Robert. "Trends in American Labor History." *Labor History,* 21 (Fall 1980), pp. 513–521.

Peterson, Joyce Shaw. "American Automobile Workers and Their Work, 1897–1933." *Labor History,* 22 (Spring 1981), pp. 213–226.

————. "Auto Workers Confront the Depression, 1929–1933." *Detroit in Perspective,* 6 (Fall 1982), pp. 47–71.

————. "Black Automobile Workers in Detroit, 1910–1930." *Journal of Negro History,* 64 (Summer 1979), pp. 177–190.

Porter, Harry Franklin. "Giving the Men a Share: What It's Doing for Ford." *System,* 31 (March 1917), pp. 262–270.

Rankin, Lois. "Detroit Nationality Groups." *Michigan History Magazine,* 23 (Spring 1939), pp. 129–205.

Reitell, Charles. "Machinery and Its Effect Upon the Workers in the Automotive Industry." *The Annals of the American Academy of Political and Social Science,* 116 (November 1924), pp. 37–43.

Ross, Arthur M. "Do We Have a New Industrial Feudalism?" *American Economic Review,* 48 (December 1958), pp. 903–920.

Rumely, Edward. "Mr. Ford's Plan to Share Profits." *World's Work,* 27 (April 1914), pp. 664–669.

Showalter, William Joseph. "The Automobile Industry: An American Art that has Revolutionized Methods in Manufacturing and Transformed

Transportation." *The National Geographic Magazine,* 44 (October 1923), pp. 337–414.

Skeels, Jack. The Background of UAW Factionalism." *Labor History,* 2 (Spring 1961), pp. 158–181.

————. "Early Carriage and Auto Unions: The Impact of Industrialization and Rival Unionism." *Industrial and Labor Relations Review,* 17 (1963–1964), pp. 566–583.

————. "Oral History Project on the Development of Unionism in the Automobile Industry." *Labor History,* 5 (Spring 1964), pp. 209–212.

"Standard of Living of Employees of Ford Motor Co. in Detroit." *Monthly Labor Review,* 30 (June 1930), pp. 1209–1252.

Steiger, Andrew J. "Autos and Jobs." *Nation,* 126 (May 2, 1928), pp. 505–506.

Stone, Katherine. "The Origins of Job Structures in the Steel Industry." *Radical America,* 7 (November-December 1973), pp. 19–64.

Street, Julian. "Detroit the Dynamic." *Collier's,* July 4, 1914, pp. 8–10, 23–27.

Stricker, Frank. "Affluence for Whom?—Another Look at Prosperity and the Working Classes in the 1920s." *Labor History,* 24 (Winter 1983), pp. 5–33.

Sugar, Maurice. "Bullets—Not Food—For Ford Workers." *Nation,* 134 (March 23, 1932), pp. 333–335.

Sweezy, Paul M. "Cars and Cities." *Monthly Review,* 24 (April 1973), pp. 1–18.

Thomas, Robert P. "Business Failure in the Automobile Industry, 1895–1910." In J. Van Fenstermaker, ed. *Papers Presented at the Annual Business History Conference.* Kent, OH: Kent State University Bureau of Economic and Business Research, 1965.

Thompson, Paul. "Crawling from the Wreckage: The Labour Process and the Politics of Production." Paper prepared for the 4th ASTON/ UMIST Conference on Organization and Control of the Labour Process, April 1986.

Tolles, N. A., and La Fever, M. W. "Wages, Hours, Employment, and Annual Earnings in the Motor Vehicle Industry, 1934." *Monthly Labor Review,* 42 (March 1936), pp. 521–553.

Touraine, Alain. "The End of the Road for the Skilled Worker: Automaking at Renault." In Edward Shorter, ed. *Work and Community in the West.* New York: Harper and Row, 1978, pp. 80–100.

"Wages and Hours of Labor in the United States." *Monthly Labor Review,* 9 (September 1919), pp. 176–189.

"Wages and Hours in Automobile, Car, Electrical Apparatus, Foundry, Machinery, Machine Tool, and Typewriter Industries." *Monthly Labor Review,* 10 (June 1920), pp. 82–94.

Watkins, Myron W. "The Labor Situation in Detroit." *The Journal of Political Economy,* 28 (1920), pp. 840–852.

Wilson, Edmund. "The Despot of Dearborn." *Scribner's Magazine,* 90 (July 1931), pp. 24–36.

Wolman, Leo. "The Extent of Labor Organization in the United States in 1910." *Quarterly Journal of Economics,* 30 (May 1916), pp. 486–518.

Wright, Thomas H. "Why Ford's Men Strike." *Christian Century,* 50 (November 29, 1933), pp. 1501–1504.

Wyatt, S. "Boredom in Industry." Personnel Journal, 8 (1929), pp. 161–171.

Zieger, Robert. "Memory Speaks: Observations on Personal History and Working-Class Culture." *The Maryland Historian,* 8 (Fall 1977), pp. 1–12.

United States Government Documents

Bernstein, Irving. *The Automobile Industry, Post-War Developments, 1918–1921.* U. S. Department of Labor. Bureau of Labor Statistics. Historical Study No. 52, September 1942.

Brissenden, Paul F. *Earnings of Factory Workers 1899–1927.* U. S. Department of Commerce. Bureau of the Census. Census Monograph 10, 1929.

Dublin, Louis I., and Vane, Robert J. *Causes of Death by Occupation.* U. S. Department of Labor. Bureau of Labor Statistics. Bulletin No. 507, February 1930.

National Recovery Administration. Research and Planning Division. Evidence Study No. 1. *The Automobile Manufacturing Industry.* Prepared by Frank Evans, Jr., September 1935.

Peterson, Florence. *Strikes in the United States, 1880–1936.* U. S. Department of Labor. Bulletin No. 651.

U. S. Congress. House. Federal Trade Commission. *Report on Motor Vehicle Industry.* House Document No. 468. 76th Cong., 1st sess., 1939.

U. S. Congress. Senate. Commission on Industrial Relations. *Efficiency Systems and Labor.* Senate Document No. 415. 64th Cong., 1st sess., 1916.

U. S. Department of Commerce. Bureau of the Census. *Twelfth Census of the United States: 1900, Population,* I.

U. S. Department of Commerce. Bureau of the Census. *Abstract of the Twelfth Census of the United States: 1900.*

U. S. Department of Commerce. Bureau of the Census. *Thirteenth Census of the United States: 1910, Population,* I.

U. S. Department of Commerce. Bureau of the Census. *Abstract of the Thirteenth Census of the United States: 1910.*

U. S. Department of Commerce. Bureau of the Census. *Census of Manufactures: 1914,* II.

U. S. Department of Commerce. Bureau of the Census. *Fourteenth Census of the United States: 1920,* IV.

U. S. Department of Commerce. Bureau of the Census. *Abstract of the Fourteenth Census of the United States: 1920.*

U. S. Department of Commerce. Bureau of the Census. *Fifteenth Census of the United States: 1930, Population,* IV.

U. S. Department of Commerce. Bureau of the Census. *Abstract of the Fifteenth Census of the United States: 1930.*

U. S. Department of Commerce. Bureau of the Census. *Fifteenth Census of the United States. Manufactures: 1929,* II.

U. S. Department of Commerce. Bureau of the Census. *Biennial Census of Manufactures: 1935.*

U. S. Department of Commerce. Bureau of the Census. *Sixteenth Census of the United States: 1940. Manufactures: 1939,* II.

U. S. Department of Labor. *Job Specifications for the Automobile Manufacturing Industry.* June 1935.

U. S. Department of Labor. *Negro Migration in 1916–1917,* 1919.

U. S. Department of Labor. Bureau of Labor Statistics. *Industrial Survey in Selected Industries in the United States, 1919.* Bulletin No. 265, May 1920.

U. S. Department of Labor. Bureau of Labor Statistics. *Wages and Hours of Labor in the Automobile Industry 1922.* Bulletin No. 348, October 1923.

U. S. Department of Labor. Bureau of Labor Statistics. *Wages and Hours of Labor in the Motor Vehicle Industry 1925.* Bulletin No. 438, May 1927.

U. S. Department of Labor. Children's Bureau. *Minors in Automobile and Metal-Manufacturing Industries in Michigan.* Bureau Publication No. 126, 1923.

Labor, Company, and Miscellaneous Newspapers and Journals

Auto Workers News, 1929–1933.

Carriage and Wagon Workers Journal, 1899–1908.

Detroit Council of Trades and Labor Unions Labor Day Review, 1901–1903, 1905–1906, 1908, 1910.

Detroit Forum, 1919–1921.

Detroit Labor News, 1914–1933.

Detroit Leader, 1933.

Detroit Worker, 1930.

Dodge Worker, 1926–1927.

Factory Facts from Ford, 1915, 1917.

Fisher Body Workers' Bulletin, 1926–1927.

Flint Labor News, 1917–1918.

Ford Industries, 1924, 1927.

Ford News, 1918–1929.

Ford Worker, 1926–1927.

Forum Folks, 1917–1919.

Helpful Hints and Advice to Employees (Ford Motor Company), 1915.

Industrial Union News, 1919.

Michigan Federationist, 1928–1931.

Michigan Socialist, 1916–1918.

Michigan Union Advocate, 1904–1910.

Michigan Worker, 1932–1933.

Pipp's Weekly, 1920–1933.

Proletarian, 1918–1931.

Wage Worker, 1901–1903.

Young Recruit, 1932–1933.

Reports and Proceedings

Carriage, Wagon and Automobile Workers' International. *Proceedings of Convention.* September 1915.

Detroit, City of. *Journal of the Common Council.* January 8, 1929–January 13, 1930.

Detroit Board of Commerce. The Americanization Committee of the Detroit Board of Commerce. *Annual Reports 1918–1930.*

Detroit Board of Health. *Report to the Health Officer on Housing and Health in Detroit.* 1916.

Detroit Department of Health. *The Detroit Industrial Worker and His Health.* 1939.

Detroit Housing Commission. *First Annual Report.* 1933–1934.

Detroit Mayor's Inter-Racial Committee. *The Negro in Detroit.* Prepared by Detroit Bureau of Governmental Research, 1926.

Detroit Mayor's Non-Partisan Committee. *Report of the Mayor's Non-Partisan Committee on Industrial Disputes (The Fact-Finding Committee) in the Matter of the Strike of the Workers at the Briggs Manufacturing Company, Detroit, Michigan.* February 21, 1933.

Detroit Mayor's Unemployment Committee. Sub-Committee. *The Effect Upon Detroit of the Three Years of the Depression.* 1932.

Detroit Youth Study Committee. *What of Youth Today?* 1935.

Michigan Employer's Liability and Workmen's Compensation Commission. *Report.* 1911.

United Automobile, Aircraft and Vehicle Workers of America. *Convention Proceedings.* September 2–6, 1918.

United Automobile, Aircraft and Vehicle Workers of America. *Convention Proceedings.* September 13–19, 1920.

United Automobile, Aircraft and Vehicle Workers of America. *Convention Proceedings.* September 13–18, 1926.

Theses, Dissertations, and Other Papers

Bailer, Lloyd M. "Negro Labor in the Automobile Industry." Ph.D. diss., University of Michigan, 1942.

Barrule, Orry (Leslie McDonnell). "Life With Uncle Henry." 1945, FMCA.

Bernstein, Blanche. "Hiring Policies in the Automobile Industry." Works Progress Administration National Research Project on Reemployment Opportunities and Recent Changes in Industrial Techniques. WSU.

Blackwood, George Douglas. "The United Automobile Workers of America 1935–1951." Ph.D. diss., University of Chicago, 1951.

Carlson, Glen E. "The Negro in the Industries of Detroit." Ph.D. diss., University of Michigan, 1929.

Chalmers, William Ellison. "Labor in the Automobile Industry: A Study of Personnel Policies, Workers Attitudes and Attempts at Unionism." Ph.D. diss., University of Wisconsin, 1932.

Cole, Raymond. "The Immigrant in Detroit." Prepared for the Detroit Board of Commerce, May 1915. UM.

Court, A.T. "Age and the Automobile Worker." 1939. DPL.

———. "Men, Methods and Machines in Manufacturing Motor Vehicles." Automobile Manufacturers Association, 1939. DPL.

Davidson, Gordon W. "Industrial Detroit After World War I, 1919–1921. M.A. thesis, Wayne University, 1953.

Faigin, Henry. "The Industrial Workers of the World in Detroit and Michigan from the Period of Beginnings through the World War." M.A. thesis, Wayne University, 1937.

Genzeloff, Leo. "The Effect of Technological Changes Upon Employment Opportunities in the Automobile Industry." M.A. thesis, University of Wisconsin, 1939.

Krivy, Leonard Philip. "American Organized Labor and the First World War, 1917–1918: A History of Labor Problems and the Development of a Government War Labor Program." Ph.D. diss., New York University, 1965.

Kruesi, Walter E. "Hamtramck: A Survey of Social, Educational and Civic Conditions with some Recommendations." 1915. DPL.

———. "Report Upon Unemployment in the Winter of 1914–1915 in Detroit and the Institutions and Measures of Relief." 1915. DPL.

Levin, Samuel M. "The Ford Unemployment Policy." Address to 25th Annual Meeting American Association for Labor Legislation, December 28, 1931.

Lewis, David L. "Henry Ford: A Study in Public Relations, 1896–1932." Ph.D. diss., University of Michigan, 1959.

Lowery, Joel John. "Labor Relations in the Automobile Industry During the Nineteen Twenties." M.A. thesis, Michigan State University, 1958.

Mayer, Albert. "A Study of the Foreign-Born Population of Detroit 1870–1950." Department of Sociology and Anthropology, Wayne University, 1951. DPL.

McDonnell, James Richard. "The Rise of the CIO in Buffalo, New York 1936–1942." Ph.D. diss., University of Wisconsin, 1970.

Parker, John. "A History of the Packard Motor Car Company from 1899 to 1929." M.A. thesis, Wayne University, 1949.

Solin, Jacob A. "The Detroit Federation of Labor, 1900–1920." M.A. thesis, Wayne University, 1939.

Wakstein, Allen Morton. "The Open-Shop Movement, 1919–1933." Ph.D. diss., University of Illinois, 1961.

Whalen, Cecile. "Detroit Shifting Scenes and Population." n.d., ca. 1943. DPL.

Wengert, Egbert S. "Financial Problems of the City of Detroit in the Depression." Detroit Bureau of Governmental Research, 1939. DPL.

Index